Resonare Christum

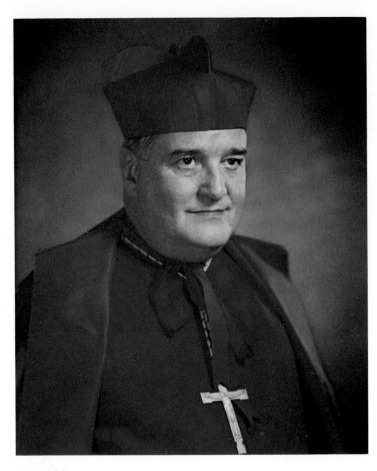

Portrait by Jonas

Resonare Christum

Volume I
1939–1959

A Selection from the Sermons
Addresses, Interviews, and Papers
of

Cardinal John J. Wright

Prepared and Edited by
R. Stephen Almagno, O.F.M.

Ignatius Press   San Francisco

Imprimi Potest: Alban V. Montella, O.F.M.
                       Minister Provincial
                       Provincial Curia
                       New York City

Imprimatur: + John R. Quinn
                       Archbishop of San Francisco

Cover by Victoria Hoke

All monies accruing to the editor from the publication of this book
will be paid to the Catholic Institute of Pittsburgh, Inc., for works of
religion, charity, and education.

Memoriae et Laudi

Iohannis I. Wright

Cardinalis

Sanctae Romanae Ecclesiae

Summis Honoribus Functi

De Humanis Pariter et Christianis Litteris

Optime Meriti

Acknowledgments

Publication of this book was made possible by the generous donation of Mr. and Mrs. John Haverty.

The literary executor is grateful to the following for permission to reproduce copyright material:

The Annals of Saint Anthony Shrine for "Our Patriotic Debt to Our Dead".

The Delta Epsilon Sigma Bulletin for "The Aims and End of Catholic Education".

Fides/Claretian for "The Church in the Sputnik Age", "The Common Good", and "The Philosophy of Responsibility".

The J. B. Lippincott Company for "Gutenberg's Bible", "Catholic Veneration of the Bible", and "Conversations with Bishop John J. Wright".

The Journal of the South Carolina Medical Association for "A Clergyman Views Medicine".

The Society of Jesus, Maryland Province, for "Jesuit Centennial in Boston".

Spiritual Life for "Christocentric Humanism".

The Thomas More Association and *The Critic* for "Joan of Arc and the Christian Conception of Personal Vocation".

Contents

Preface

The task of preparing for publication this selection from the sermons, addresses, and papers of Cardinal John Wright (1909–1979) has been an entirely pleasant affair. Pleasant, because of the trust placed in me by the Wright family and by the Cardinal's executors. Pleasant, because I was able to work in the congenial atmosphere of this university, which was an object of Wright's love and concern. Pleasant, because of the encouragement and cooperation from so many of his friends and admirers. And, finally, pleasant, because "to be reminded" of Cardinal Wright "is always the greatest delight to me, whether I speak myself or hear another speak of him." (*Phaedo*)

The Cardinal's words are presented with as little intrusion as possible. This is his book. Each text speaks for itself. The notes endeavor, simply, to put a background to the text.

I know that this text will be welcomed by Cardinal Wright's friends, and I hope that this book may possibly be of interest and give insight to someone who had not the privilege of knowing him.

It remains only for me to thank President Wesley W. Posvar, Ph.D., Dean Thomas J. Galvin, Ph.D., the Most Reverend Anthony G. Bosco, the Reverend Alban V. Montella, O.F.M. (my Minister Provincial), the Very Reverend Leo V. Vanyo, J.C.D., Professor Roy B. Stokes, Dr. Ellen G. Detlefsen, Ph.D., Melody Mazuk, Deborah Lordi Silverman, Brenda Gail Kenny, Audrey Daigneault, Charlotte Tancin, Patrice Kane, and especially JoAnn Hartz, my secretary, for their cooperation and assistance.

R. Stephen Almagno, O.F.M.

The University of Pittsburgh
School of Library and Information Science
November 9, 1984

Part One

The Boston Years
1939−1950

Introduction

John Joseph Wright was graduated from the Boston Latin School in 1927 and entered Boston College. The then headmaster, Patrick T. Campbell, had likewise been headmaster during my student days. He was later to become Superintendent of Schools. He told me the following story while Cardinal Wright was a student in Rome. A well-to-do alumnus waited upon Mr. Campbell and stated that he would be happy to pay all expenses, if John Wright saw fit to go to Dartmouth. John Wright did not care to go to Dartmouth and so Mr. Campbell went immediately to Boston College where he asked for a scholarship for a young man who had a vocation to the priesthood, but did not yet know it. It was granted, and the journalist that John Wright dreamed of becoming gave way to the priest, bishop, and cardinal who cast such a long shadow over a whole generation.

John Wright was a loyal alumnus of the Latin School. Many times when he felt that some adverse influences were conspiring to bring down the School's high standards, he would do that which he best of all the alumni could do: he would write and talk until the danger was over. See, for example, the address *Haec Studia*—published in Volume II—which he delivered on April 25, 1960, at the Three Hundred Twenty-Fifth Anniversary Dinner of the Boston Latin School. Many years ago the custom was started of giving a Paul Revere bowl to the Latin School Man of the Year. No one was surprised, nor did anyone cavil, that the first recipient was Bishop Wright.

He was likewise to be a loyal student and alumnus of Boston College. He first came to public attention when, in his senior year, as leader of the Boston College debating team, he shone in a victory over Oxford University at Symphony Hall. In

13

addition to excelling in his studies, he worked for the *Boston Post*, doing such things as a column of advice for the lovelorn. He taught public speaking and debating at one of the Catholic high schools. And all the time the decision toward the priesthood was maturing. During his time of study in Rome, I had occasion to visit his family's home. I noticed eight prayer books on top of a radiator cover just inside the door. I asked one night: "Whose is that? Whosoever it is—he needs a new one!" I was told it was John's *Father Lasance Prayer Book for Men*, heavy with wear. Its appearance told how many times he had carried it to Saint Angela's Church and turned its pages while following the Mystery of the Mass.

John Wright entered Saint John's Seminary in the fall of 1931. I had been appointed to the faculty a few months before, and it fell to me to instruct him in his major courses, Psychology and Natural Theology. He was an apt student; and I took it for granted that he would spend the rest of his course in Rome.

One day the following July, at our seminary villa, the priest in charge, Father Kelleher, who was to precede John as auxiliary bishop of Boston, said, "Both John Wright and I have turned down going to Rome." John had left on the noon train to work in a boy's camp. However there was the opportunity to discuss the matter with John Wright; and the upshot was that he changed his mind and took off for Rome in October.

Rome was in every sense a delight. As was to continue all his life, John Wright was the person things happened to and he was in the midst of rare occasions. When I visited him in 1938 he had just learned that Pope Pius XI had inquired of all the universities in Rome whether there was a doctoral thesis on nationalism to be defended the following spring. If so he wished it defended in his presence, as he had some remarks to make on that occasion. As it happened, John Wright's thesis, *National Patriotism in Papal Teaching*, was the only such thesis up for defense. He was working very hard at it, among

14

difficulties, because that year he was made acting vice-rector of the North American College.

He answered a phone call early one morning in February to learn that Pope Pius XI had just died. He called the chauffeur and went to the Vatican. Without difficulty he entered the papal apartments where prayers were being said for the deceased Pontiff lying on the bed. There was to be no defense *coram Pontifice*.

However, the defense of his thesis was photographed in cinema with sound track, and for his defense he received *full points*—a straight A. In Rome "he won golden opinions from all sorts of people", to quote Macbeth. Equally golden were the accolades he won for his pastoral work after his ordination in 1935. With the exception of a summer spent in northern England, all the other summers were spent in Corbiac, a village in the Dordogne. The Dordogne is famous throughout France for its truffles, but not for much else. Father Wright stayed at the home of Colonel de Corbiac, and made friendships which lasted until his death. I met the Colonel de Corbiac at London in 1948 with Bishop Wright. He was a man of profound traditional piety, and he spoke of the love that Father Wright had left behind him in France.

In the Dordogne he perfected his French the better to converse and preach, and he pursued an avocation which had been with him since Latin School days—collecting memorabilia concerning Joan of Arc. Over the years his interest and his collection grew, until he was invited to give the panegyric at Orléans, on the anniversary of the lifting of the Siege. This address, *Joan of Arc and the Christian Concept of Personal Vocation*, is published in Volume II. And see also R. Stephen Almagno, "Entrevue avec le Cardinal John J. Wright relative au don de sa collection johannique à la Bibliothèque publique de Boston," *Bulletin de la Société des Amis du Vieux Chinon*, (1977): 17–22.

But it was time now to return to Boston. As rector of the seminary I had requested Father Wright as a member of our faculty. There was, however, another request for his services which might be hard to overlook. Bishop Spellman, the auxiliary, asked for his services in Sacred Heart Church, Newton, where he was pastor. All things worked out for the good, however, since Bishop Spellman was named archbishop of New York several months before Father Wright's return. He was assigned to teach logic to the students in junior-year Philosophy. Now, logic tends toward a certain dullness, and I recalled how surprised I was that each time I passed Father Wright's classroom, his students were laughing. I said to myself that there is a good pedagogue, and wondered why I got no laughs from Psychology.

Father Wright was homesick for Rome. I recall speaking to him once about Rome and he said: "That is far away and long ago." My reply was: "You were there less than three months ago."

As if to breathe again the air of Italy, he spent hundreds of hours in the North End of Boston. In a few days, I shall start to reassemble a crèche he bought for my mother in his first year as a professor—bought in the North End and lugged to Brighton by trolley, for Cardinal Wright never learned to drive a car. He began to give talks on the flowers of Rome, the shrines of Rome, the smells of Rome, and so on. Within a very short time he became a speaker in great demand. His *romanità* was always in evidence.

There was one task which he found unrewarding, and to which he had to be pushed. That was the publication of his thesis, which had an historic value by reason of the Second World War then raging. It was finally completed and, unlike most, was published, by the Newman Press, Westminster, Maryland, in 1942, with second and third reprints in 1943 and 1956. On the occasion of Cardinal O'Connell's funeral, a few years later, I presented the faculty of Saint John's Seminary to the Apostolic Delegate. He shook hands with each one, uttered a pleasant phrase and shook hands with the next. He had done

16

this with Father Wright, when I interrupted to mention that his thesis had just been published. "Oh, the book!" said Archbishop Cicognani, and took Father Wright into the corner of the dining room for a five-minute conversation. All Wright would say afterward was: "That was a good idea, having the thesis published."

Within a year he was assistant chaplain to the League of Catholic Women, and in a few more years became their chaplain. His time in Boston were the golden years for the League, all the older members attest. I am pleased that two of his major addresses to the League—*Christendom and Heresy* (May 15, 1946) and *The Holy Father's Historic Appeal to Women* (delivered several times during 1946)—are included in this volume.

I have been asked to say something about his family, who were always loyal and supportive of every endeavor. His parents were the salt of the earth. And his mother, in particular, had a dynamism which he inherited. There is a phrase that he and I often bandied back and forth: "Leave the best unsaid."

When it came time for Father Wright to leave the seminary he had two filing cabinets—each with four drawers—filled with nothing but thanks and praises for his sermons, talks, and spiritual direction. This is the true encomium on his seminary years.

On September 14, 1943, Monsignor Jeremiah F. Minihan was named chancellor of the archdiocese of Boston. He had been for the previous twelve years secretary to Cardinal O'Connell. In his place Father Wright was named, and acted as secretary until the following April when Cardinal O'Connell died. During these months Monsignor Minihan continued to live at the archbishop's house, while Father Wright moved to a suite in the chancery. It was an obvious wrench for him to leave the seminary and the continued intellectual stimulus which the faculty and the students provided. However, he was soon at home in his new post, taking care of the mail with the

Cardinal each morning, and accompanying him on a two-hour walk each afternoon. His evenings and weekends were free, due to Monsignor Minihan's presence with the Cardinal. This gave him time for his intellectual interests and for speaking and preaching. Many of his best efforts of this period will never see publication—outlined as they were on the back of an envelope or some such. His command of vocabulary, and his skill at English grammar, honed through debate and classroom teaching, put forward his thoughts in admirable array.

On April 21, 1944, Cardinal O'Connell died after a brief illness, at the age of eighty-four. The Consultors of the Archdiocese a few hours later selected Bishop Richard J. Cushing as administrator of the archdiocese, until a new archbishop should be chosen. The new administrator continued Father Wright in his post, and invited him to live in the archbishop's house. Thus began a collaboration which was to last for many years—speeches delivered by Cushing, but with the bred inflections of Wright. One of these, *I Belong Here*, delivered before the National Convention of the Congress of Industrial Organizations, was reprinted by the labor union in more than a million copies. This collaboration continued during the Worcester years and, in lesser fashion, during the Pittsburgh years.

Father, later Monsignor, Wright continued to speak and preach everywhere; and in this he was encouraged by the new Archbishop. Once, preaching at Saint James' Church, in downtown Boston, on civic virtue, he offered as an example a local politician who had recently declared: "Sure, I'll take a buck." After Mass, the same politician—who had been in the congregation—confronted him in the sacristy to state that he was about to complain to the archbishop. Father Wright replied that he would not wish to work for a superior who would reprimand him for preaching as he had.

After only a few years as auxiliary bishop, Louis F. Kelleher died suddenly, and Monsignor Wright was appointed to the post.

Cardinal Cushing was open in his admiration of his new Auxiliary Bishop. They shared much of the same Boston background, but were of very diverse personalities. Nonetheless they were drawn to each other and remained friends until Cardinal Wright was able to perform the last good offices of the eulogy at Cardinal Cushing's funeral.

During his period as auxiliary bishop, Cardinal Wright began his patronage of many activities in which he was to interest himself for many years. For example, the day following his ordination as bishop, there was a national meeting at Saint John's Seminary of priests and lay people interested in Catholic Action. The new Bishop spent the whole day and into the evening with them. He became the National Moderator of the Laywomen's Retreat Movement concerning which after a few years he gave an annual report at the meeting of the American bishops. He started the practice, which continued in his Worcester years, of giving a Day of Recollection to the students of Saint John's Seminary on the day before Christmas.

Cardinal Cushing had made a practice, even as Auxiliary Bishop, of informally greeting everyone in the church at times of Confirmation. Bishop Wright carried on this practice, making himself known to parishioners everywhere, and drawing closer to the clergy who already knew him.

His knowledge of the archdiocese made it natural for him to become a species of Vicar General, without the title. From his office in the chancery went forth admonitions of justice, of appointment, and though they were signed only "Auxiliary Bishop" no one questioned their authority, least of all the Chancellor, an old seminary colleague. His office and his heart were open to all, and it was with a profound sense of loss that Boston learned in 1950 that Bishop Wright was to be the ordinary of the new Diocese of Worcester.

In addition to his work as priest and bishop, John Wright became what no bishop since the early days of Cardinal O'Connell had managed to be. He was adopted and loved by Establishment Boston. He early became involved in the work of the Boston Athenaeum and in his mid-thirties was named a Fellow of the American Academy of Arts and Sciences. He frankly admitted to pleasure at being mentioned as "another Cheverus"—the first bishop of Boston who was so universally loved that when he was summoned back to France to become bishop of Montauban (and later cardinal archbishop of Bordeaux) a hundred and fifty Protestant Bostonians signed a petition to have him remain. See, in this regard, John Wright's address: *Channing and Cheverus*, published in "The Worcester Years" section of this volume. When a few years before he died, Cardinal Wright gave his magnificent collection of Joan of Arc books and artifacts to the Boston Public Library, he was shown the room where they would be displayed and he asked that it be called the Cheverus Room. See R. Stephen Almagno, *Cardinal John Joseph Wright the Bibliophile* (Pittsburgh: The Pittsburgh Bibliophiles, 1980).

He loved Boston next to Rome. One of the most difficult weeks of his life was when he had to decide whether to accept the proffered archbishopric of Boston, and felt, for reasons with which I did not agree, that he must say no. He was proud of Boston and her history and he never doubted but that his last repose should be where it is—in Boston.

Edward G. Murray

I

The Religious Inspiration of Massachusetts Law

Each year this votive act of adoration brings to the altar of the living God the representatives of our judiciary, and unites them in spiritual fellowship with those who, across the ages, have called down the blessing of the Almighty on the evolution of our law in the universities and halls of justice of Bologna, Paris, and Oxford, and in the London Inns of Court. You do well so to associate yourselves with these holy men who, out of the past, still bow with you before their God and yours, and answer, I have no doubt, their devout "Amen" to the prayer for you intoned at this altar these few moments ago: "Deus qui corda fidelium—Father, you taught the hearts of your faithful people by sending them the light of your Holy Spirit. In that Spirit give us right judgment and the joy of His comfort and guidance."[1]

You need, as did they who centuries ago first planned this Votive Mass, the guidance of the Holy Spirit of God. But it is no less true that in a very literal sense God needs you. God works through secondary causes. It is by men, not angels, that the kingdom of God is brought to pass on earth. Wherever the truth is made manifest and by whatever man, wherever the good is vindicated and in whatever cause, wherever the beautiful is brought to perfection whoever be the worker, there God Himself is at work. "Now there are varieties of gifts, but the same God, who works all things in all . . . and all these things are the work of one and the same Spirit."[2]

The gifts which your vocation requires of you and the

This sermon was preached at the Church of the Immaculate Conception, Boston, Massachusetts, on October 9, 1943, on the occasion of the Third Red Mass in New England.

21

works you do are so close to those of God Himself as to give them some adumbration, however faint, of the divine Majesty and awesomeness. You are the wielders, in varying degrees of sovereignty; you interpret and apply, you bind under and loose from, the positive civil law which is the codification in this Commonwealth, and as God has given us to achieve it, of that natural law which the Creator has implanted in the innermost hearts of men. The authority you wield belongs so intimately to God that Bossuet could call those who hold authority and administer the law men like unto God. You attain your offices and commissions by democratic election or by duly prescribed appointment; you are answerable to those who designate or elect you. But your sovereignty is still of God; there is no true authority which is not divine, no trust which is not sacred, no stewardship which is not answerable ultimately to God.

In a democracy those who hold divine authority, for however brief a time, are responsible to God for the liberties of the people whom they rule. Liberty, no less than authority, is a divine perfection. Indeed, perfect liberty is proper to God alone for only in God does there exist, in absolute degree, that self-dominion which is implied in all liberty. The mastery which in God makes perfect His liberty is identified with the divine sovereignty—and so in God freedom and sovereignty, liberty and authority are flawlessly integrated, wonderfully harmonized. Among men, however, mastery whether of self or of society is never complete and never without challenge, and so freedom among men is never perfect. Among men authority, too, is always shaded with imperfection; it is frequently suspect and sometimes defied. Liberty and authority, so perfectly reconciled in God, are, even among men, correlative attributes. But in point of historical fact there usually exists in all forms of society a disturbing tension between the claims of authority and the pursuits of liberty.

Our fathers in this Commonwealth of Massachusetts knew

that the divine attributes of liberty and authority, analogously present among men, could only be reconciled in our topsy-turvy world if God Himself would somehow work among us unto their reconciliation. Our fathers did not believe that it is enough for God to be in His Heaven in order that all be well with the world. They knew that Heaven and earth must work together if the earth is ever to achieve something, at least, of the order which prevails in Heaven, and if the sons of men are finally to win the freedom of the sons of God.

Our forefathers, for reasons of prudent realism, provided in their constitutions for the separation of the organized Church and the organized State; but their idealism, even in temporal matters, was nonetheless informed and inspired by the Judaeo-Christian tradition, and especially by the Revelation transmitted by the Church; and so there is reflected in the wise laws which they wrote for the preservation of liberty and authority alike a blend of the divine and the human, a happy medley of the hopes of earth and the will of Heaven.

The men who made this Commonwealth realized that in God's holy Providence all society, religious and civil alike, and all legal traditions, both of authority and of liberty, exist for the perfection of human personality. They would have understood the magnificent implications of the doctrine which our late Holy Father Pope Pius XI so wonderfully summarized: "It is therefore according to the dictates of reason that ultimately all material things should be ordained to man as a person, that through his mediation they may find their way to the Creator. In this wise we can apply to man, the human person, the words of the Apostle . . . 'all things are yours, and you are Christ's and Christ is God's.' "[3]

Hence the obligation, clear from Reason and confirmed by Revelation, for the law to weigh all things in the scale that measures their effects on human personality. The celebrated *Declaration of the Rights of Man*, despite its debatable premises and its lamentable omissions, enunciated at least one proposition

23

that, so far as it goes, is beyond dispute, namely that ignorance of and contempt for the rights of man are the chief causes of public evils and the corruption of governments.[4]

The men who wrote the laws of our Bay State were not thus ignorant nor thus contemptuous. Our legal tradition so respects human personality that even before a child is born our state is consecrated to protecting his human rights, his right to life, his right to be born; even, in accordance with the famous decision of a century ago, his right to inherit; indeed, the rights of the unborn child are sacred to our state under a double title: they are the rights of a human, and of a human incapable of pleading his own right, and therefore with a greater claim, not a lesser, on the protection of the state as our fathers understood it.[5] The law's insistence on the right of a child to be born has demanded, in our medical and moral tradition, certain acts of heroism which many in our day profess to find superhuman; but our forefathers considered heroism to be a duty when there is question of the inviolable rights of human personality.

The child is not born immediately into civil society. Logically, at least, he enters that society, as our forefathers understood it, through the medium of his parents, or more precisely, through his family. In the Massachusetts tradition of law the family is the elementary social unit; for our forefathers democracy meant a plurality of families, cooperating by consent, for the collective protection and promotion of those God-given natural rights which the family by itself might be powerless to secure for the individual person. But democracy meant, even more, sovereignty of the family in its own essential work of the rearing of children.

The development of the child's faculties, the formation and refinement of his character, his initiation to the requirements and the discipline of existence in society—all these are the work of the family, and no agency could supplant the parent, our fathers considered, in these works. The consequent amount of legislation in our state protecting the right of the parent over the child is impressively large. Our forefathers followed Blackstone in his suggestion that the positive precepts of the law should correspond accurately to a natural necessity decreed by that divine Providence which has provided for the welfare of children, as never could the state, by implanting in the breast of every parent an insuperable affection, more imperious than any written law, and which not even the wickedness, ingratitude, and rebellion of children can totally suppress or extinguish.[6]

And so, Massachusetts always has recognized that the normal family is, in its own way, sovereign; only the abnormal inadequacy of a particular family places its members within the competency of our courts. Even then, whenever possible, it is the tradition of our state to do all that artifice can do to supply the defects of Nature by providing the homeless child with the nearest possible approach to a family life and training. Our state was the first in the Union to provide legislation which abolished, as far as possible, public institutional and *wholesale* bringing up of children. Our state preferred the plan of foster homes where foster parents could in some degree supply for natural parents in the training, within a family, of the human person.

The noble concept in our law of the central position and the sanctity of the family is further and emphatically reflected in our marriage legislation. Decry as we may the spread of divorce in our Commonwealth, decry as we must the factitious efforts so frequently made to condone divorce under the law, the men who made our Massachusetts judicial tradition are not responsible for these unhappy conditions.

Our forefathers recognized the ends and the purposes of matrimony; they considered it the creative cause of the social unit, the family. Mr. Justice De Courcey, of the Supreme Judicial Court of Massachusetts, interpreted the tradition of our forefathers concerning the special dignity of the marriage contract in these rational and exalted words: "By the law of this Commonwealth marriage is regarded as more than a civil contract. After cohabitation, at least, it ripens into a status which affects the parties thereto, their posterity and the whole community . . . it is a change which, for important reasons, the law recognizes, and it inaugurates conditions and relations which the law takes under its protection."[7]

In an earlier case, authoritatively described by Mr. Justice De Courcey as a basic case in Massachusetts jurisprudence, Mr. Justice Bigelow used no uncertain language. He said: "The law, in the exercise of a wise and sound policy, seeks to render the contract of marriage, when once executed, as far as possible indissoluble. The great object of marriage in a civilized and Christian community, is to secure the existence and permanence of the family relation, and to ensure the legitimacy of offspring. It would tend to defeat this object if error or disappointment with personal qualities or character were allowed to be the basis of proceedings on which to found a dissolution of the marriage tie."[8]

For the strength of the state, for the sake of the child, and in order to guard his personal right to a home, our forefathers legislated in such wise as to protect the family as the school where personality comes to perfection. Inevitably, however, there comes that day when his parents must delegate to others, usually outside the home, the specialized work of providing the child with the knowledge to which our law recognizes his strict right. In our Commonwealth this further and specialized work of education is done in schools, public and private, which are universally esteemed.

Our fathers in the Bay State possessed an extraordinary appreciation of the manner in which the power of education to perfect personality makes education the right of every person. In our state constitution they wrote, in homely and historic words, their shrewd reasoning: "Wisdom and knowledge, as well as virtue diffused generally among the body of people, being necessary for the preservation of their rights and liberties

26

. . . it shall be the duty of legislatures and magistrates, in all future periods of this Commonwealth, to cherish the interests of literature and the sciences, and all seminaries of them . . . to encourage private societies and public institutions, rewards and immunities, for the promotion of agriculture, arts, sciences, and a natural history of the country; to countenance and inculcate the principles of humanity and general benevolence, public and private charity, industry and frugality, honesty and punctuality in their dealings, sincerity, goodhumor and all social affections and generous sentiments, among the people."[9]

Archaic phrases, these, and redolent of a more placid age, but God save this Commonwealth when it pursues educational objectives contrary to this constitutional directive and the ideals, human and Christian, which inspired it. Despite all the considerations of public welfare which dictated the phrasing of this article in our constitution, note with what care our fathers, by insistence on the possibility and privileges of private schools, protected the prior rights of the family, of the parent over the child, and of the individual person.

Once in our land, though outside our Commonwealth, these rights were challenged, and it became necessary for the United States Supreme Court to rule in protection of educational and family rights which our Commonwealth not merely respects, but sedulously defends. In the so-called *Oregon* case the Court spoke in words which our forefathers needed never to be told. It said: "The fundamental theory of liberty, upon which all governments in this Union repose, excludes any general power of the state to standardize its children by forcing them to accept instruction from public teachers only. The child is not the mere creature of the state; those who nurture him and direct his destiny have the right, coupled with the high duty, to recognize and prepare him for additional obligations."[10]

The graduate from our schools finds himself protected on every hand by the legislation which our forefathers wrote to

27

guarantee his right to choose his own work, to contract at will for payment, to acquire property and otherwise to enjoy the fruits of his toil. If these personal rights be struck down or arbitrarily interfered with, there is a substantial impairment of liberty in its long-established constitutional sense.

Something of that sense, as our forefathers understood it, is expounded by Mr. Justice McReynolds in a classic decision interpreting, among other things, the constitutional understanding of personal liberty. He said: "Without doubt, it denotes not merely freedom from bodily restraint, but also the right to engage in any of the common occupations of life, to acquire useful knowledge, to marry, establish a home and bring up children, to worship God according to the dictates of his own conscience, and, generally, to enjoy those privileges long recognized by common law as essential to the orderly pursuit of happiness by free men."[11]

This is a decision in the letter and spirit of the legislative tradition in which your predecessors in this Commonwealth wrote. Behind that tradition is the testimony of human reason in its highest moments and the racial remembrance, at least, of the revelation which God made to Israel of old through the prophets, and which He perfected in the teachings of Jesus Christ. No one can read these cases and fail to recognize that the men who wrote our law were the products of a tradition of religious faith, a tradition whose genealogy goes back through the great Scholastics, to the Fathers of the Church, to the Mount of the Beatitudes, and to the heights of Sinai. The law of this Commonwealth, as our forefathers wrote it and as our courts have transmitted it, is Christian in its inspiration and in its letter.

The United States Supreme Court, speaking by Mr. Justice Brewer, has permitted itself to declare in remarkably direct terms the religious, indeed, the organized Christian character of the American tradition. The Court said: "If we pass beyond these matters to a view of American life as expressed by its

28

laws, its business, its customs, and its society, we find everywhere a clear recognition of the same truth. Among other
matters note the following: The form of oath universally
prevailing, concluding with an appeal to the Almighty; the
custom of opening sessions of all deliberative bodies with
prayer; the prefatory words of all wills, 'In the name of God,
Amen'; the laws respecting the observance of the Sabbath,
with a general cessation of secular business, and the closing of
courts, legislatures, and other similar public assemblies on that
day; the churches and church organizations which abound in
every city, town, and hamlet; the multitude of charitable
organizations existing everywhere under Christian auspices
. . . these and many other matters which might be noticed add
a volume of unofficial declarations to the mass of formal
utterances that this is a Christian nation."[12]

So far the words of the Court; nor is their import obscure.
Without prejudice to the strict religious tolerance that obtains
for all faiths, without disparagement of the notable influence
on our national life of the devout members of other faiths, this
nation is in its law and its life a Christian nation; the traditional
habits of mind and attitudes of our people, as well as their
institutions and laws, are those which have been developed
under the dominance of the Christian faith, embryonic in the
promises made to Israel, born together with the Church on
Pentecost two thousand years ago, and coming to maturity
with a strength so vital that it communicated itself to the
cultures of those peoples who once made Europe great and
America possible.

Nowhere is the Christian character of our nation better
typified than here in Massachusetts. The men who most
contributed to the early building of our state subscribed to a
theology which the ancient faith was bound to eschew as
heretical; they preached certain moral conventions which their
own sons and daughters have felt free to relax as excessively
austere. But lament as one may their dogma and fret as one

may at their restraints, for this may their names never die: The men who wrote our law feared God, and they were resolved never to fear any man.

They feared God with a holy and a wholesome fear, and because they did, they wrote into the Preamble of the constitution of this state devout words of homage to their Creator, a recognition of their dependence on Him, and a prayer for His direction in the mighty task of building here their Commonwealth. They feared God, and so they did not talk glibly of a freedom to worship God, a freedom which they had no intention of exercising or implementing. Rather, they wrote in the Second Article of their constitution words of right and duty: "It is the right as well as the duty of all men in society publicly and at stated seasons to worship the Supreme Being the great Creator and Preserver of the universe. . . ."[13]

But they were resolved to be in no necessity of ever fearing man, and so they wrote into the Thirtieth Article of the state constitution their high resolve that this was to be a government of laws, not of men—of objective, constitutional statutes not subjective, arbitrary impulses, however high-minded, however immediately beneficial. They resolved that the moods and passions of the people must never be permitted to overthrow the institutions which represent their own deliberate development and their own deepest convictions. Our written laws, basic among them our constitution as interpreted by the judiciary, constitute at once the fruit of our deepest convictions and the safeguard of their survival. And these objective, constitutional controls our forefathers committed to the judiciary—to you. By your oath you are bound to preserve them.

It was an act of almost superhuman prudence so to place in the hands of judges the security of our liberties. Elsewhere, even in constitutional governments, the judicial power is invariably subordinate to the legislative. Even in England, as Chief Justice Taney once remarked, the courts are bound to enforce the acts of Parliament, even should they believe them to conflict with the Magna Charta or the Petition of Rights. But our forefathers built more wisely; they acknowledged in the executive and legislative branches of government only those powers specifically delegated to them in the constitution. Many of these men had long since ceased, for reasons of sad history, to catch the overtones of divine authority in the pronouncements of the Roman Pontiff; but all of them, I think, would have endorsed with full understanding the declaration broadcast recently from the Vatican, a declaration directed primarily, of course, against the dictatorships of the moment, but setting forth a principle inconsistent with all arbitrary and totalitarian government. The Pope, said this broadcast, indicts attempts to subordinate juridical and leg-islative activities to the requirements of particular groups, classes or movements, as these must be subordinated only to the establishment of justice and to the service of society as a whole. . . . The Pope condemns those who dare to place the fortunes of whole nations in the hands of one man alone, a man who as such is the prey of passions, errors and dreams. . . . It is essential that a preestablished set of laws be placed above the governor and the governed alike, far outside the reach of arbitrary action.

Mindful of such salutary truths, our forefathers providently empowered their courts to test, in accordance with well-settled and familiar principles of law and equity, every demand for further power, for political action, for departure from tradition made by any executive, however wise or however popular, or by any legislature, however capable or however representative. Through their courts, as our forefathers constituted them, the American people themselves protect themselves against them-selves. Our courts represent, as one critic has said, the settled habits of thought and action of our people. An executive might easily be influenced powerfully by the disillusionment or the dreams of the moment; he might be deluded by the siren

31

song of the elusive future and forget the warning voice of the sane past. A Congress might be stampeded by a madcap outcry, and even a majority might be found to demand crude and cruel legislation.

And so our forefathers looked to the judiciary to decide whether a popular and passing whim has resulted in political action which contradicts the constitutional guarantees of personal liberty and political security. If so, even the majority must withdraw its demand, or give its apparent wish the time for patient meditation and cautious procedure required in order to revise the Constitution. But to override the Constitution, to despise the tradition—this would be revolution, and our forefathers, though they might and did revolt against men, permitted no revolution against the law. For them no political dream could be so dazzling, no social need so urgent, no executive so capable, no majority so overwhelming, that our forefathers would permit any or all of these to put aside the codified tradition of the Constitution and its authentic interpretation. That is what the men of Massachusetts meant when they planned a government of laws, not of men.

These prudent provisions were typical expressions of the shrewd conservatism of New England men, a conservatism sometimes gently mocked, sometimes bitterly derided, but a conservatism for which this nation has more than once had cause to bless New England. Thanks to it our forefathers accumulated in the corner of the world committed to their care a cultural and political heritage well worth conserving, so well worth it that all subsequent peoples who came here, however otherwise they may have differed from the original colonists, speedily acquired, as with the air they breathed, the typical conservatism of this Commonwealth. It is not a static, reactionary mold of mind; it is a dynamic conservatism, the result of enlightened convictions, a conservatism bent on losing nothing of the good which the past has preserved for us, and resolved to add to that good in transmitting it to those who, please God, may build a better future.

The conservatism of our forefathers was not designed to enslave us in the name of the past, but was calculated to save us from enslavement in the name of the future. It recognized that hard-won liberties can be speedily lost under the seduction of easily promised future freedoms, that the God-given heritage of the past and the sacred liberties of the present can be sacrificed in the name of a future which may never be, which perhaps were better not.

The conservatism of our forefathers is particularly saving in time of crisis; it reminds us that there will be, when the tumult and the shouting dies, no new heaven and no new earth. It reminds us that the citizens of the brave new world-to-be will still be men, not gods. It reminds us that any future world can only be built out of whatever good survives from the old. It warns us never to hold lightly the good which our forefathers built so patiently here in this Commonwealth; never to gamble with the liberties which are the heart and soul of that good; never to permit the religious faith to grow cold which taught us those liberties; never to forget the blessings on this Commonwealth by which Almighty God has confirmed the wisdom of those who, building it, honored Him and His chief creature, the human person.

Yet even in our land are sometimes heard the voices of new prophets who spread a teaching forgetful of our fathers' God and of their reverence for the dignity of the human person. These new teachers write their laws without reference to God and, ignorant of His Scripture with its warning that we put not our trust in princes, they propose, sooner or later, a government of men, not laws. They talk little of the family, less of the sovereignty of parents, and not at all of the dignity of personality. They speak rather of race, of tribe, of class-consciousness, of nationalism. They hold in contempt or violently assail the earthly beginnings of the Kingdom of God, and they boast of their readiness to build, without the help of Heaven, a self-sufficient City of Man. They preach a gospel alien to ours, and dire in portent.

It may be that you do not always discern the blessing of God on the faith of our fathers. But if you doubt the wrath of God on those who thus propose to forget that faith and to desert its social corollaries, then I invite you to advert once more to the military, economic, and political preoccupations which you left behind you at the doors of this church and to which too soon you must return.

No defense of Christianity and of the values which it taught our forefathers could be more effective than the present straits to which these new prophets, contemptuous of the faith, have reduced the world. Should contemplation of the disasters which infidelity to God and to the Law has released upon us dishearten you in your effort to cleave to the ancient traditions of our people, know that as God was with our fathers, so will He be with us. Take heart from the memory of how our forefathers made possible the fulfillment, on these New England shores, of the prophetic word of the Psalmist: "Blessed are the people whose God is their Lord."[14] Learn from the history of this Commonwealth and never forget it, that for those who love God all things work together unto good.[15]

The Diocesan Priesthood

On the Feast of Corpus Christi, twenty-five years ago today, a bishop long since dead raised to the holy priesthood more than a score of young men who sought to serve the Church of Christ in the archdiocese of Boston. One of those young men is the priest with whom today we join in jubilee, a man of God to whom so many present here this morning owe countless contacts with Divinity, from the initial contact by which the Divine life is begotten in us at Baptism through all the wondrous system of sacraments by which we are kept close to Christ, or brought back to Him, during all the years of our lives.

We say that on this day a quarter century ago the Church gained twenty-six new priests. Yet, in a very fundamental sense, when we speak thus we speak inaccurately. There is but one priest of the New Law, and He is Jesus, the Christ. All priesthood is in its essence a share in the single and unique priesthood of Christ, a participation in His vocation, a perpetuation of His mission. There is but one priesthood, the priesthood that Christ Jesus exercised; and there is but one priest, in any adequate sense—Christ Jesus, High Priest of the New Law.

Pope Pius XI, in the magnificent letter to all priests by which he commemorated the jubilee of his own ordination, reminds us that in every nation, pagan and Christian alike, there has always existed a priesthood.[1] There have always been men apart, men held in special esteem by the people and striving to

This sermon was preached at the Church of Our Lady of the Presentation, Brighton, Massachusetts, on June 3, 1945, on the occasion of the twenty-fifth anniversary of the ordination of the Reverend Daniel J. Donovan.

accomplish the natural desire of mankind to bring human things within the compass of things divine and to bridge the chasm between men and their Maker. Jesus Christ, precisely because He is at once God and Man, is equally at home in Heaven and on earth; He is the sole figure in human history qualified to fulfill literally the office of *pontifex*, of bridgebuilder 'twixt heaven and earth, which is the essence of the priestly office. Christ is the only priest of the Christian Church because by His Incarnation He brought into human affairs the fullness of Divinity and by His redemptive death He offered a sacrifice capable of being offered on earth, yet worthy of being received in Heaven.

Christ, then, is the perfect priest Whom the men and the nations of all places and all times awaited. He was darkly present in all their temples, and whatever offerings the clean of heart once made in the ancient temples of Italy, of Greece, of the Druids, or of the Orient—these offerings were entrusted to Christ, though He was unknown by name to those who prayed. Whoever, in all the history of human craving after love, has craved a love higher than human, has craved Christ; whoever sought truth higher than reason, sought Christ; whoever hungered after life more perfect than nature, hungered after Christ; whoever prayed for peace, prayed for Christ. Wherever any man, in his desire for these blessings, sought the ministrations of his priests, that man bore witness to the need of himself and of mankind for the priesthood, the unique and the perfect priesthood of Jesus Christ. Christ is our only priest, and all priesthood is His.

So Father Donovan, whom all these years we have loved and venerated as our priest, is not a priest as Christ is a priest. Saint Paul perfectly describes and places all our priests, and conspicuously our beloved jubilarian, when he calls them *ministros Christi et dispensatores mysteriorum Dei*—"servants of Christ and stewards of the mysteries of God."[2] Through all the years of his clerical career, from tonsure when first he

36

entered the seminary to the day of his ordination and through all the years since, that is all Father Donovan has been, or, say better, he has been all that, for the servant of a king is himself a king and the steward of a God himself does things divine. Any supernatural power which Father has wielded, any supernatural character that he has possessed, to the extent that it is truly supernatural is not his; it is Christ's. It abides in him only because he is somehow identified with the priesthood of Christ.

When first he entered the seminary, the clipping of his hair at tonsure made him share Christ's demarcation from the world. Later, in the office of porter he was given symbolic charge over the doors of Christ's church. In the lectorate he came to share something of the authority with which Christ on one unforgettable morning rose up to read the lesson from the prophet in the synagogue and with the accents of conscious divinity applied to Himself the words of the lesson of that day: "The spirit of the Lord is upon me, wherefore He hath anointed me to preach the gospel to the poor, He hath sent me to heal the contrite of heart, to preach deliverance to the captives, and sight to the blind, to set at liberty them that are bruised, to preach the acceptable year of the Lord, and the day of reward."[3]

And so all along the line to priesthood and since, Father Donovan's dignity, his office, his work, his grace, have never been his, but always Christ's. Baptizing, absolving, preaching, consoling, guiding, blessing, and consecrating—it has been his hands, his words, his lips, his gentleness, his tact, his kindness, his zeal—but Christ's power, Christ's priesthood, Christ's harvest. He had gladly lost himself in the priesthood of Christ, but, so losing himself, what dignity has become his!

The dignity of the Catholic priesthood is not the dignity of the professional class; it is the dignity of the Son of God, the heir of all the ages. The virtue of the Catholic priesthood is not the fragile virtue of all-too-human men; it is the virtue of the Spotless Lamb. The authority of our priesthood is not the

37

dubious authority of specially trained men; it is the authority of the Word of God, the Word that was in the beginning and that is God.[4] Father Donovan has brought to thousands in this quarter century the sublimity, the virtue, and the authority of this Catholic priesthood, the priesthood of Jesus Christ.

He has done so in the special vocation of the diocesan priest. This priestly vocation, the vocation to serve a diocese in obedience to a bishop, has a dignity all its own. Its apostolate is permanent and never-changing, as the essential needs of men for Christ's priesthood are unchanging. The great religious orders, with their particular vocations, come into existence in response to the peculiar needs of certain epochs and certain places; history bears witness that they dissolve and disappear when the need which first brought them into being itself no longer exists. The diocesan priest must meet the general needs of all the faithful and at all times. He is not the son of Saint Ignatius, but, like Father Donovan through all the years of his priesthood and especially, in his case, during the first seven years of his service, he must have all the soldierly obedience of the Jesuit and a readiness to swallow his pride for the sake of objectives higher than himself. He is not the son of Saint Francis, but, like Father Donovan wherever he has been stationed and especially here in Brighton with his clubs, his scouts, and his constant activities in this parish, he must be possessed of the genial joy that comes of a priestly heart unfreighted with the vulgar baggage of place and property and preferment. He is not the son of Saint Benedict, not of Saint Bernard, nor of any other of the great founders of priestly communities, but he must always find his companionship in the fraternity of his fellow-priests and share the community of their burdens, as Father Donovan has wonderfully done, officially as the scrupulously conscientious administrator of another man's parish and personally as the confidant and secret strength, as many of us well know, of numerous brother priests. The diocesan priest is not the son of Saint Dominic, but all the love of the Preachers for God's Holy Word must be his as week in, week out, he preaches the law of the Gospel and tries to remember, in daily contact with his people, what Father Donovan has never forgotten: The voice which penetrates the hearts of the hearers is the voice commended by the speaker's own life; because what his word enjoins, his example helps to bring about. The diocesan priest is not the son of Maryknoll, but all the apostolic spirit and all the zeal for souls of the missionary orders must be his, as it has been Father Donovan's from the beginnings of his priesthood to the day when he gave up a parish of his own in order to consecrate himself to his present apostolate of building up in this diocese devotion to the Holy Name of Jesus and preparing here at home a Holy Name Organization which will be ready to re-teach reverence and reconstruct the pattern of the gentle Christ in the hearts of our returning servicemen.

Such a priest, such a secular priest, is the son of the universal apostles, and Saint Paul called these the glory of Christ: "apostoli ecclesiarum gloria Christi."[5] He is constituted a priest by his obedience to the apostles in their successors, the bishops. It is by his obedience that he becomes assimilated to the priesthood of Christ, as it was by Christ's obedience that He became Himself a priest.

Christ is a priest only as Man, not as God. His glory as a priest comes not from His Divinity but from the sublimity of His human obedience. "Christ became obedient for us even unto death," writes Saint Paul, "wherefore God hath exalted Him."[6] His glory is born of His obedience. His priestly name, Jesus the Christ, is given Him, a name above all names, precisely because He was obedient.[7]

So your name, O priest of Jesus Christ, was given you by the bishop who ordained you not for your merits nor for your grace, but in exchange for your promise of obedience. Remember that day a quarter of a century ago, the bishop permitted you to rise from your knees only when he had asked: "Dost thou promise to the bishop, thy ordinary, and to his successors, reverence and obedience?" and you had answered with a promise which you have kept, kept with a fidelity to which all your brother priests this day pay tribute through the lips of a younger priest who is grateful for the inspiration of your mature example.[8]

By the act of your will by which you became one with Christ in loving obedience to Him and to His Church, your human personality became veiled before the eyes of men and even those of God. In you during these twenty-five years of your priesthood, in you henceforth forever, God sees no longer a man pleading before Him, but His own Son, the co-sharer of His own nature. To His altar you daily bring bread and wine, but God still sees the Upper Room and hears His Christ blessing these species: This is My Body! This is My Blood! Daily you pray in union with the universal Church in the recitation of the Divine Office, but the prayer that God hears is that of His Son, for every psalm and every petition proclaims Him and recalls His mercy. From the pulpit you preach, and the accent is yours and all the style, but God, listening to you, hears the voice of His own Son, our only Teacher, the Master, Christ. All your life you work (and you have always prayed that the work would be hard!) so that when your priestly apprenticeship on earth is done God may find in the palms of your human hands the traces of Christ's work divinely done.

Then if in joy you come to Him finally with a lifelong priesthood manifestly fruitful in triumphs won for Christ, God will see you resplendent with a glory happily not yours alone, for the Creator of Light is not dazzled by the brilliance of any creature, but rather Christ's, the Light of His own light, *lumen de lumine*.[9] And if, mayhap, you come to Him somehow defeated, beaten, or betrayed in all that you strove to do to bring His Kingdom to pass on earth, then you may still lift your confident gaze to Him, for He will see in your eyes, since you are one with Christ, the blended tears of two: yours and those of His Son!

So, today, in the maturity of your priesthood, we kneel before you as twenty-five years ago they knelt who first sought the fair, fresh blessing of your priestly hands. We beg of you a place in your memento for the living together with your beloved father, here present to rejoice with you. We join with you in your prayers for your beloved dead, especially for her whose flesh and blood still live at God's altar in you. We pray now, as they did then, that God may prosper all your priestly works and transmute the silver of your human merits into the fine gold of His eternal glory.

III

The Pope and the War

According to last year's newspapers, a Petty Officer of the British Royal Navy, one Albert Penny, was captured by the Italians in August 1940, and interned at Viterbo, forty miles from Rome. A year ago he returned to England with a wondrous tale to tell.

After two years' internment Penny escaped from the Italian concentration camps, purloined a bicycle belonging to some good citizen of Viterbo, and pedaled forth to Rome. Knowing Italy and Italian, he was able to hail passers-by with a cheery "buon giorno", and to nod cordially to occasional Italian soldiers. He spent several days in brazen sightseeing in Rome, and after having thrown a coin into the Trevi Fountain (as must all good tourists who hope to return to Rome), he pedaled across the city to the Vatican State. Acting as if he had always lived there, he passed plain-clothed Italian police and gorgeously adorned Swiss guards, to enter the confines of the Sacred State of the Vatican. Safe inside its walls, he revealed his identity to an astonished British diplomat and to embarrassed prelates who finally arranged his exchange at Lisbon for an Italian sergeant held by the British.

Now back to England, the recollections of the Vatican which Petty Officer Penny has brought to his dominantly Protestant nation are what you might expect. "Of all my adventures," said he to the British press, "the most wonderful was my audience with the Pope. He received me in a small throne room, gave me a rosary for my wife and a silver crucifix for our home. Then he sent me on my way with his blessing."

This address was delivered on June 28, 1945, on the occasion of the fiftieth anniversary of the Quincy Council (no. 96) of the Knights of Columbus.

This news-story provides a sign and a symbol of the place in a world at war of the Vicar of Jesus Christ and of that Vatican City which is his home. As Petty Officer Penny quit the streets of Rome in flight from an enemy nation and crossed Saint Peter's Square, he found himself surrounded by a forest of great columns, the famous colonnades of Bernini, colonnades which stretch out in front of Saint Peter's arm-like to embrace the world. And as he threaded his way through their sheltering quiet, he passed, all unheeding no doubt, under the inscription which proclaims their purpose and makes them symbols of the Holy See itself in time of war. For over each arch of the colonnades appear these words of Isaiah: "And there shall be a tabernacle for a shade in the daytime from the heat, and for a security and covert from the whirlwind, and from the rain."[1]

The case of Officer Penny is not the only symbol since the outbreak of hostilities of this pacific role of the Vatican in time of war. Mr. Herbert Matthews, ace correspondent for the *New York Times*, reported from Rome recently the stories of nineteen other Allied soldiers who in diverse ways found safety as *guests* in the neutral territory of the Holy See during the Nazi occupation of Rome. In that same period, the special character of the Vatican was symbolized as well, indeed even more so, by the advent to the Vatican, with free passage through the streets of the Italian capital, of Mr. Myron Taylor, of the Ambassadors to the Holy See alike of China and Japan, of Great Britain and of Germany, and of the forty other sovereignties, including every political and other alignment, which still are represented at the Holy See.

In all these incidents may be seen a recognition on the part of the world at large, and even on the part of a regime which, we are told, recognizes little else that is lawful, a recognition of the manner in which the Papacy, sovereign in the Sacred City of the Vatican, has created in the modern world something akin to the medieval right of sanctuary, a place where even the most guilty can seek refuge and state their case and where even the most just are forced to recognize some ultimate limit to the prosecution of their claims.

That the Holy See has thus been able to become a place of sanctuary in the world at war, a center of sanity in a world of chaos, should serve as complete justification of the so frequently criticized refusal of the Sovereign Pontiff to espouse completely the cause of either of the alliances between which this dreadful war is being fought. One uses the word *justification* here very reluctantly, and with great reservation. Catholics find it difficult to admit that there is any need for apology, or in that sense *justification*, for the Holy Father's refusal to become a partisan in this or any conflict which involves on both sides, even though in varying proportions, an admixture of truth and error, of good and of evil, of ideals and of intrigues.

In speaking thus, we are guilty of no lack of patriotism, no lack of loyalty to the true cause of our nation and its allies. We are simply facing realities with that humility which keeps due patriotism from becoming nationalism, and true loyalty from becoming arrogant blindness. In this same spirit we must be prepared to find a like reserve, a like detachment, on the part of the Holy See even now that our forces have occupied Rome, a reserve on all political or military matters, broken only if and when the prospect of promoting a true peace justifies anything less than reserve. This detachment is no merely negative moral neutrality; it is dictated by a positive moral obligation, the obligation acknowledged by Pope Pius XII in these Christ-like words pronounced at the height of the war:

"We love—and in this We call upon God to be Our witness—We love with equal affection all peoples, without any exception whatsoever, and in order to avoid even the appearance of being moved by partisanship, We have maintained hitherto the greatest reserve."

The determination of the Holy See to maintain an attitude of neutrality no matter who may be the military authorities actually in control of the city of Rome was stressed in an

44

official statement issued on behalf of the Vatican June 7, just after our troops entered the Eternal City:

> The Holy See from the very beginning of the present war has always maintained an attitude of strict impartiality in regard to the actual armed conflict, remaining outside and above purely material interests and the competitions of contending parties.
>
> Conscious of its universal mission of peace and charity, the Holy See in the exercise of its spiritual ministry left nothing undone to prevent the outbreak of the war not only through its intense diplomatic activity directed to this end but also by solemnly recalling to all nations the eternal and unchanging principles of the moral teachings of Jesus Christ on the basis of which it would not have been difficult to have avoided the conflict and to have found a peaceful solution for the international controversies involved.
>
> With the outbreak of this terrible war which before long spread to all continents, the Holy See employed every means at its disposal to bring relief to all peoples without distinction of nationality or race, from the miseries and sufferings consequent upon the war, seeking to render the conflict less inhuman. . . .
>
> It is the avowed policy of the Holy See to maintain unchanged this attitude of neutrality whoever may be the military authorities actually having control of the City of Rome and it has every confidence that it will be able to continue its spiritual activity in the world through regular and free contacts with its representatives in the various nations and with the episcopacy of the Catholic Church.
>
> It is likewise expected that the efforts of the Holy See to relieve every human misery will suffer no obstruction in their continued development.

In the Axis nations, the independent attitude of the Holy See thus far in the war has been the object of bitter attack; on our own side it has been no less bitterly criticized in certain quarters, and now that we are in possession of Rome the position of the Holy Father may be even more militantly and fiercely assailed.

Who are they who profess not to understand the detachment of the Vicar of Christ from the alliances in the war? Who are they who label this detachment *neutrality* and demand that it be justified? Well, first of all there are some who, preoccupied exclusively with political considerations, fail to recognize that the Holy See is not a contender among the political sovereignties of the world, nor a potential political ally of any one against the others, but holds, in the ancient phrase, the "presidency of charity" amongst men, and seeks objectives independent of and superior to the fortunes of political systems.[2]

Then there are some who with their eyes fixed solely on the maps which chart mere earth and water forget that the Rome of the Popes is not the Rome of the Caesars, far less the mere capital of Italy, youngest of European national states. It is not the property of the people of Rome, certainly not the property of the Axis nations, nor of the Allies. It is the common patrimony of all children of God, of all who have been enrolled by Baptism and supernaturalized by grace as citizens of that true Rome of which Christ Himself is foremost citizen.[3] That Rome is the second fatherland of every Christian heart, and the mother of all the faithful.

How beautiful a thought it is in time of peace—how comforting in time of war!—that as one by one the chanceries and palaces of the political world close their doors to nation after nation and race after race, the Vatican, our Universal Father's House, keeps wide its gates and remains the spiritual home of all who look with loving eyes from the four corners of the earth to the white-clad Vicar of the Universal Christ.

Finally, there are those who fail to understand that Roman Catholicism is not, like Established Anglicanism, for example, or Eastern Orthodoxy, a department of the State within which it finds itself. Neither is it, like Unitarianism and kindred creeds, an aspect of the culture prevailing for a time and a space among a people, and intrinsically bound up with the fortunes, prosperous or perverse, of that culture.

Catholicism is a universal and transcendent faith; in every State, even in its least happy condition, it inevitably eludes the confines within which any political system seeks to imprison it. Even those nations to which the Church gave birth and strength and maturity, she constantly outlives. It is her perennial destiny to watch decline and die and be supplanted cultures to which originally she gave form and spirit. And so the Papacy, as Macaulay so clearly recognized, shares the permanence and universality of the Church. Indeed, in the phrase of Saint Francis de Sales, the Papacy and the Church are one, and the characteristics of Christianity are those of the Pope, including a detachment and supranationalism proper to the religion of Jesus Christ.

So in this war when the Papacy is criticized, when it is said that the Holy See is out of touch with the world of politics, with the world of political realities, and the world of the modern spirit, we have no difficulty in answering. The Church does not exist upon the earth to receive directions from the world of politics and political realities, nor to receive impulses from the modern spirit. The Church exists, in modern times, as in ancient, to refine and to sanctify the spirit of the age, to transmit to men the unvarying impulses of the spirit of God. With the Christ Whose Vicar he is, the Roman Pontiff, oracle of the Church of God, must say in time of war as at all time: "ego cogito cogitationes pacis et non afflictionis—my thoughts are of peace and not of affliction."[4]

In fidelity to these thoughts of peace the Roman See during the Middle Ages saved Europe from the abyss of barbarism. In fidelity to these thoughts of peace the Roman See fostered understanding among the most widely separated and most hostile nations and created the unity that for a thousand years was Christendom. In fidelity to these thoughts of peace today, while every other institution in the world plots war and takes sides in war, the Holy See serves as the safeguard of the things which pertain to peace, and refuses to take any side, however

47

justified, so long as taking sides might limit her work for peace.

In an age of nationalism such a vocation becomes extraordinarily difficult to fulfill. A foreign writer has eloquently described how the Church as bride, as mystical body of the Prince of Peace, must be the peace of men. Her head can only think thoughts of peace, her heart can only pray for peace, as her Liturgy unceasingly does. But the world-wide body of the visible Church not only *embraces* the States and citizens of this world, it also *consists* of them. There is no Catholic who is not at the same time either a German or a Frenchman, an Englishman or an Italian, or a member of some other nation. There is no Catholic Church in any of these many States which has not grown together with that State, breathed its air, and shared enough of its fortunes to come somewhat to resemble it.

Hence the bitter practical problem which torments the Chief Shepherd of Christendom in time of war. In the conflicts of States one with another the German Catholic thinks and feels not only Catholic, but also German, the French, French. And so the temptation for Catholics within the nations, sometimes almost the compulsion for them, is to compromise the detached spirit of Catholicism with the partisan spirit of national and transitory demands. Nevertheless the Papacy, at least, must be firm in this matter. However much Catholics within the nations may be swept along the way of war, the care for peace still belongs to the elementary duties of the Holy See.

There is no war that is not ushered in, accompanied and followed by a veritable flood of deadly sins; every war, whatever its origins, stands in crying contrast to the peace of Christ in the reign of Christ, and must therefore be resisted by the Vicar of Christ before it begins: and resisted in its sad consequences on the human spirit and on human values during its prosecution and in its aftermath.

In time of peace the enunciation and defense of universal, human, and international values is a chief task of the Holy See.

The fact of war, far from diminishing that task, actually increases it, and together with it increases the obligation of the Roman Pontiff to preserve that freedom from partisanship which is so required if he is to serve as the stay and the guardian of international values.

The Holy See is the sole international force left on the face of the earth. There is no other. All others have failed. The League of Nations, Socialism, Freemasonry, international commerce, scientific relations, cultural and artistic cosmopolitanism, the memories men have of the beauties of one another's countries, the very sense of human fraternity, all these have been shattered under the impact of the war. Yet the Holy Father remains, while the nations rage, the sole herald of universalism, prophet of the *beata pacis visio*, the blessed dream of eventual peace. He remains the voice of those caught within the opposing arms of the pincers of war, the voice of all those silenced on every side and whose thoughts are thoughts of humanity and brotherhood and peace.

Do you not recognize how essential it is that such a voice be left? When men, even good men, are talking with detached calm about the necessity and desirability of sending waves of planes to decimate the Japanese people, and to destroy in a few weeks the work of centuries in Europe; when on the one side Nazi spokesmen are prepared to say that should they find their cause doomed they will abandon it with such a slam of the door that the world will reverberate in ruins for centuries to come; when on the other side allied leaders are talking more discreetly and smoothly but no less ominously of the process of burning and bleeding and bombing all over the world by which they are resolved to obtain their every last objective; when national spokesmen are talking in these terms, how very important it becomes that there be someone above the lines of partisan division to speak in the interests of sanity, of humanity, and of God.

Providentially, such a voice does exist. It speaks through the

49

lips of our Holy Father, Pope Pius XII, and it pleads, as did he in his Christmas message of a year ago, for the recollection by all parties of those international agreements which once made war less inhuman by confining it to combatants, which regulated the occupation of conquered lands and moderated the treatment of the vanquished.

Should his voice be silenced, or should he abdicate his detached supranationalism, who then would protest against the progressive abandonment by both sides of these human-itarian traditions? Shall he keep partisan silence and no one be left to speak for the innumerable dead who lie buried on the battlefields between the opposing armies?

Shall no one speak for the endless, sorrowful army of mothers, widows and afflicted who have been deprived of hope, comfort, and support? Shall no one speak for the host of exiles, torn from their homes by the hurricane of war, and through no fault of their own, sometimes only owing to nationality or descent, doomed to death or to slow destruction? Shall no one speak for the multitudes of non-combatants, women and children, the ailing and the aged, whom aerial warfare, the horrors of which the Pope has almost alone among public leaders repeatedly denounced, indiscriminately robs of possessions, homes, charitable institutions, places of prayer, and even life? Shall no one interpret, no one give voice to the torrential tears and unfathomable bitterness which are the results of the destructive fury unleashed on every side?

Shall no one speak for peace? But peace is the principle and the end of all individual, national, and international life. Every human action, be it private or social, is ethically sound only so far as it tends toward peace. The battle of the soldier, the very war a nation declares, is justified morally only when, on Saint Augustine's principle, we go to war in order that we may restore peace. Shall no one in time of war prepare for that peace? Shall no one rise above the blinding battle of men to watch for the dawn of God's hour and to do battle for God?

Thank God, one shall do all these things. One does dare speak as did our Holy Father on Christmas Eve two years ago: "Over the ruins of a social order which has given such tragic proof of its inadequacy to serve the good of people and preserve the peace, we summon to a crusade for peace and justice the hearts of all those who are magnanimous and upright. We summon them to share our solemn vow not to rest until, in all peoples and all nations of the earth, a vast legion shall be formed of those handfuls of men who are bent on bringing back society to its center of gravity, the law of God and who aspire to the service of the human person and of his common life ennobled in God!"

Pope Pius XII is not the first Father of Christendom to preach this crusade for a world order, to raise his voice for international reconciliation, for disarmament and for whole-hearted cooperation in the works of peace. Pope Benedict XV, when last a fratricidal war ravaged humanity, preached this same crusade. It is, however, the tragedy of the last generation that the voice of the Pontiff found no echo in the hearts of those who could by propaganda and organization have converted the Pope's prayer into the people's program. It may be the hope of our generation, that since the last war the Holy See can number in every land men and women who have become conscious of the social implications of the Catholic faith that is in them.

It is not primarily in rulers or in diplomats that the Holy Father places his hopes for peace. Rather, it is to the devout throng of the faithful that he prefers to address himself. The Vicar of Christ bids his faithful to begin the building of world peace by seeing in every neighbor a member of the universal human family and in every local crisis a chance to kindle the charity of the universal Christ!

Thus can we help build a better world. Thus can we hasten the advent of that truly Christian world order the hope of which, the struggle for which, shapes the Pope's policy in this unhappy interlude of war. We must teach men, as does our Shepherd, that the world is not made up of abstract political theories; it is not made up of senate houses, and market places, and arsenals, and factories. It is made up of men and women and children—of men looking for work, of women seeking food, of children looking for opportunity. It is made up of men shivering in the squares of Moscow and Milan, of women crying in the silent places of Italy and America, of children bewildered in the streets of Barcelona, London, and Cologne. The world is made up of these, and these are held together by charity or they are not held together at all.

But if they be bound by charity, O how beautiful is the world that they can share! A world in which patriotism is preserved, for patriotism is human and necessary and must be preserved. It survives every effort to uproot it, and even those who are sent abroad to fight for *one world*, come back loving more passionately the corner of it that they left. "Dear Mom," one boy in the service wrote home recently, "I have been all over most of the world. I have been in Jerusalem and have even stood at the place where Christ was born, and I still wish that I was back in North Carolina where I was born!"

Christ would have understood that preferential love; He, the perfect Man, Who gladly died for all men and for every race, wept with holy affection for the capital City of His own nation. Christ must gladly bless a like patriotism in ourselves. His Vicar warns us, however, that this sentiment must never become exclusive or monopolize our hearts. We must learn from reason and faith what Edith Cavell learned from suffering unto death: that patriotism is good and noble and necessary, but that patriotism is not enough. We must broaden our minds, open our hearts, to every man, woman, and child whom God has placed upon this earth to seek Him together with us.

Thus can we build a world in which the sons and daughters of the several nations bring no longer their special genius for destruction to the misery of mankind, but rather their national gifts to the greater happiness of all: a world in which the young people of France and Spain bring their sane philosophy of life to build a more humane world for all to enjoy; the young people of Poland and Lithuania and the East bring their devout and indestructible faith to build a more holy world for all; the young people of England bring their practical genius to build a more efficient world for all; the young people of Germany and the nations of the North bring their stalwart hearts to build a more brave world for all; the young people of Ireland and Scotland bring their mellow humor to build a more tolerant world for all; and the sons and daughters of America, no longer sent across the seven seas to die for a future scheme which may never be and which perhaps were better not, bring their characteristic gift of generous and enthusiastic initiative to the building of a more abundant world for all to enjoy.

This is the world for which the Pope is working, and his solicitude that nothing be lost by any nation which might be brought to the building of this world, is what determines the attitude of the Holy Father to the war. "May the Lord preserve him and give him strength and never suffer him to fall into the hands of those who hate him!"[5]

IV

Christendom and Heresy

Christendom involves a magnificent ideal, the most sublime social ideal in human history. It could scarcely be otherwise, of course, since it is the historical by-product of the vision of a God-Man, Our Lord and Savior, Jesus Christ. Still, the ideal of Christendom suffers from serious menaces in this present moment of human history. And the question is which of these is the greatest menace actually impeding the social realization of Christendom.

Whatever may be the greatest menace to Christendom, this, at least, is certain: *the greatest scandal in Christendom is its division*. The radical principle of its division is heresy; the first tragic consequence of its division is the existence of that hydra-headed monster, sectarian Christianity. Christianity has become relatively impotent in the social order, almost incapable of shaping the course of social history because of its theological and moral shattering to bits under the impact of heresy.

There are increasing grounds to hope that heresy has almost spent its force as a principle of division. Time was when Western Protestantism, like Eastern Orthodoxy, added to the scandal of sectarianism by canonizing, so to speak, the very idea of divided Christendom. Even within the memory of living man, Protestant apologists have customarily contended that the divisions of Christendom proved its vitality, its healthy development. Fallacious comparisons with the natural order and with the level of individual personal differences have been used to justify a multiplicity of conflicting creeds as if they were the divinely intended condition of Christendom. It has

This address was delivered at the Hotel Statler, Boston, Massachusetts, on May 15, 1946, on the occasion of the tenth Diocesan Congress of the League of Catholic Women.

been ingeniously argued that uniformity of belief would be unfortunate, uninspiring, and deplorable; in matters of belief, as in those of diet or recreation, variety should be the spice of life!

The division of Christendom was particularly applauded by traditional Protestantism when it coincided with lines of national loyalty. Nationalism as a principle of sectarianism was accepted by many heretical divines as normal, natural, and even providentially pre-ordained. Catholics had talked of *Christendom*, of the Church *in* Italy, the Church *in* France, the Church *in* England, the Church *in* the United States, the Church *in* China. But Protestants talked in terms that not merely declared the *fact of nationalism* but implied the sacredness and the permanence of that fact. Protestants spoke proudly of the established Church *of* England, the Waldensian Church *of* Italy, the Lutheran Church *of* Germany, the Church *of* Scotland, the Church *of* Ireland, the Protestant Episcopalian Church *of* America.

Recently, however, Protestant thought and expression seem to have taken a new direction. *The Christian Century*, one of the more literate of Protestant periodicals, has begun to feature articles on the possibility of Protestant ecumenism; lesser Protestant publications carry like essays. These are chiefly exploratory at the moment, but their significance, one thinks, is very great. True, even the friendly observer will wonder how much of this ecumenism is due to positive theological considerations and how much of it is merely a negative acknowledgment of the futility of divided religion in a society economically and politically headed (it sometimes seems) toward *one world*. An article in the current *Reader's Digest* by Dr. Harry E. Fosdick, for example, pleads for a world religion in view of the increasing world unity on every other level.[1] A few weeks ago we had here in Boston an Ecumenical Meeting which was intended, at least, to bring together the representatives of almost all the Protestant sects. It was calculated to demonstrate the possibility of realizing on the level of worship the modern Protestant craving for unity, social and religious. On that occasion a Protestant bishop (who does not particularly like us) discussed some aspects of the problem of unity among religions as he sees that problem.[2] We shall return to a consideration of Bishop Oxnam's effort to secure a united Protestantism on the basis of a common opposition to Catholicism. Suffice it for the moment to note at least the desire for unity, however unworthy or unstable the grounds offered by individual apostles of Protestant unity. Only yesterday in New York another Protestant bishop (who does not particularly dislike us) spoke on this same point of the reunion of Christendom. He said:

> More than ever today, when the whole world is one, we must think of Christian unity in its true world-wide meaning. Christian reunion means the reunion of all of us, all who are baptized into Christ and can accept Him as God and Savior. It means the reunion of all Christians both Catholics and Protestants in the one great Church of God. The reunion of the Church will come and today there are many signs of its coming . . . in Protestantism there is a great movement back to Orthodoxy and away from humanism. Reunion will come, not by compromise of faith and conviction, not by throwing aside creed and doctrine, but by a fuller appreciation of the truth revealed in Christ.[3]

All persons who love God and who lament the divisions of Christendom will welcome the high-minded aspirations of this good man. They will particularly approve the positive and fundamentally spiritual content of his appeal as contrasted with the highly political and negative position of the Methodist bishop who assailed traditional Christendom, Catholic and Orthodox alike, here in Boston. We might make certain reservations with regard to other parts of Bishop Manning's pronouncement but we must recognize in his last sentence a perfect statement of the Catholic position. Since first heresy divided the flock of Christ, Catholics have prayed and tried to work for the restoration of the unity that was in the beginning. But they have consistently argued, particularly as against their Protestant neighbors, that "reunion will come not by compromise of faith and conviction, not by throwing aside creed and doctrine, but by a fuller appreciation of the truth revealed in Christ."[4]

The abiding conviction of the Catholic Church is that a fuller appreciation of the truth revealed in Christ and taught by Christ and transmitted from Christ will lead, under God, to the reestablishment of Christendom within that single, sacred, universal, and ancient city of God which we know as the One, Holy, Catholic, and Apostolic Church.

The new Protestant tendency toward ecumenism is indubitably good. It represents a tardy but altogether welcome recognition on the part of Protestant Christians that religious division is not healthy and not desirable but pernicious and unnatural. Some individual and isolated Protestant souls have always sensed this. Matthew Arnold comes to mind. He said: "If there is a thing specially alien to religion, it is division; if there is a thing specially native to religion, it is peace and union. Hence the original attraction toward unity in Rome and hence the great charm when that unity is once attained."[5] Thackeray sensed the same thing, I think, when he wrote about the beauty of that unity under a single spiritual authority which has always been the Catholic dream.

It may well be that these sensitive men spoke in advance of their times and that, as Dorothy Thompson observed a few weeks ago, the hideous social and political consequences of a Christendom torn asunder by heresy may lead many to seek security under what she called Christendom's oldest roof.

But in the light of these recent Protestant emphases on the necessity of religious unity, both those which are sympathetic and those which are hostile, we should review our own position on the question of the unity of Christendom. We should review it with especial reference to the attack on our position by contemporary heresy. There is no great point any longer in pointing out the absurdity of Protestant nationalism or racialism; in all probability that is a spent force save as it may find tedious expression in the snobbery of individual Protestants preoccupied with the fancied religious superiority of their Nordic, Anglo-Saxon, or even American sensitiveness, profundity, or piety. Heresy bids fair to perpetuate religious division from a new direction, especially now that heresy is seeking to establish itself on an ecumenical basis. A man like Bishop Oxnam, for example, is no longer likely to present (publicly at least) his case for heresy and against Catholicism on the basis of the supposed superiority of Nordic cultural and religious institutions to the corresponding Latin institutions. He might have done this at the time of the last war; his prototypes did. He is not likely, especially given his world vision and his ecumenical aspirations, to prate of Anglo-Saxon independence of thought and Mediterranean servility, of North American religious initiative and South American religious degeneracy. In the present mood of the Protestant liberal, at any rate, his *political* positions will preclude any of the more shallow theological nonsense to which his predecessors even a half generation ago used to treat us when they talked of the sublimely individualistic Germanic access of the lonely soul to God as contrasted with the debased, institutionalized Latin fumbling of the Roman Catholic after his God. The libraries are filled with this type of Protestant attack, but it is all a little old-fashioned now.

The new defense of heresy is on a totally different basis. It has been developing during these last several years. It takes its vocabulary from the political conflicts of the hour; it can be reduced to this summary of Bishop Oxnam's attack at Trinity Church last month. The contention is this: Protestantism is *dynamic*, Catholicism is *static*; Protestantism is *democratic* and consistent with liberty, Catholicism is *hierarchical* and *authoritarian*. Accordingly, the mood of the hour being progressive and democratic, Catholicism stands condemned as reactionary and Fascist.

This is not the first time that the Church has been condemned for its refusal to *change*, to accommodate itself to the moods of the hour. The heretic has always protested against the intransigence of Catholicism and so this point need not long detain us. Father Lacordaire tells the story of this conflict beautifully:

> They (the Ages) have come, one after the other, to the door of the Vatican; they have knocked there with buskin and boot, and the Faith has appeared under the frail and wasted form of some old man of threescore years and ten. The Faith has said, "What do you desire of me?"
>
> "Change."
>
> "I never change."
>
> "But everything is changing in this world. Astronomy has changed, chemistry has changed, philosophy has changed. Why are you always the same?"
>
> "Because I come from God, and because God is always the same."
>
> "But know that we are the masters; we have a million of men under arms; we shall draw the sword; the sword which breaks down thrones is well able to cut off the head of an old man, and tear up the leaves of a book."
>
> "Do so; blood is the aroma in which I recover my youthful vigor."
>
> "Well, then, here is half my scepter, make a sacrifice to peace, and let us share it together."
>
> "Keep thy purple, O Caesar! Tomorrow they will bury thee in it; and we will chant over thee the *Alleluia* and the *De Profundis*, for these also never change."[6]

The efforts to damn us as the slaves of an authoritarian system are more dangerous, however. This is the principal purpose of Bishop Oxnam in his recent address. It takes two forms: it represents us as antagonistic to our neighbors because of their religious opinions and it represents us as incapable of *political democracy* because of our *theological Faith*.

We are told that our theological faith is inconsistent with the spirit of democracy; Protestant theology, on the other hand, breeds democracy. Bishop Oxnam offers in his recent speech certain considerations which, he asserts, demonstrate the congenial atmosphere which Protestant theology creates for democracy, and in a series of sometimes subtle and more often snide passages he attempts to establish a like congenial relationship between the spirit of Catholicism and that of political authoritarianism or even Fascism.

After studying the speech in question, a Catholic might easily ask himself whether a democratic political system in Bishop Oxnam's understanding of the world would tolerate us at all. Bishop Oxnam so describes the idea he has of democracy and its relationship to Protestantism as to make it perfectly clear that in his democracy one would have to be a Protestant, in fact, a liberal Protestant denying not merely Catholic theology but Anglican, Orthodox, and all hierarchical churches as well. But fortunately for America, its idea of Democracy has never borne any slight resemblance to that of Bishop Oxnam.

The particular instances which the Methodist Bishop accumulates in his effort to bolster his case against Catholicism as a religion congenial to democracy are largely contemporary and topical, but the fundamental charge is not new. The Methodist Bishop sings an old song to a new tune: it is the classic Protestant case against Catholicism. Sabatier compresses it into the very title of the book in which he gave it much more scholarly and sensitive expresson than our reviler in the pulpit at Trinity could possibly have done. Bishop Oxnam popularizes the alleged problem by implying that the conflict between Protestantism and Catholicism is a conflict between religious democracy and religious Fascism. This is simply a politically-minded Methodist bishop's misleading way of saying what

60

has always been said by the heretic, i.e., that the conflict between Protestantism and Catholicism is the conflict between the religion of liberty and the religion of authority. It is the religious form of an alleged general conflict between *authority* and *liberty*.

Freedom, the heretic has always argued, is the refreshing note of primitive Christianity. The early Church was characterized by an untrammeled spirit of liberty, liberty in discipline and liberty in doctrine. In this it reflected its kinship with the mind and purpose of its Founder.

The so-called liberal Protestant argues this way: Jesus Christ came into the world to restore the spirit of liberty; He came to free men from all bondage, from the bondage of sin, of course, but also from the bondage of the old law. Indeed, the most obvious difference between the new law which Christ established and the old law which He annulled is the absence in the one of that legalism and ecclesiasticism which had reduced the other to mere slavish routine. Jesus Christ protested against the intolerable manner in which the religious life of the people had been hampered by pyramiding hierarchies, minute legislation, and the petty sanctions of organized religious authority. As against this, Christ preached no binding dogmas, no prescribed ritual and no authoritative hierarchy. He preached the *spirit of liberty*. His dogmas, if indeed we can call them such, were few and very simple; He taught the Fatherhood of God, the Brotherhood of Man, and salvation through the acceptance of His leadership. He expressly forbade the recognition of any religious authority lesser than that of God Himself: "Call no man father for one is your Father, God."[7] Christ may have provided for a very few simple rites, probably Baptism and possibly the Eucharist in some form, but the whole point of His teaching both in faith and in morals is that it is *free*. It can best be understood in terms of contrast with authoritarianism.

This is how the liberal Protestant represents primitive Christianity to have been.

The liberal Protestant concludes that this spirit of liberty and the essential Christianity which it informs are to be found nowadays only in Protestantism. The Protestant is perfectly free in the realm of dogma. He may choose, accept, reject, or make his own those doctrines which his private interpretation, his emancipated intellect, his religious experience, or his theological sense dictate. In matters of morals and of religious discipline he is largely free to choose for himself in accordance with the demands of his spiritual development or the voice of his autonomous conscience. Private interpretation is not limited by the modern Protestant to dogma, the Apostles' Creed, and the passages of the Bible. It extends to moral matters, to the Ten Commandments and even, as in the cases of race suicide, abortion, and divorce, to the natural law itself. In matters of worship, the Protestant is particularly free. He may attend any church he prefers unless he happens to be a somewhat *snooty* high Anglican or an unduly cantankerous Evangelical. He may eat or not eat fish or flesh, and Friday for his wife presents no special problem of a rubrical kind. He may order his day, Sunday included, much as he pleases and his calendar is not complicated by feasts of precept and fasts of imposed penance. He considers that he lives and moves and has his being in the very spirit of primitive Christianity. He tells us that he has the truth and the truth has made him free!

Not so with the benighted Catholic! Bishop Oxnam, with merciful restraint, does no more than suggest our pathetic plight. It needs no great development: the Protestant observes it with pity, you Catholics know it all too well. In liturgical discipline you are hemmed in on every side; your diet, the disposition of your days, your Sunday morning goings-in and goings-out, your access to the sacramental system, your risings and sittings and genuflections, your Signs of the Cross, your takings of holy water, all these seem to the Protestant to be rigidly set down for you. You must worship in this church and not another; when you are baptized it must be in this fashion and not in another, and only sponsors of these qualifications may stand for you. If you be married it must be in this season and not in that, in this church and not in that, and all manner of questions and restrictions and regulations and conditions must be bravely met before you are finally privileged to hear the strains of the "Wedding March". Alas, if your parish priest be too scrupulous a disciple of Pius X even the "Wedding March", if you prefer that from *Lohengrin*, will probably be denied you. Once married, even the most intimate aspects of your wedded life are regulated by moral laws which many Protestants now reject; your children must be educated under this code, sedulously protected from that other. When finally you come to die you may not be buried on certain days and you must be buried in certain places. A whole web of canonical disciplines imprisons you at every turn.

In matters of Faith your lot is no less tragic. In the opinion of men like Bishop Oxnam, the simple teachings of Jesus Christ have been enormously complicated for you by a vast theological system, a system largely spun by professional theologians or ecclesiastical councils. Not only that, but this entire superstructure, elaborate, intricate, and enormously technical, is imposed upon you in its every detail as binding at the peril of your soul. According to him, you are allowed little or no room for speculation, scant opportunity for choice, only one alternative: *believe or be anathema*. You cannot reach your own conclusions with regard to the number of the sacraments in the primitive Church; you cannot allow your personal mystical sense to decide for you what attitudes you are to take toward the dogmas concerning the Mother of Christ, the fact of the Incarnation, or the manner of Christ's presence in the Eucharist. This sobering conclusion appears to impose itself: in the spirit of its teaching and the manner of its discipline the Catholic Church (and at this point if you be Bishop Oxnam you must carefully remember to say the *Roman* Catholic Church) has gone back to the spiritual tyranny of the old law, the very

63

system against which Christ so vehemently protested. The liberal Protestant might just as well be honest about it: the Catholic, unlike his Protestant neighbor who lives and believes in the spirit of liberty, is almost as badly off as was ever the son of Israel in the days of the Pharisees, the phylacteries, the burdensome minutiae of the law, and the bondage of priestly castes. He binds his own limbs, as the old phrase says, by his Act of Faith, and he puts the other end of the chain into the hands of the priest. Such is the situation as between the free spirit of Protestant democracy and the tyrannical authoritarianism of Catholic theology. So, the liberal Protestant decides, Catholics live in a theological atmosphere that is not congenial to political democracy!

Much of this is so false that it calls for no refutation before a Catholic audience; more of it is irrelevant. Some of it is conscious malice. It is not easy to see what political democracy has to do with the acceptance or rejection of revelation which is presumed to come from God. It is hard for the humble mind to see why one could not debate which of several candidates for public office are the most competent and choose among these in democratic fashion and yet at the same time believe that there is no debate with regard to the rights and the authority of God, *if* He exists, or rather *since* He exists. One can very reasonably maintain that the democratic theory of government is by far the best under which to run the City of Man and yet continue to recognize that the *Kingdom* of Heaven is still just that. One can passionately believe in democratic processes and parliamentary government without supposing that this has anything to do with God's eternal counsels and conditions for the supernatural order. The only elections ever held in Heaven ended disastrously in the eternal fire which was prepared for the devil and his angels![8] The will of the people may well be sovereign in temporal matters; temporal matters have been given into our stewardship and so in them we can accept, nay claim, popular responsibility. But matters eternal, the things

64

of God with which theology is concerned, are quite another problem. Only God can tell us about them and this He does by *revelation* and that revelation is *authoritative* or it is without point.

Theology is the study of God and there is nothing *simple* about God. It is entirely false to pretend that New Testament theology is simple. It is preposterous to suggest that Protestant theology is simple. No one could possibly read the dismal, tortuous speculations of Luther or Calvin or Boehme, or any of the classic Protestant theologians, and then complain of the intricacy of Catholic theology. We are not so much concerned, however, with the comparison of our theology with that of the Protestants: We are concerned with the liberal Protestant effort to contrast our theology with that of the New Testament. Compared with the systematic and carefully defined theology of the Church, New Testament theology is hopelessly complex and puzzling; the proof of that is the hundreds of creeds into which Protestants have become divided in their effort to explain what the New Testament teaches. Dogmas such as that of the Blessed Trinity, of Original Sin, of the Redemption, of Eternal Damnation, of Supernatural Life—whatever else you may say of these, they are none of them *simple*. Yet the New Testament is replete with them and Jesus Christ not merely talked about them. He talked about little else! Certainly Saint Paul, whom a generation ago Protestants used to claim for some completely unintelligible reason as their own, has little or nothing in his writings save *dogma*, the dogmas of Justification, of Predestination, of Redemption, of Ecclesiology. You may say anything you choose about Saint Paul, but you cannot accuse him of being simple in his theology. I beg you to read the prologue of Saint John's Gospel and tell me whether it has that clarity and simplicity and air of indifferentism which our liberal Protestant friends regret that they cannot find in the Church. Yet it and all the later pronouncements with regard to the Faith (the decrees of the Councils and the like) will prove

65

masterpieces of lucidity if you compare them with the traditional and to date unrepudiated Protestant theologians and professions of faith.

And yet, Bishop Oxnam seems to have a point. It remains true that on the whole the Catholic is bound to believe a certain set of dogmas while the Protestant is free to accept or reject them. It is true that the Catholic accepts religious authority in matters of Faith, though he is usually temperamentally wary of authority in all other matters. It is also true that the Protestant can claim a tremendous liberty in matters of faith, though he, oddly enough, is usually most deferential to authority in other matters. This brings us straight to the consideration of the relationship between *authority* and *liberty*.

Are liberty and authority irreconcilable? Is there not a level on which they complement one another? Are they not correlative rather than mutually antagonistic? Perhaps their relationship one to the other may be suggested by this paradox: liberty can only be secured by laws, and laws, in the moral sense, can only exist among things endowed with liberty. Where there are no laws or too few, not liberty but slavery exists. Even the vast and complex legislation of our political society represents a development which, in the main, guarantees greater liberty. Most of our pyramiding legislation has been written precisely in order to provide more and more protection to liberty. The so-called economic royalists and others who protest the inevitable development of political authority do so because they recognize that this growth of authority means, para-doxically, an extension of *liberties* in which, since they are not their own, they are not interested. Only that man is free, then, who lives under law: The highest measure of liberty in our complex lives requires an ever more highly developed authority.

In the field of knowledge, moreover, liberty does not consist in the absence of scientific dogmas, but in their presence. All truth has its dogmas, and ignorance of them brings with it no

66

real liberty. If I am ignorant of the dogmas of mathematics, or the dogmas of physics, or the dogmas of geography, I am, perhaps, more free in one sense than the man who is handicapped by his knowledge of them. I am free to believe that two and two make five; I am free to jump without protection from an airplane; I am free to set forth in any direction in the hope of reaching the North Pole, but this is not liberty in any reasonable sense. Thomas Edison submits his intellect to the dogmas of electrical science and he thereby becomes free to avail himself of them and to use them for his perfection and our utility. In the field of religious faith, the believer submits his intellect to the dogmas of God's revelation and accordingly he becomes free to use them for his perfection and the benefit of mankind. This is what Christ meant when He said: "You will know the truth and the truth will make you free."[9]

Monsignor Benson used to develop this point most effectively. He used to point out that the soul, like the body, has its proper environment. This environment has its proper laws and these laws are discoverable. Revelation provides the most detailed knowledge of them but reason is able to discover much in their regard. Prayer, for example, elevates the soul, base thinking degrades it. Many truths with regard to the spiritual order were perfectly familiar long before Christ came. Christ came with this object among others: that He might reveal the laws of Grace and instruct men in the dogmas essential to the right use of those laws. *He came, then, to increase men's liberty by increasing their knowledge*. He did on the level of the spiritual and in the realm of Grace what the scientist does on the level of matter and in the realm of material energy: by providing us with the truth in their regard, by increasing our knowledge, He makes us more free both to seek and to attain our perfection. What Christ did in transmitting to the Church the wisdom of Heaven, the Church does in transmitting to us the wisdom of Christ. The Catholic Church has for its divinely established functions to take the revelation of Jesus

Christ and by her dogma and her discipline to popularize it, rendering it comprehensible and effective. The Church does this *systematically*, and the system under which she lives and works and teaches is that which Jesus Christ provided.

Christ did not condemn the Pharisaic system because it was a *system*; indeed, He Himself founded a *system*, a sacramental system, a hierarchical system, a dogmatic system. Christ condemned the Pharisaic system because it was *Pharisaic*. He gave us liberty, to be sure, but it was the liberty of the sons of God—*and it is only by dogma that we come to understand what it is to be a son of God.*

Ours, then, is a dogmatic faith but it is not on that account the enemy of the freedom which Christ came to bring. Yet Bishop Oxnam and his followers try to make their point by another route: They argue that, however free our dogma may make us, it compels us to adopt a tyrannical and persecuting attitude toward those of our neighbors who believe otherwise than do we. Not all non-Catholics so misrepresent our position. Dr. W. H. Mallock, a distinguished Protestant theologian, was able to write these words:

> Never was there a religious body, except the Roman, that laid the intense stress she does on all her dogmatic teachings, and had yet the justice that comes of sympathy for those that cannot receive them. She condemns no goodness, she condemns even no earnest worship, though it be outside her pale. On the contrary, she declares explicitly that a knowledge of "the one true God, our Creator and Lord", may be attained to by the "natural light of human reason"; meaning by *reason*, the mind unenlightened by revelation; and she declares those to be anathema who deny this. The holy and humble men of heart who do not know her, or who in good faith reject her, she commits with confidence to God's uncovenanted mercies; and these she knows are infinite, but except as revealed to her, she can of necessity say nothing distinct about them. It is admitted by the world at large that of her supposed bigotry she has no bitterer or more extreme exponents than the Jesuits; and this is

what a Jesuit theologian says about this matter: "A heretic, so long as he believes his sect to be more, or equally, deserving of belief, has no obligation to believe the Church . . . and when men who have been brought up in heresy are persuaded from boyhood that we impugn and attack the work of God, that we are idolaters, pestilent deceivers, and are therefore to be shunned as pestilence, they cannot, while this persuasion lasts, with a safe conscience hear us."[10]

Thus for those outside her fold the Church has one condemnation only and it is one which any upright man would make: the condemnation of insincerity in religion, the refusal to seek God's will while professing to revere it, the refusal to follow God's word while professing to have found it. Catholics are guilty of insincerity when, claiming to have the authoritative revelation of Christ's law of love, they nonetheless withhold their charity from men of good will. Protestants, and especially *liberals*, appear to us insincere when they proclaim their readiness to defend the right to their Faith even of Catholics, and then, within the selfsame speeches, vilify us for defending that Faith ourselves!

We began noting the repeated expressions of a widespread desire for religious unity. There is little hope in the thinkable future of the dogmatic union of Christendom, but there should be hope for a greater cooperation on a moral basis among the decent members of our community. Protestant leaders constantly assert that plain speech should precede that cooperation. Perhaps a little plain speech on our side will do no harm. It should be frankly stated that many Catholics have become alarmed by the menacing tone of antagonism that some Protestant leaders have sounded in our community. Catholic young people are scandalized by the unworthy publications, frequently obscene, distributed by apparently flourishing Protestant organizations—vile publications, many of them lampooning our nuns, our sacraments, and our moral code. Older Catholics are disturbed at the recrudescence of a malicious *political* attack on the Church which they recognize from its earlier manifestations in the days of the little Red School House, the A.P.A., the refined legalism of lawyer Marshall's attacks on Al Smith and the rude forays of Tom Heflin against the Pope. Echoes from all these were recently blended in the antagonistic and ungenerous blast which Bishop Oxnam made against us here in Boston. These things disturb Catholics because they remember the unhappy social, economic, political, and religious difficulties anti-Catholics of this kind can create and have created for our people in the past.

I think we need not worry, however. Good Protestants are also good neighbors, and the great majority of our Protestant lay people do not share the suspicion and the hatred in our regard of occasional bigoted spokesmen. If we, on our side, keep the laws of Christ's charity, if we are conspicuously faithful to the corporal and spiritual works of mercy, then we shall not alienate these millions of friends further from us. We shall have and deserve their good will—and faithful to our Catholic heritage, we shall continue to give them ours.

V

The Holy Father's Historic Appeal to Women

In October of last year, 1945, our Holy Father the Pope delivered a historic appeal to Catholic women to recognize and utilize their potential influence on the reconstruction of the social order.[1] The pronouncement of the Holy Father has been widely commented upon alike in the Catholic, the non-Catholic, and the secular press. It has, however, been the object of no little misunderstanding on the part of some, and positive misrepresentation on the part of others.

Many people, among them perhaps some Catholics, appear to believe that the recognition of the social and political role of women is a peculiarly modern phenomenon. Some even seem to suppose that the notion of women's rights is bound up with the rise of Protestantism or of the secularism which followed the Protestant disruption of Christendom. Nothing could be theoretically more absurd or historically more inexact.

Among the major premises of Catholic social teaching from Apostolic times has been the idea of the absolute equality of all humans as *persons*, and in the life of the supernatural society which is the Catholic Church, sight has never been lost of Saint Paul's definitive declaration: "There is (in the Church) neither Jew nor Gentile; there is neither bond nor free; there is neither male nor female; for you are all one in Christ Jesus."[2]

A very little reflection on their own history will suffice to remind Catholic women of the great place their sex held in the religious life of the Church during the period of European history when that now unhappy continent was dominantly Catholic. The great Religious Orders of women are perhaps the most unique example of strictly feminine idealism being

This address was given at the 1946 Area Days of the League of Catholic Women.

71

brought to achievement under strictly feminine organizations, set up and administered exclusively by women. One has only to recall the names of Saint Monica, Paula of Rome, Saint Scholastica, Saint Clare, Dame Julian of Norwich, Saint Teresa of Avila, Saint Jane Frances de Chantal, Saint Bridget of Sweden, and countless other holy foundresses of our Religious Orders in order to appreciate the Church's recognition of the talents, the dignity, and the leadership of women in the life of the Church.

In the secular life of the days when society was guided by Catholic idealism, the leadership of women—even in political and social matters—was similarly taken for granted. Again, one has only to recall the place in public life of Catholic queens in the age of united Christendom to realize the Catholic recognition of the aptitude of women for public life. Mary R. Beard, non-Catholic author of a recent book on *Women as Force in History*, has substantially recorded, despite occasional inaccuracies, the place of Catholic queens in building the political, social, and cultural foundations of Europe.[3]

The enormous work of converting and civilizing the barbarian nations fell largely to Catholic queens—to Saint Clotilde, the wife of King Clovis in early France; to Bertha, the wife of Ethelbert, King of Kent in primitive England; to Ingunda in early Spain; to Theodelinda among the Lombards in early Italy. These women head a glorious line of Catholic women who dedicated their talents and their strength to public life; who employed, in the phrase of Henry Adams, "terror and tenderness to tame the beasts around them"; and who built, in amazing part, the foundations and the fabric of European civilization.[4]

It is preposterous to talk of feminism as a modern phenomenon or of women in public life as a Protestant contribution to history when we remember women like Joan of Arc, a Catholic girl in her late teens who galvanized a defeated nation and guaranteed its survival; or women like Queen Eleanor of

Guienne, Queen Blanche of Castile, or Mary of Champagne; queens like Elizabeth of Hungary, Margaret of Scotland, Isabella of Spain, or Maria Theresa of Austria. Neither Protestantism nor secular democracy have yet produced a Who's Who of women in public life comparable to this galaxy of magnificent Catholic queens, the political, social, cultural, and, in a sense, religious leaders of their nations.

Public opinion in the Catholic Middle Ages was entirely on the side of so-called rights of women. As Father Gerald Walsh has reminded us, when the Crusaders went to the Holy Land it was the most natural thing in the world for the Crusaders' wives to *take over* and to run the great baronial estates and the local popular assemblies of medieval Europe, the true breeding-places of our democratic traditions. Women met on terms of equality with the men, and in many of the codes of customary law man and wife acted as equal partners in all matters of family business.[5]

I mention all this to discount the point of view of those who represent as *revolutionary* the Holy Father's appeal to women to take a more conspicuous place in public life. In fact, the Holy Father's message restated, in contemporary terms perhaps, but with fidelity to the great Catholic tradition, the constant place the Church has expected women to fill in the life of society at all times. That place has never been exclusively the home, let alone the kitchen. Catholicism has always recognized that there are three great spheres in which women can save their souls, perfect their personalities, find their happiness, contribute to the building of the social order, and spread the Kingdom of God.

To each of these spheres the women who choose it bring the same feminine qualities and instincts; in all of them, however they may differ superficially, the woman has the same essentially feminine function. Some women are called by God to consecrate themselves to Him under religious vows; most women are clearly intended by God to dedicate themselves to

73

Him in marriage; a third group are called by God to serve Him by careers in the world. But whether as a consecrated nun, or as the founder of a home, or as a person seeking her career in the world, the social contribution of the woman is always the same: she brings into society, religious and secular, the creative, constructive, and maternal instincts peculiar and natural to her sex.

Even Catholics sometimes fail to appreciate the social significance of nuns; non-Catholics are almost always completely ignorant or weirdly misled in their regard. Some people suppose that the cloister offers a girl a place, perhaps even the best place, in which to work out alone her personal salvation; indeed, many might assert that a girl enters the convent in a kind of flight from the world and in the hope of saving her soul by dying to society.

For all I know, even some nuns may so interpret their vocations. But such an asocial concept of the religious life is utterly at variance with both theory and history. No one has a right to die to the world in any such individualistic and self-centered fashion; even the most cloistered nun by her life of prayer and penance necessarily helps vitalize that Communion of Saints which is the principal supernatural factor in human social solidarity. One need only read the intentions for which the hallowed souls pray who immolate themselves among our Carmelites, our Trappistines, and our Poor Clares to appreciate how social-minded and socially fruitful are the sacrifices of these privileged religious, than whom no one is more dead to society.

The nun makes her influence in society in two further ways. The virgin consecrated to God under a vow of chastity sets a standard which, by a curious indirection, enables us to gauge the true position of women other than nuns in any given civilization. Consecrated virginity diffuses throughout the society which includes it a fragrant atmosphere of purity and of spiritual integrity which, again by a curious indirection, enhances the sanctity of marriage and the dignity of women. Here is a strange paradox, but it admits of historical check: *The greater the respect and esteem shown by a society to consecrated virginity, the higher the position of other women in that society invariably will be.*

Ireland for example holds in equal and simultaneous veneration virginity and maternity; the cloister and the home; the nun and the mother. So, on the other hand, it is significant that the Protestant revolt, which was to have so many unfortunate consequences for the dignity and the position of women, began with attacks on virginity by Martin Luther and liquidation of convents by Henry VIII. Nor should it surprise you that the only State in our day which sends women into the front-line trenches equally with men is a State which still outlaws convents, encourages the contempt of consecrated virginity, and degrades maternity to the level of a factor in the military program of its political regime.

The second way in which the nun makes felt her influence in society is more direct. Despite their other-worldly vows and despite the supernatural heroism required for the renunciations which they make, our nuns are still women. They have all the instincts of women and these instincts, though sublimated, are not destroyed by the vows which nuns make. The creative, constructive, and maternal instincts of the woman in the nun are, on the level of nature, part of the secret power of the Church to renew the face of the earth after such periods of violence, destruction, and degeneracy as the one through which we have just passed. Our nuns must be the mothers of millions of other people's abandoned children all over the world. They must be the governesses, the guides, of hundreds of thousands of children who have been left morally diseased by the ravages of war. In Italy, France, Germany, Poland, Austria, Belgium, and elsewhere the souls of a whole generation of girls and of children depend in great part on our nuns for their eventual salvation.

75

Sublimely consecrated to God and supernaturalized by His grace, the feminine influence of our nuns finds its way into society through our teaching Orders, our hospital Orders, our social service Orders, and our missionary Sisters. These women are not dead to the world. Rather, they are the chosen channels through which the God of life continually renews a dying society; they give the world their lives that the world itself may live. The girl who chooses to become a Catholic nun claims little of life or liberty or love for herself, but more today than ever before in history she is the best hope that abandoned children have that they may live useful lives, may become capable of liberty and worthy of love.

Most women are destined to achieve their perfection through marriage. The young woman who chooses for her career the building of a home and the founding of a family, who seeks her happiness in the sacramental vocation that is marriage, is a mature person no matter what her age. That is why in a normal society the Catholic Church always favors relatively youthful marriages. There is no more disturbing proof of the abnormality and the perversity of our social and economic system than the manner in which it obliges young people who wish marriage to delay indefinitely their plans for military, economic, political, and other kindred reasons.

In the Catholic scheme of things the girl who chooses marriage for her vocation becomes the central person in society, the chief influence for good or evil on society's well-being. The obligations of her vocation should make her the perfect member of society. It requires of her that she develop a solicitude for others, a selflessness and a tenderness which cannot but produce in her all the so-called other-regarding virtues so needed in the good citizen.

The Church considers the mother the central person in society, however, not so much because of what her vocation does to her as because of what she does in the social order. We said that our Catholic theory of consecrated virginity seems almost unintelligible to the non-Catholic world; sometimes one feels that our Catholic concept of the dignity of the mother is similarly unintelligible to the contemporary Protestant mentality. A man like the Methodist Bishop Oxnam, for example, shows little or no comprehension of the Catholic moral philosophy in these matters when he presumes to represent our position in his public presentation of his own theories.[6]

Not long ago Bishop Oxnam gave one of his typical talks before the Planned Parenthood group in New York; their name indicates the new line of the Sangerite birth prevention crowd. The Methodist Bishop implied that the Catholic position with regard to race suicide is dictated by our desire to *outbreed* our neighbors in political and religious strength! Could a cruder or more cruel caricature of the Catholic position be imagined? Could anyone be guilty of a more callous insensibility to the valiantly accepted worry and the secret tears, the frugal planning and the heroic self-sacrifice in the lives of those decent married people who strive to live up to the moral idealism of their faith in an economic society for which they are *bitterly* indebted in no small part to the theology and the social institutions of the ancestors of this Bishop who maligns us?

Bishop Oxnam's followers point out that our Catholic philosophy looks to women as the source of the nation's *biological* strength. It does, of course; to whom else could it look? But in our theory of things the mother is far more than the mere source of a nation's *biological* strength. She is the source of its *economic* strength, for all markets depend on her and she is the principal purchasing agent for all a nation's customers. She is the source of a nation's *cultural* strength, for she is the first teacher of its citizens and plans most of their subsequent education. She is the source of a nation's *moral* strength for, even more than the clergy or the pedagogues of a people, the mother provides that formation of mind and

77

character in the young which is the foundation of personal and public morality in the adult.

If our children have strong bodies and decent characters, if they are cooperative citizens and prepared to live in civilized society, if they are devout Catholics and trained in the virtues which make for their perfection and the happiness of those who live with them—then we have their mothers to thank. No other influence is as strong as that of the mother in forming and preparing human beings for life. She molds the men and women of every society and no society will be better than she makes it. She controls the tone and temper of society on its every level. A nation can flourish only to the extent that it is composed of flourishing families; the family is hers and it is likely to reflect her physical, moral, and mental qualities.

A girl who plans to find her career in this vocation cannot possibly secure too much liberal education; we should have courses designed precisely to prepare our girls for the tremendous personal responsibilities and social influence which they will have as mothers of families and builders of homes. When society again becomes normal they will be the most important people in the world!

A principal part of the Holy Father's message is dedicated to those great Catholic women who are destined to achieve their personal happiness and the service of God by vocations outside the cloister or the founding of a family. The task of the Catholic woman who chooses to seek a career in the world is to carry out the dedication of her womanhood to God through the loving service of her fellow man. In our day opportunities for these women are tremendous, but in all of them the contribution they must make is still, like that of the nun, essentially feminine. The Church and society need women in the professions and in public life in order to bring into these the creative instinct which, as we said, is always the characteristic contribution of the woman. Women must restore to political and professional life the emphasis on the spiritual, an emphasis now so sadly lacking.

We need Catholic women lawyers, Catholic women doctors, Catholic women social service workers, Catholic women journalists, Catholic women in the administration of public institutions. No one can visit a modern courtroom, hospital, directors' meeting, or public institution without realizing how cut-and-dried, how technical, the professions at work in these have become; how insensible, all too frequently, to spiritual realism. We may need women in these fields in order to restore Christ and His values to them.

Here in Massachusetts we have recently witnessed in connection with our Parole Board an example of how legislation written to control delinquency and potential delinquency among women and children can easily become pharisaical and inhuman. There is one passage in the Holy Father's historic appeal to women which almost sounds as if it had been written with our local legislation on this point in mind. The Holy Father says:

Associated with men in civil institutions, the woman in public life will apply herself especially to those matters which call for tact, delicacy, and maternal instinct rather than administrative rigidity. Who better than she can understand what is needed for the integrity of woman, the integrity and honor of the young girl, and the protection and education of the child?

And in all these questions, how many problems call for study and action on the part of governments and legislators. Only a woman will know, for instance, how to temper with kindness, without detriment to its efficacy, legislation to repress licentiousness. She alone can find the means to save from degradation and to raise in honesty and in religious and civil virtues the morally derelict young. She alone will be able to render effective the work of protection and rehabilitation for those freed from prison and for fallen girls. She alone will reecho from her own heart the plea of mothers from whom the totalitarian state, by whatever name it be called, would will to take away their children.[7]

In the light of this urgent need for Catholic women in the professions, our parents might well meditate the new obligations which the times impose with regard to the advanced education of their daughters. Our typical Catholic families have usually proceeded on the assumption that opportunities for advanced and professional education should be sought for our boys, but not necessarily for the girls. Indeed, most hard-pressed Catholic families have come to consider it perfectly natural that the girls go to work as soon as possible precisely in order to help with the advanced and specialized education of the boys. In prosperous families it seems frequently taken for granted that advanced education for the girls should be taken no more seriously than as a kill-time between their high-school education and marriage.

We must rethink this whole matter. A realistic recognition of the de-spiritualized, de-Christianized state of the professions and of public life, together with an understanding of the influence which Catholic women could have on the rehabilitation of these, will, please God, cause parents to plan with as much solicitude and even sacrifice for the specialized education of their bright daughters as they do for their bright sons, particularly when the former show any interest in finding their happiness and saving their souls through careers as women in the world.

To all three groups of women the Holy Father makes one general appeal for cooperation in the building of the peace and the reconstruction of the social order. His basic premise in this appeal is again the essentially creative, constructive, and maternal instincts of the women, no matter what her special vocation. These instincts are outraged by the antagonisms and the war-breeding divisions of our society.

Generally speaking, men have displayed an inability to heal

these divisions, or else an indifference to the sufferings of which they are the causes. It is a truism that even in the animal kingdom the female of the species is instinctively aroused to action when the lives of her young are in danger. Among humans this instinct is lifted to the level of the rational and spiritual safeguarding of the family; it finds its highest expression in the Catholic woman's almost unique jealousy for the safety and sanctity of human life. That life was never in greater jeopardy than it now is. Its sanctity is despised by many who seek to change our fundamental laws: by the Communists, by the racists, by the eugenicists, the birth-controllers and the abortionists. Its safety is menaced by the militarists, the war-breeding politicians, the malevolent diplomats who will most likely write the treaties on which our hopes for peace depend.

The plots of the militarists and the schemes of the others are all aimed at the family, and the woman is ultimately the most valiant defender of that divinely instituted unit. Hence the ringing challenge of the Holy Father: "Your day is here, Catholic women and girls! Public life needs you. Your destiny is at stake. On your social and political activity may depend the legislation and administration of the State. Accordingly, let the electoral ballot in the hands of a Catholic woman be her most important means toward the fulfillment of her strict duties in conscience, especially at the present time."[8]

Our society at home is divided by political partisanship; it is divided abroad by conflicting economic and political Imperialisms. The prospects for peace are almost hopelessly diminished by armament races and by tensions arising out of matters which have nothing to do with the security of the family or the sanctity of life. Women, more concerned with these fundamentals than our male citizens, will cut through the pretensions of political parties and the absurdities of rival Imperialisms in order to promote the basic human values which make for peace. They know its monetary cost and its

81

staggering material sacrifices; even more vividly they know its cost in blood and heartbreak and the shattering of decent human dreams. Because they know these dreams as few men can, the Holy Father depends on them to repudiate policies which obstruct the peace, and politicians who promote division. He depends on them to stand firm against flag-wavers or demagogues who seek to exploit their religious, racial, national, or class loyalties. I beg you to remember in times of elections, or whenever public policies are being formulated, these words of the Holy Father: "No wise woman favors a policy of class struggle or war. A woman's vote is always a vote for peace!"[9]

So women will demand of the politicians who seek to be our peacemakers that they put aside armaments, conscription, balances of power, and the other techniques by which too long the peace has been made impossible. Not long ago Dorothy Thompson published an open letter to the international politicians in which she pretended to speak for all women everywhere. The letter so closely reflects the attitude which our women should have, if they are to fulfill the social destiny to which the Holy Father has summoned them in the international order, that I quote it to you in its entirety.

"Gentlemen of the United Nations Security Council, I would like to present my credentials and I crave a hearing.

"I come from Mary Doe. She did not tell me to come and yet she sent me. She said 'Someone must speak up.' She has been saying that over and over again for centuries. So I have come. For I am, myself, Mary Doe.

"Gentlemen, we have given you our sons. Some are dead, and some are wounded, and some gibber behind bars, and some walk without feet and work without hands, and each of these is as precious to one of us as all the world we gave them to you to save.

"We did not distrust you in those days, gentlemen. We believed in you.

"We said, 'Soon there will be a victory over the forces of evil, and then our good leaders will take the destruction out of the world, and the children of all future mothers will be tucked into bed with laughter, and we will be able to look, then, into the eyes of the photograph, under the Purple Heart, and say softly, You died, beloved, that this good world might be.'

"Now comes the second heartbreak.

"I speak quietly, gentlemen. But we are mothers who cannot look into our dead sons' eyes. When we look we see an accusation in them more terrible than your bombs.

"Their eyes say, 'It is a lie that we died to free humanity of fear and found the world forever on peace. Already new armies are forming, of nations and within nations, and already there is a quarrel between those who speak or pretend to speak for their peoples, as to who shall have the most dreadful war weapon ever invented, and under what circumstances it can be released to glaze the earth it strikes, to evaporate men, women, and children into air. Already spheres of influence, all highly armed, are marked out into which others may not penetrate.'

"Gentlemen, all spheres of influence are inhabited by people. And all these people are bound together, each with the other, into families of fathers who support, mothers who protect, and children upon whose growth in love depends all civilization and culture.

"Gentlemen, all these families in all the nations and in all the regions and spheres, have identical needs, hopes, and yearnings. All, without exception, seek freedom for their own development, as persons and societies, free of pressures from other *powers*, and free of terrorization from parties within. And all, without exception, pray for the security of peace.

"There may be at times states, or ambitious leaders of states, who are not *peace-loving*, but there are only peace-loving mothers, fathers, and children. In the societies they create for themselves and around themselves, within yet apart from the States, Powers, and Parties you gentlemen represent, they live in mutual trust.

"Nowhere must the peace of families be *enforced* by instruments of indiscriminate terror.

"All you gentlemen represent states organized in the name of these families.

83

"You, Leader of the Union of Soviet Socialist Republics, speak for a state that proclaimed less than a generation ago the world-wide solidarity of all people who work. Yet you have not once raised your voice against the slaughter of the children of the vast majority—the workers—if only it be called *enforcing peace*.

"You, Mr. President, represent a country that proclaims liberty under law, the equal rights of all men. Yet you have collaborated with programs establishing one law for the victor and another for the vanquished, one law for the powers and another for the powerless.

"You, Mr. Prime Minister, represent a people rich in tolerance, so peaceable amongst themselves that your police carry no weapons. Yet so fragile is your peace that you do not dare permanently to dissolve your air-raid wardens or shelters, and you too have raised but a weak and unconvincing voice for the controlled prohibition of the race-destroying weapons that have usurped the last free zone of the globe, the air.

"Gentlemen, speak no more to the mothers about your peace and its *enforcement*. Your peace seems almost more terrible to us than was the war. For beyond the war we saw the rainbow of peace, but beyond your peace we see the lightning flashes heralding the thunders of war. Speak to us, gentlemen, of law; speak to us of liberty; speak to us of justice; speak to us of humanity; speak to us of truth.

"Report to us what you are doing to create these. Speak no more to us of your terrible enforcements, not of peace, but of national power.

"Speak to us of charity, and mercy. While you make your speeches and lay your plans, little children and their mothers are dying in the millions because they have no bread.

"Nurtured in confidence and love, no child of mankind knows fear.

"Yet you, gentlemen, whose policies are the outcome and recreator of fear, dare promise to free the world of fear by means of mighty armies. And as a result of your policies, declared to the world with unexampled smugness, the war against the children goes on after every arm has been laid down.

"Some of you are Christian gentlemen. Each of your mothers

84

had but one ambition for you—that you should grow up to be a good man. Each of them taught you to pray, not 'Make me a leader of the world!', but, 'Make me a good boy.' Do you think your mothers were silly? Sentimental? Ah no, gentlemen, they were deeply wise. For goodness is the only source of beneficent power.

"Gentlemen, this is all I have to say now. But it is not the last word. We, gentlemen, are one-half of the human race. We were put into this world to brood and nurture, train and protect humanity. We form the greatest International in the world. You try, gentlemen, to keep us apart. You, sir, will not let us freely communicate with our sisters. You, Mr. President, will not let us reach out our hands to a child elsewhere. You, Mr. Prime Minister, seem to fear more for the British Empire than care for the people in its far-flung parts. But in spite of you we shall find each other.

"Gentlemen, beware! I come from Mary Doe, not to beseech but to admonish and warn. For I am pushed forward by the hosts of the mothers for whom you first groped in the dark, and without whom you wander now in the dark, a darkness shot through with nightmares and terrors.

"We would relieve you of your fears, gentlemen. But first you must lay aside your guns. You must come into the room of your mother unarmed. Then we will show you that the healing power of the world is not where you search for it, is not in the earthquake and the fire, but in the still, small voice; is not in the intellect even, but in the emotion of the ideal—the unquenchable faith in life, the indestructible power of love."[10]

Clearly the vocation of women in our society is a challenging one! The Holy Father declares that it can be fulfilled only under the patronage of the Perfect Woman, the Mother of Christ. She should be for you a symbol of the fact that in all His plans for humanity and at every crisis in history God depends upon the cooperation of women. Even when the work of our redemption was at issue, a work which only God could do, it waited on the free and intelligent cooperation of a woman, the

Jewish girl who became the first and best of Catholic women. She is the patroness of all types of Catholic femininity. A consecrated virgin, she is the queen of our nuns. Mother of Jesus in her home at Nazareth, she is the inspiration of every home builder and founder of a family. The constant companion of her Son in His public life, she is the ideal of those Catholic women in the world who, in every profession and type of career, live so close to Jesus and bring Him so close to society. May she inspire each of you, whatever the vocation God has given you.

VI

Jesuit Centennial in Boston

Browsing through the library not long ago, I came upon the Court Stenographer's record of a trial which took place in Boston from March 17 to April 6, 1859. It was the trial of a schoolmaster, by name McClaurin F. Cooke, submaster of the Eliot School of the City of Boston, for an assault and battery upon Thomas J. Wall, a pupil of that school.[1] It was charged, and at no time denied, that Cooke, whose age the report does not indicate, beat with a rattan stick for thirty-five minutes a boy named Thomas Wall, whose age is given as ten years. The reason for this amazing beating was that young Wall refused to recite the Lord's Prayer, the Ten Commandments, and other passages of Sacred Scripture in accordance with Protestant forms, although, as the evidence on both sides makes abundantly clear, he was ready and willing to recite them in accordance with the Catholic forms of his fathers and his Faith. In a pathetic passage of the Court testimony we learn from Cooke himself and from his sympathizers that young Wall, ten years old, gave no other offense whatsoever, that he acted as he did only after consultation with his father and his priest, and that he made his position clear with dignity and decorum even to the point of repeating quietly, without tears at the age of ten and after the beating had been going on for about fifteen minutes, that he would gladly recite the Commandments and the Lord's Prayer provided he could do so in a form consistent with his conscience. This was not considered adequate, however, and the beating continued until the boy's hands were, as the Protestant doctor testified, swollen, sodden, livid, and with the skin broken in two or three places.

This sermon was preached at the Church of Saint Mary, Boston (the North End), Massachusetts, on October 19, 1947. The church was razed in 1978.

87

It is an amazing document, this Court record, and almost unintelligible after more than ninety years to those of us who live in these more free and favored days. The perfervid flights of oratory of schoolmaster Cooke's attorney, the unconcealed bias of the judge, the evidence of compact solidarity among the youthful witnesses, ranging in age from eight to twelve years, all these would make amusing reading after these many years were it not that even now, almost a century later, there fairly leaps from the yellowed pages of the pamphlet the malice and the bigotry and the perverse narrowmindedness of Judge Maine, of schoolmaster Cooke, of some Miss Shephard who appears as one of the teachers, and of the extraordinary master of bombast, H. F. Durant, Esquire, who was the attorney for McClaurin F. Cooke.

I need not tell you that Cooke was acquitted. Whatever became of young Wall, I do not know, nor of his father, described as a laborer at T Wharf, with whose brogue Cooke's lawyer and the Judge himself had so much fun during the trial. To what end Cooke came or Miss Shephard or Mr. Mason or Judge Maine or H. F. Durant, Esquire, again I do not know. There was one figure in the background of this trial, however, who is very much in my mind tonight. We do know what became of him and of his work and of that of his brethren. We are gathered here to commemorate it. H. F. Durant, Esquire, in the course of one of his many speeches defending Mr. Cooke's bigoted and sadistic beating of young Wall, tells us that the true villain in the cast was not in the courtroom. He says that he was a priest, a member of the Society of Jesus, and he describes him as coming from a foreign land, as speaking with an alien accent, as striving to foment rebellion against the Protestant traditions of Boston and the free institutions of the Commonwealth by influencing in seditious fashion the minds of young Irish boys at secret meetings held, according to his description, in a dark basement of a church in Endicott Street. The meetings, of course, were of St. Mary's Sunday School

88

and the secrecy of these meetings may well be doubted in view of Mr. Durant's own assertion that there were nine hundred young Irishmen present at them; they ranged in age, the Court was informed, from eight to about sixteen.

The nefarious priest in question was, of course, Father Wiget; the Rector of Saint Mary's was Father McElroy. Mr. Durant informed the Court in his blazing peroration that the foreign agents at Saint Mary's in Endicott Street would live to regret the day that he, H. F. Durant, appeared in Court for Mr. Cooke and against their Sunday School pupil. He frankly prophesied that in encouraging boys like young Wall not to be cowards about their religion, as young Wall testified at the age of ten was one of his ideals, the alien Jesuits had overreached themselves and he issued a stern warning that they desist from training boys like Wall, whom he described, the Court concurring, as a very small and somewhat dirty little martyr, a very abominable and altogether absurd little cherub to be sure. And Mr. Durant encouraged the Judge to find satisfaction in his verdict, even if the Irish might resent it, by fixing his attention on the radiant thought that by his decision against young Wall, age ten, and for McClaurin F. Cooke, he would be hastening the end of the work but recently begun on Endicott Street and would silence forever the voice of the Vatican in our fair city.

My thoughts go back tonight to Father Wiget, to Father McElroy and to those who, one hundred years ago, began in a moral and mental clime typified by Judge Maine, schoolmaster Cooke, and Miss Shephard, the parochial, sodality, and educational work which the Jesuits have done in these parts since first they came to Boston, to Saint Mary's on Endicott Street in 1847. By 1859 when young Wall stood in the Police Court before Judge Maine and spoke like a theologian on the difference between the Catholic and the Protestant version of the Ten Commandments, the Fathers had nine hundred boys in their Sunday School here in Saint Mary's. Ten years before that, in 1849, the number of girls in Saint Mary's parish warranted the coming to Boston from Cincinnati of the Sisters of Notre Dame to establish the Girls' School in Stillman Street. By 1860, the year after Judge Maine, goaded on by H. F. Durant, Esquire, had taken the legal steps which would break forever the power of the Jesuits in Boston, Father Wiget had established the parish school for boys and had begun, at the corner of Traverse and Portland Streets, the work of Jesuit education in Boston. Since that day, beginning in a sense with young Wall, in addition to the hundreds of thousands of boys to whom the Jesuits have been Mission preachers, Retreat masters, and Confessors, it is safe to say that the Society of Jesus here in Boston has taught an army, growing larger each year, of more than fifty thousand boys in their parochial schools, high school, College, and allied institutions.

As one of these, and in the name of all the others, I would like this evening to center your thoughts on the Society of Jesus itself.[2] During these days of anniversary each of the elements in the history of the parish will be recalled and eulogized. His Excellency, the Archbishop, pointed out this morning the place of the parish church in the life of the parish and he recalled with praise how old Saint Mary's since the coming of the Jesuits has been the House of God, the Spiritual Home of its parishioners, the Gate of Heaven for priests and people alike. Tomorrow and the day after our thoughts shall turn to the work of the laity, living and dead, to whom we owe the present and the past, and to the work of the parish nuns, who, as the teachers of the children, are the mothers of God of the future to the parish.

I make it my privilege this evening to speak of the Fathers who have been the Spiritual Leaders of Saint Mary's, the centenary of whose coming to Boston occasions this celebration. They are, of course, the Fathers of the Society of Jesus. I shall not limit my consideration to those who have personally shaped the history of Saint Mary's: I urge you all to read their names in the Souvenir program book and to recall, as you do so, the worthy manner in which the parish priests and assistants and missionaries of Saint Mary's have walked in the tradition of piety and patriotism, of priestliness and wholesome public influence established one hundred years ago by the heroic, saintly Father McElroy, Father Bernadine Wiget, and their associates. The priests of Saint Mary's have been great men, great priests. But the only greatness after which they have aspired personally has been the complete and faithful fulfillment of the formula by which they would be great Jesuits. They were men, these priests at Saint Mary's, of the traditional Jesuit pattern, leading lives like to those which, among their confreres in the Old World, so edified their students that even Voltaire, who defamed most other things and persons, said that he would not stoop to the meanness of defaming the Jesuits. More, he added that the best years of his life had been spent in Jesuit schools and that while with them he had never listened to any teaching but what was good nor ever witnessed any conduct but what was exemplary.

What has been the secret of the success of the Society of Jesus in teaching young men? I suppose a score of answers might be given and each would be different and each would have its truth. Certainly, among other characteristics of the work of the Society in the education of young men, these have been present from the beginning: their approach has been positive, rational, conservative, conciliatory, and, above all, spiritual.

It has been positive. Contrary to a popular misconception, the Society was not founded by Saint Ignatius, nor approved by Pope Paul, in order to oppose anything. It was founded and fostered to achieve something. It flourished in the days of the Counter-Reformation, but it did not set forth to overcome any group so much as it did to win over another group. The Society was not founded to oppose Protestantism; nowhere in its letters of approbation nor in its Constitution is there any reference to such a purpose. The original hope of Saint Ignatius, as Europe fell into heresy all about him, was to train men to bring the Faith into areas where it could breathe fresh air and acquire a new beginning. He hoped to convert the Mohammedans, especially the Moors, and, while it is true that his followers were to become famous for their universities and for their disputations with heretics, it is even more significant that Saint Ignatius himself and his companions first sought of the Holy Father permission to teach the Catechism to children and to provide religious instruction to the poor and the ignorant of Italy, Sicily, Spain, France, Germany, and the African and Asiatic missions.

The positive approach of the Society, so fresh in the early years and foremost among the elements of its inspiration, led to its emphasis on reason and the cultivation of reason by education in behalf of the cause of religion. Because of this rational, intellectual element in its tradition, the Society grew rapidly; within two hundred years it had twenty-five thousand members and had established almost eight hundred colleges. By the middle of the eighteenth century, in a period which we think of as de-Christianized and almost completely secular, the Jesuits had two hundred thousand students in their schools and colleges in Europe alone and had established educational centers of every type throughout the missionary world. It was of some of these missionary schools that Senator Vest of Missouri spoke when he told the United States Senate that in his inspection of the Indian schools at the request of the Senate, "I did not see in all my journey a single school that was doing any educational work worthy of the name unless it was under the control of the Jesuits", and he added to his tribute these words: "No man ever went among these Indians with more intense prejudice against the Jesuits than I had when I left the city of Washington."[3]

The conservatism of the Society has frequently been criticized even by their friends. It is, however, the conservatism of people who have something worth conserving—a tradition so closely identified with all that is best in Christianity itself that those who seek to damage Christianity usually begin by attempting to discredit the Jesuits. In our day, as in centuries gone by, the first act of revolutionary governments which seek to cripple the Church is the confiscation of the schools and institutions of the Jesuits; the Society continues to be what Saint Ignatius prayed they would always be: the favorite target of anti-Christian forces.

Despite the conservatism of the Society in matters of faith and in the essentials of the Christian tradition, the Jesuit Fathers have always striven to be the conciliators between the Old Faith and whatever new science may commend itself to each age. Conservative but conciliatory, the genius of the Society of Jesus has made it cordial to new ideas and to new movements. Thus, in the age of the great explorers, in the sixteenth and seventeenth centuries, the Jesuits became the most ambitious and adroit of missionaries in all the newly opened corners of the world. This was the time of Xavier, of Aquaviva, of De Britto, of Ricci, and of Father Avril. Thus, too, in the seventeenth and eighteenth centuries during the Renaissance, the Jesuits sponsored a Christian Humanism which blended the fundamentals of the Faith with the best of the new learning. This was the age of Bourdaloue, of Segneri, and of the Jesuit poets, historians, philosophers, theologians, and court preachers. Thus, in the eighteenth and nineteenth centuries, as science began to dominate the thoughts of men, the Jesuits were among the foremost of Catholic priests and scholars to enter that seemingly remote field of priestly interest. The *Biographical Dictionary of the Exact Sciences*, published in the middle of the last century, lists almost nine thousand names of scientists. Of these, more than ten percent are the names of Catholic priests, and about half of the priests who are listed in the *History of the Exact Sciences* are Jesuits. Most of these did their work as missionaries in the study of geography, of agriculture, of medicine, of botany, of anthropology, and

93

of astronomy; but others, a truly distinguished list, have done their work in the great Jesuit laboratories and observatories for meteorology, astronomy, and seismology, originally in Europe and in South America, but nowhere with greater distinction than here in America, at Georgetown, in California, and in New England, under men like Father Hagen, Father Secchi, Father Tondorf, Father Ricard, and our own Father Ahern here at Weston.

So in our own day as new problems beset the human mind and new formulae, especially in the social, the political, and the economic order, must be found for human living, the Jesuits are in the vanguard of the peace movement, the study of the social question, the new journalism, the possible contributions of psychiatry, and the needed restatement of questions of Church and State, of inter-faith cooperation, of interracial justice, and of international order. To name any men of the Society of Jesus who are working in these critical fields as conservers and conciliators would be to do an injustice to dozens of others of the same Society who are no less hard at work in these same fields.

Above all, the secret of the success of the Jesuits has been in the spirituality of their system. It is a system which produces professional men, scientists, business men, and citizens of the good society; but it produces these almost as by-products. Its essential purpose has been from the beginning the production of saints. The Jesuit saints are known and loved by all Christendom. Each one is different from the others; each is a type of the many classes whom the Jesuits have influenced and guided. There are young noblemen like Stanislaus Kostka and Aloysius Gonzaga; there are young plebeians like Saint John Berchmans. There are lay brothers like Saint Alphonsus Rodriguez; missionaries of the most extraordinary zeal like Saint Francis Xavier or Saint John Francis Regis, and of extraordinary abnegation like Saint Peter Claver and Saint Francis de Hieronymo; there are theologians like Saint Robert Bellarmine and martyrs like those

94

of Elizabethan England, of Asia, and of North America. More than two score of Jesuits have been canonized by the Church; more than six score are listed among the Blessed; countless others bear the title Venerable, the Church's recognition that they truly lived to the greater glory of God.

Here in America the history of the Jesuits is one of the most proud chapters in the story of Catholicism. It has been told with admiration by Protestants like Francis Parkman and with pride by priests like Fathers Hughes, Garraghan, and Harney, or by laymen like Doctor James J. Walsh. The Jesuits have made felt their zeal in the missionary history of America, their learning in the educational history of America, their gifts as conciliators in the political history of America, and especially in the difficult question of religious toleration and civil liberty. It has been said and proved that whenever religious toleration was put forward as a policy of government in the American colonies—with the sole exception of Rhode Island—it was due in essential degree to the Jesuits or to the students of Jesuits.

It may be said that all these considerations are far removed from a local anniversary like the one we celebrate tonight. That is not true. Saint Mary's was the initial point of contact between the Society of Jesus and the organized life of the Catholic Church in these parts. Beginning at Saint Mary's, the Jesuit Fathers have made a contribution to the life of the Church in Boston which includes the qualities we have reviewed here this evening: their positive and rational approach to the education of youth, their conservative instinct together with their readiness to assimilate and adopt to Christian purposes whatever is new and modern and useful, and above all their characteristic spirituality. If there are grounds for pride in the past, they should only serve the more to inspire our prayer for the future: that God may give the Church in Boston through the Society of Jesus even greater services in education, in Catholic thought and in the spiritual inspiration of all our people.

We are privileged to live in times not less but much more challenging than the times which saw the Jesuit beginnings in Boston. We always live in missionary times, we always encounter opposition, we always need new courage, new ideas, new methods. Together with all of us, under the new and challenging leadership of our Archbishop and in the face of ever ancient, ever new, obstacles to the progress of the faith, the Fathers of the Society of Jesus still have a mighty work to do in Boston.[4] We pray God that they will do it; the last one hundred years prove that they will do it well.

VII

The Historian
In the Service of Peace

I count it a privilege to speak to you on the particular subject assigned to me: The Historian in the Service of Peace.

I assume that we are all equally aware of the unhappy fact that peace remains an object of wistful longing rather than of confident enjoyment. The dawn of the mid-century year still finds the forces which work for division as active and as powerful as ever they have been in our times, more active, one still fears, than the forces which work for peace.

These respective forces vary but little from generation to generation. Vocabularies and nomenclature change and so do the alignments of states and regimes. But the causes of war remain constant and equally permanent are the principles of peace. The antagonisms which constitute *cold war* and which lead to armed differences still polarize around the centrifugal loyalties which divide mankind into conflicting cultural, racial, or national camps. The fairest hopes which nourish the dream of peace are those which aspire after some centripetal social loyalties capable of transcending national, racial, or cultural lines and thus achieving a human community—a world organized in peace because united by common bonds.

Division is the work of men. Unity is the Will of God. The divisions fostered by men yield their fruit in war. The unity commanded by God has peace for its social corollary. Both spring from intellect—division from the conflicting counsels which are the thoughts of men, unity from the single thought which is the plan of God.

This address was delivered at the Hotel Statler, Boston, Massachusetts, on December 29, 1949, at the luncheon meeting of the Catholic Historical Society Convention.

Thoughts are the stock in trade of the scholar. Hence the reliance of those who seek peace on all who as scholars write or speak or teach or otherwise influence thought. Historians particularly, it seems to me, are bound by an obligation to be peacemakers, an obligation flowing from the peculiar power of their thoughts to inflame or to discipline national and other group passions.

Doctor Herbert Bell, in his Presidential Address before the eighteenth annual meeting of your association, discussed the obligations of Catholic historians in a world where loyalties are turned into divisive instruments and history is used of set purpose to make nations into bitter enemies.[1] Doctor Bell's observations, made on the eve of the Second World War twelve years ago, are well worth repeating now that the war has ended without any appreciable correction of the conditions which produced it.

Having sketched the manner in which human loyalties had been perverted by the totalitarian regimes of the prewar period, Doctor Bell declared:

> Considering all this, it seems to me that one obligation which rests on Catholic historians stands out clearly. In a world where loyalty is turned into an instrument which helps to darken men's intellects and souls; to reconcile them to the loss of all freedom; to make nations and even groups of fellow citizens into bitter enemies, Catholic historians must do their best to see that loyalty comes into proper use again. They must strive to see that it is placed at the service of Christian civilization and the institutions by which Christian civilization is exemplified; and they must strive most of all to see that the services and the real principles of the Church are understood by Catholics and non-Catholics alike. They must bring back to Christendom the realization that the Church, apart even from its divine nature, is in the highest sense an institution of international utility; that it offers practical reconciliation between order and freedom, patriotism and worldwide brotherhood, tradition and adaptability to men's present needs. Such, indeed, is the duty of every educated Catholic; but it is

the very special duty of Catholic historians. For who does not know the power of history to deepen loyalty? The enemies of Christianity know it so well that they have been at the greatest pains to distort history in their service.[2]

If a layman, Doctor Bell, pleaded as he did for historians to emphasize the historical role of the Church as an agent for peace and as herself a bond of unity in the peaceful society, then perhaps it is appropriate that a priest make, as I now do, the plea that history utilize *every* level of nature and grace, *every* aspect of the history not merely of the Church, but of civil society as well, in order to provide ever more and ever stronger bonds of human unity.

The historian will properly point out the powerful, the unique energies which the Gospel and the earthly City of God bring to forging the unity of mankind. But he will no less certainly prompt his students to reflect on the myriad ways in which the City of Man and the universal voice of Reason cries out for human unity, and he will realize that in the building of peace, in the organization of a sane international order as in all things else, "gratia non tollit naturam, sed perficit et supplet defectum naturae."[3]

In order to enter the service of peace, history, as Lord Acton observed, must be made our deliverer not only from the undue influence of other times, but from the undue influence of our own, from the tyranny of environment and the pressure of the air we breathe. It must help promote the faculty of resistance to merely contemporary surroundings, however compelling, providing a saving familiarity with other ages and other orbits of thought.

If historical studies are so to function unto the liberation of humanity from divisive influences and as a means to the peaceful unity of the race, then somewhere there must be achieved a happy blend of the scientific and the humanistic spirit in the writing, the teaching, and the study of history.

The scientific spirit will be preserved by Catholic historians who render prompt and complete obedience to the oft-quoted admonitions of Pope Leo XIII in his letter announcing the opening of the Vatican archives: ". . . the first law of history is not to dare to utter falsehood; the second, not to fear to speak the truth; and, moreover, no room must be left for suspicion of partiality or prejudice. . . ."[4]

The humanistic spirit is less easy to define. Moreover, in our age of arid *Wissenschaft* on the one hand and the sweating rhetoric of propaganda on the other, it is even difficult to achieve. Perhaps, however, it is likewise among the modern Popes that we will find apt formulae for the development of a worthy humanism in all teaching and particularly in teaching the historical sciences in the service of peace. Obviously if we are to integrate the letter of strict science with the spirit of sane humanism, we must make a distinction between *education* considered as mere instruction or factual stocking of the mind and *education* considered in the full sense of the harmonious development of all the faculties distinctive of man.

The late Pope Pius XI added to his declarations on the devotional and sacramental means to the establishment of the peace of Christ in the reign of Christ an observation which might well be the watchword of the historian in the service of peace: "We now add that this reign can be brought to pass on earth in no other way than by the labor and industry of the Church engaged in the work of educating men."[5]

The Church is engaged in the work of educating men when she speaks authoritatively through the Supreme Pontiff or the Hierarchy in communion with him. She is engaged in the work of educating men when she interrupts or defines through the councils or the ordinary channels of her teaching. But she is also engaged, in due measure, in the work of educating men when she expounds or explains or records or reflects through her scholars, her professors, her poets, her scientists, her historians.

Hence the crucial importance that our historians be themselves motivated by Christian humanism as well as the *scientific* spirit and that they transmit to those whose personalities they shape a truly *humane* as well as a *scientific* understanding of themselves, their race, and their world.

Purely secular attempts to educate for internationalism have suffered almost as much from their lack of genuine *humanism* as they have from the lack of supernatural elements; indeed, the two defects are interrelated. No one will have an adequate understanding of human personality or human history who lacks an appreciation of their spiritual elements, and the very talk of spiritual matters speedily becomes gaseous unless it be firmly founded on an understanding of that Pure Spirit which is God.

In the period between World War I and World War II much honest but wholly inadequate effort went into attempts to provide some species of education for what was called *worldmindedness*. It would be unjust, very unjust indeed, to offer World War II as necessary evidence of the futility of these efforts, but it is the part of truth to declare that they were foredoomed to failure. It is not merely the absence of any creed concerning *God* which vitiates most such studies in international relations; it is also the absence of any concept of *Man*, of the tremendous possibilities as well as the pathetic limitations of man's nature and of human personality, which precludes their effectiveness.

A typical survey of such educational efforts is provided by John E. Harley in his book *International Understanding*, published by the Stanford University Press in 1931. Completely secular in its emphasis, Harley's study provides what he apparently considers an exhaustive list of those educational, social, athletic, and recreational interests which, he tells us, "will train an elite to think, feel, and act internationally."[6]

God finds no place among the interests listed—but neither does the study of *man*, which was once announced to be the proper study of those interested in *mankind*. Significantly enough, neither is there any place given a *philosophy of history* as a means of training an elite "to think, feel, and act internationally."[7]

The Catholic historian will not be surprised by such an omission from a list of interest which does not include either God or man. For him, again as for Acton, Philosophy and History, indeed History and Theology, will always reflect reciprocal light on one another. Said Acton: "History will aid you to see that the action of Christ Who is risen on mankind whom He redeemed fails not, but increases; that the wisdom of divine rule appears not in the perfection but in the improvement of the world. . . . Then you will understand what a famous philosopher said, that History is the true demonstration of Religion."

And so education, if it is to produce citizens of the world in any civilized sense, must be scientific. But it must also be spiritual and therefore truly humane. Historical studies provide in many respects the most important means of making it both. Typical of the divisions underlying the antagonisms of *cold war* and the brutalities of armed conflict are those identified during these recent centuries with aggressive nationalism. Aggressive nationalism has been the product of education, and no course in the curriculum of modern schools has done more to propagate false nationalisms than has the teaching and study of history; conversely no course can render more effective help in correcting the excesses of pagan nationalism and in promoting the wider loyalties which make for peace than the same study of history.

Carlton Hayes points out lucidly in his *Essays on Nationalism* how nationalism is a cultural phenomenon, not at all physical.[8] It is not *in the blood*; it cannot be transmitted biologically from one person to another; it is an *acquired character* and the method of its acquisition, as of any cultural product, is *education*. Hayes likewise confirms the contention that the most dangerous zone of infection is the history classroom.[9]

A wise Frenchman, appealing for a more widespread emphasis on God's part in history and on the broadly human aspects of the pageant of history, speaks of the appalling damage done by *l'histoire dirigée* which has been the principal weapon of the nationalist and the imperialist in promoting divisive loyalties in modern times.[10] His conclusions are confirmed by a typical investigation into the history courses provided national groups which was carried on by a commission of German and French historians who met in 1935; a translation of their findings was published in the *American Historical Review*, January 1938.[11] Like evidence concerning the causes of international and interracial hatred in children has been supplied through the joint study of Baumgarten and Prescott in the *Journal of Educational Psychology*, May 1928.[12]

He is a blind jingoist indeed who fails to recognize to what a great extent our American children have become the victims of a no less crass if usually less militaristic *histoire dirigée*. Surely we can somehow improve certain emphases in our history classes and thus do our part in helping build a more *humane* world order by developing in our children an historical perspective which includes some glimpse of *all* the earth against the background of eternity. Our children must think of local or national elections in 1920 or 1932 or 1948 or 1952 in terms of the places these years will have in the total story of mankind. There must be less thinking of the history of the world in terms of 1066 and 1215 as mere preparation for 1492 and 1520—as these dates in turn were simply a preparation for 1776 and 1812 and the other great years which brought history to its logical culmination in the White House, Radio City, the Chicago World's Fair and the Little Church Around the Corner.

Somehow we must manage to teach the history of every local wonder and national way in terms of the great human adventure. We must give our students a healthy pride in their own particular bypath or pilgrimage under the stars, but at the same time we must develop their sense of the broad highway of history—of the place of their tribe or nation in the human caravan as, having set forth from God in the beginning, it finds its way back to Him at the last, through all the slow stages, the blunders and blessings of the mysteries joyful, sorrowful, and glorious, which are the stuff of history.

VIII

The Philosophy of Responsibility

The trials of the so-called war criminals have been subjected to thoughtful criticism by commentators, legal philosophers, and historians. The opinion has been expressed that these *trials* may eventually cause our Nation and our allies very real embarrassment because the courts which conducted them functioned without previous written law and with the doubtful competence of conquerors. Quite possibly, too, apart from these considerations the cases of individual *war criminals* may have involved injustices or inequities because of passion or partisanship or misrepresentation.

Whatever of all this, there was one refreshing aspect to the determination to bring to trial the *war criminals* and to demand an accounting before some bar of justice from some of those who by deliberate plan and conscious choice brought about the appalling evil that was World War II. This determination constituted a dramatic affirmation before all the world and under the most solemn circumstances of a seriously neglected truth, the truth that political, social, and other moral disasters do not merely happen. They are not the blind results of inexorable fate. Even the most complex of these calamities are not the work of irresponsible, mechanical forces alone. Just as great movements forward in the social history of mankind may be accurately attributed to the honorable actions of upright men, so the moral disasters which overtake men and nations must be attributed to the unfortunate use by responsible men of that freedom in which God created mankind from the beginning.

This sermon was delivered at the Saint Matthew Cathedral, Washington, D. C., on the occasion of the 1949 Red Mass.

In the rise and fall of societies as in the personal salvation or damnation of individual men, the old truth enunciated by the Sacred Scripture remains valid. It is a law of social history as well as a condition of individual salvation: "He shall have glory everlasting who was free to transgress but did not; who was free to do evil things, but did not do them."[1] This is the clue to man's perfection: "Before man is life and death, good and evil, that which he shall choose shall be given him."[2] "Behold I set forth in your sight this day a blessing and a curse: a blessing if you obey the commandments of the Lord your God . . . a curse, if you obey not."[3] This is the key to a nation's progress, its use of the freedom in which God made man from the beginning: "Jerusalem, Jerusalem, thou who killest the prophets, and stonest those who are sent to thee! How often would I have gathered thy children together, as a hen gathers her young under her wings, but thou wouldst not!"[4]

The determination to bring to justice the so-called war criminals constitutes, I repeat, a dramatic reaffirmation of the reality of free will and of personal responsibility for the moral consequences of individual actions. I speak of a *reaffirmation* because the philosophy of responsibility had lost something of its appeal, certainly in social thinking and possibly in legal thinking, in the generation immediately preceding the war.

There had always been the temptation to shuffle off responsibility for moral defect. Shakespeare described and refuted it: "This is the excellent foppery of the world, that, when we are sick in fortune—often the surfeit of our own behaviour—we make guilty of our own disasters the sun, the moon, and the stars; as if we were villains by necessity, fools by heavenly compulsion, knaves, thieves, and treachers by spherical predominance, drunkards, liars, and adulterers by an enforced obedience of planetary influence. . . ." But, "The fault, dear Brutus, is not in our stars, but in ourselves, that we are underlings."[5]

The philosophy of responsibility in modern times has

further suffered from the impersonal, collectivist theories of society and of history which found favor during and since the last century. These linked human action more often to material forces and mass controls than to spiritual personality and individual responsibility. An earlier generation of devout and God-fearing people had recognized the challenge of some environments and the limitations of certain heredities, but they still acknowledged that the generality of men remains free to make conscious choice between moral life and death, good and evil. But then social theory followed new lines along which it has attempted to lead legal theory and application. As against the old philosophy of responsibility there has grown up the theory that misconduct is always abnormal, that what the law calls crime and what the conscience calls sin are to be explained largely in terms of causes beyond the control of the sinner or the criminal. The philosophy of responsibility has been replaced by the philosophy of excuse.

Under the newer concept, it is no longer a question of being able to transgress, but refusing to do so; it is more a question of acting in accordance with the characters which, without our asking, we have received. Character is considered a product of circumstances, and delinquency and crime are simply other names for conflict and maladjustment. Criminals are sick people, like the insane. They should be dealt with as sick people and far from seeing in their criminal actions anything for which they are responsible, we must learn to recognize in criminality the existence of something for which society is responsible. This has become the typical doctrine of a whole school of psychology and sociology. Hence the familiar captions under pictures of young criminals, "Who is the real delinquent, this boy or society?" Hence, too, the frequent statements of sociologists and other experts who announce, "We believe in the responsibility of society, not of the individual."

Last month I listened to a broadcast over a national network of an extremely effective radio drama. It was clearly conceived by its author and presented by its broadcasters as setting forth a profound and cogent point. Its scene was the cell of a condemned murderer. Every device of skillful radio-theater drove home the idea of the play as stated by the players:

> Tonight I am sitting on the edge of a prison cot in the cell of a condemned murderer. Between him and the rope which will break his neck and choke the breath from his throat are nine hours of tortured darkness. Soon the collective hand of society will reach out and pull the lever that will spring the trap and send his feet kicking in mid-air in the death struggle. Perhaps the collective conscience of society will permit itself a slight qualm. As I write the murderer watches me. He is nothing more than a big-boned, hulking, somewhat dull kid who continually trembles. He will die in the first light of the morning. I shall write then about the court which should have tried him. It is a purely imaginary court (a court which sits in judgment on ordinary people who lead what might be called a blameless life.) A court established by a law which reads in part: "Whereas the state decrees that no one lacking twenty-one full years in age, can now alone be held responsible for any murder, it is ordered that a minimum of six shall then be hanged if one such minor is condemned to die." And so this court has been called to quickly find the necessary five; the five additional nooses which await along with the one society has decreed for the young murderer.

The five extra nooses, as the play developed, were fashioned for the necks of the boy's school authorities, his parents, a political leader in his community, a representative of organized entertainment, and an average member of the general community. The broadcast was extremely effective. It undoubtedly left in the minds of millions the impression that thus responsibility was placed where it always belongs: not with the individual criminal, but with the total society—and therefore with no one. It was a dramatic example of the *philosophy of excuse* as opposed to the *philosophy of responsibility*.

Judge John Perkins, former Justice of the Boston Juvenile Court, tells how one morning a probation officer came into his court room and said: "I went to the prison association dinner last night. The principal speaker made a moving address. At the end of it, after describing how a parolee had committed an atrocious murder, he burst into a dramatic peroration. Raising his eyes to the ceiling and with his voice trembling with emotion he exclaimed dramatically: 'Somehow, somewhere, some one of us failed this man.' " The judge remarked ironically: "You mustn't object to that argument. As a matter of fact, it is a wonderful idea for us, too. All these cases we have been worrying about, because they turned out badly, were not our fault. We never failed. Whenever we thought we had failed, someone else had always failed *us*."

This is the *philosophy of excuse—the philosophy of ultimate irresponsibility*. For more than a generation it has undermined the moral and legal and individual social responsibilities upon which the stability of society must repose.

The linking of misbehavior to maladjustments and to forces beyond the control of the individual offender may frequently be justified, but not so often as to warrant a general philosophy of law which loses sight of the normal facts of individual responsibility and of personal freedom. Misbehavior, whether sinful or criminal, always includes an element of maladjustment, but sometimes there are adjustments which the *individual* must make on the level of the spiritual in order to meet the test of the material and the trial of the evil.

We must ameliorate bad conditions. We must strive by social action to lighten the load where it is unjust or unsafe, but we must recognize that in all this adjustment there are adjustments expected of the individual as well. We have rationalized too many ruthless tyrants in terms of their adolescent frustrations. Too many maladjusted criminals have been explained in terms of the conflicts and tensions of potentially great artists who were forced to be obscure paperhangers in Austria or of

109

potentially great leaders of social movements who were destined to become gangsters and leaders of anti-social rackets which tore American communities apart. Too much gangsterism and sheer criminality on the obscure levels of the underworld and on the higher levels of international action and diplomacy have been encouraged by this *philosophy of excuse* in the realm of conscience and on the level of courts. The war crimes trials have caused to resound in our century some echo, at least, of that voice of responsibility which spoke centuries ago with accents divine: "This night do they require thy soul of thee."[6] They have reminded public servants of that accountability which is imposed on every free agent: "How is it that I hear this of thee? Give an account of thy stewardship, for now thou canst be steward no longer."[7]

It is good for civilization that the *philosophy of responsibility* should be reaffirmed and that the *philosophy of excuse* should be subordinated to it, cut down to size. Civilization was not achieved by any such philosophy as that of excuse, by vagueness about accountability. Mankind did not emerge from recurring periods of social decline and even savagery by any such formulae. Social progress has not been accomplished by swinging along with impersonal destinies, by riding the wave of the future, by the blind operation of uncontrolled biological, economic, or social forces. It has been achieved by the vision and determination, by the self-knowledge and self-discipline of single individuals and of individuals in groups who have understood the meanings of these responsible, contructive words: *I know. I will. I do.*

" 'Lord, if thou wilt, thou canst make me clean.' And stretching forth His hands Jesus touched him saying: 'I will: be thou made clean.' And immediately his leprosy was cleansed."[8]

"And returning to himself, he said: 'I will arise, and will go to my Father, and say to Him: "Father, I have sinned against heaven and before Thee. I am not worthy to be called Thy son; make me one of Thy hired servants" '."[9]

It is for us, the living, rather to be dedicated here to the unfinished work which they who fought here have thus far so nobly advanced. It is rather for us to be here dedicated to the great task remaining before us: that from these honored dead we take increased devotion to that cause for which they gave the last full measure of devotion; that we here highly resolve that these dead shall not have died in vain; that this nation, under God, shall have a new birth of freedom; and that Government of the people, by the people, and for the people, shall not perish from the earth.[10]

Poverty is the north wind that lashes men into Vikings. What we call evils, as poverty, neglect, and suffering, are, if we are wise, opportunities for good. If I am left alone, yet God and all the heroic dead are with me still. If a great city is my dwelling place, the superficial life of noise and haste shall teach me how blessed a thing it is to live within the company of true thought and high resolves. Whatever can help me to think and love, whatever can give me strength and patience, whatever can make me humble and serviceable, though it be a trifle light as air, is opportunity, whose whim it is to hide in unconsidered things, in chance acquaintances and casual speech, in the falling of an apple, in floating weeds, or the accidental explosion in a chemist's mortar.[11]

It is easy to satirize these valiant concepts of an age perhaps more rhetorical, but also more resourceful, more self-reliant, more imbued with the *philosophy of responsibility*, more contemptuous of the *philosophy of excuse*. But the whole history of human achievement gives meaning to that rhetoric and attests to the worth of those who indulged in it, who taught their children and told their fellow-citizens and trained themselves to recognize that they could do evil, but must not, that they could transgress, but would not.

So we in our legislation, in our law courts, in our social theory, must recognize and make allowance for the inadequate and the unfortunate, but we must not treat their condition as the normal condition of mankind and we must not spin our

III

moral philosophy around their deficiencies. In our sympathy we must not place emphasis on excuse rather than on responsibility and thus spread a demoralizing social philosophy. We must make responsibility the universal norm and excuse the challenged exception. We must state the rules rather than constantly find reasons why they do not apply. We might well return to a bit of the rhetoric that glorified heroism and achievement and tone down the rhetoric lavished on those who lack the moral wherewithal by which to try or who, having it, prefer to serve themselves and blame society rather than serve society and honor themselves. We must recognize how the *philosophy of responsibility* enabled boys with withered legs to become useful citizens, leaders of their community, but above all masters of themselves—while the *philosophy of excuse* has allowed men of real intelligence and potential parts to become the instruments of society's confusion and of their own damnation. Social stability and individual salvation still depend on the recognition of the central place of individual responsibility in whatever good may be accomplished or whatever evil must be suffered on the face of the earth over which God gave man dominion.

Specifically, it was the philosophy of responsibility that made America great. It is the basis of free self-government as free self-government in turn has been the basis of American greatness. Woodrow Wilson said some wise things about the relationship of self-government to the kind of character produced by the philosophy of responsibility. He said: "Self-government is not a mere form of institution, to be had when desired, if only the proper pains are taken. It is a form of character. It follows on the long discipline which gives a people self-possession, self-mastery, the habit of order and common counsel, and a reverence for law which will not fail when they themselves become the makers of law."

I offer this as a legitimate social and political conclusion from the moral philosophy of responsibility: If we are to acquire or keep the kind of character which Wilson said was essential for self-government, we must preserve the disciplines by which that character is built and the moral philosophy which dictates those disciplines. Church, state, and home must unite in happy understanding to teach each generation the self-possession, self-mastery, the habit of order and peace and common counsel which will not fail them when they themselves become the makers of law. Thus will our citizenry become the men of glory who could transgress, but will not do so; who could do evil things, but will not do them; who use their freedom, fortified by God's grace, to do God's will on earth unto the temporal stability of their nation and the eternal salvation of their souls.

Part Two

The Worcester Years

1950—1959

Introduction

In Webster's *New Collegiate Dictionary* the word *charisma* is defined as: "1: an extraordinary power (as of healing) given a Christian by the Holy Spirit for the good of the Church; 2a: a personal magic of leadership arousing special popular loyalty or enthusiasm for a public figure (as a political leader or military commander); b: a special magnetic charm or appeal."

Certain acknowledged leaders of the world known to us in the history books of the past two centuries especially—such as Napoleon, Lincoln, Theodore Roosevelt, Churchill, Albert Schweitzer, Pope John XXIII, and today Pope John Paul II—could be said to qualify under 2a and 2b as having *charisma*.

I think that such *charisma*, with an effect upon so many people in our time, was also the gift of John Wright—as a student, priest, bishop, and Cardinal-Prefect of the Congregation for the Clergy. He used this gift, this *charisma*, throughout his life, from his entrance into the teaching body of the Church in 1935 until his death in 1979, for one purpose alone, the propagation of the Faith.

Those who knew Cardinal John Wright, and especially those who were fortunate enough to be associated with him in Worcester, and indeed wherever he lived, will never forget him. He loved all his priestly assignments; but the diocese of Worcester was his first vineyard and he its first shepherd. The zeal and affection he ever had for Worcester—called the Heart of the Commonwealth of Massachusetts, because of its geographical location—became for him truly a part of the Heart of the Church of Christ. This seemed evident to me by the way John Wright, the first bishop of Worcester, interpreted by his life the words *Resonare Christum*, his chosen episcopal motto. Otherwise I could not, then or now, explain the happy circumstances of the birth, the continual vigor, and the progress of the Church in Worcester. Indeed, the first bishop's successors, the Most Reverend Bernard Flanagan and the Most Reverend Timothy Harrington, have labored to maintain and to nourish, as their happy inheritance, the diocese of Worcester, Massachusetts.

I first met John Wright at the North American College in Rome. At that time, the college was located on the Via dell'Umiltà, near the Trevi Fountain. He was registered in the class of 1936. I was a member of the class of 1934. My acquaintance grew into a lifetime friendship and endured until his death on August 10, 1979. It was my happy experience to live with him in the bishop's house in Worcester and to work with him as his first chancellor and second vicar general in the early years of the new diocese. In later years, I enjoyed his confidences and kindnesses during friendly visits to Pittsburgh or Rome as often as my own pastoral duties allowed. Because of him I came to enjoy and to be honored by a lasting friendship with his family whom he loved dearly and by whom he was loved in return. Prelates, priests, religious, and many thousands of devout Catholic and non-Catholic friends and acquaintances also shared the Cardinal. Hence, I am honored to have been asked to write a few personal memories—as the Introduction to *The Worcester Years*—about this priest who served God with his whole heart, mind, and strength.

I remember him as a public speaker from his debating society years at Boston College and throughout his ecclesiastical career. In his day he was the equal of the best Catholic apologists in these United States. His voice was never a powerful one, in fact at the start of any sermon or address it was not attractive; yet he was able to hold an audience wherever, or to whomever, he spoke. He seemed to sense what the audience wanted and then with a joke or a story or the description of some personal experience—always very well told—he was able to teach and to accomplish what he had set out to do.

118

In Boston, Worcester, Pittsburgh, and Rome he preached and lectured—as long as his health allowed—wherever he was invited. And, as this collection testifies, he spoke all over the world. Yet somehow, at the same time, he fulfilled the exhausting, everyday, administrative tasks of diocesan business and later of national and international committee work.

I remember him as a prolific writer, often laboring throughout the night and into the early hours of a new day, preparing a sermon for the installation of a bishop or for some similar important event in the life of the Church when the doctrinal position of the Catholic Church had to be upheld or built up again in the minds and hearts of its people.

With all that work, still he was able to find time to study the life and to write about his beloved Saint Joan of Arc, a lifelong heroine. Saint Joan typified for him the country he loved and admired—France. And he admired the good that her sainthood exemplified for the world in which we live. Because of his affection for his native city, Boston, he arranged before he died that his private collection of Saint Joan books and memorabilia be donated to the Boston Public Library. Thus he insured that the Saint's life and lessons would continue to inspire and to teach today's citizens and generations yet to be born.

Like all scholars, wherever he lived, he kept a large library. It contained many old and new Bibles, biblical commentaries, the usual periodicals read and studied by the clergy, a fine collection of English classics (especially Shakespeare) and all manner of theological literature, Catholic and otherwise. He frequently used this library not only for reference, but as a research tool to provide proof and substance to the many theological papers that he enjoyed preparing and editing.

I never knew a person who was such a slave to his mail; but, again, for him it was a means to an end. He began his day, and often ended it late in the evening, by dictating the replies to his mail into a dictaphone. Efficient secretaries typed these daily for his signature. Upon his return from speaking tours, pilgrimages, meetings, or visits, one had to meet him at the airport with baskets of mail which he began to open even before the car left the airport. Indeed, until the last minute before he left his home or office for a journey the outgoing mail was always carefully read first and then signed. Copies of his letters were always kept and filed. He urged his co-workers to do the same. He used to say: "Always have a back-up man, for the Church must go on." And, "the Church must not die because of business left undone or records not kept."

The Cardinal loved music, especially classical music, although he never to my knowledge played any musical instrument. From the time he came to Worcester until his departure for Pittsburgh (1950 to 1959) his appearance was a permanent feature at the traditional Annual Fall Musical Week, sponsored by the music lovers of Worcester, in the Worcester War Memorial Auditorium. He thus became a personal friend of the *Worcester Telegram*'s music critic, Raymond Morin. He was also a friend of Worcester's truly great and highly respected music director, Harry Levinson. A lifelong friendship with Boston's world-famous Arthur Fiedler made possible the annual Pops Concert of the Boston Symphony Orchestra presented in the Worcester War Memorial Auditorium for the benefit of Saint Vincent's Hospital.

In the Bishop's house, on High Ridge Road, in Worcester, a Hi-Fi record player, playing opera records, was a daily and often a nightly event. In fact, the Cardinal seldom bothered to look at television and, as I recall, in Worcester he never owned or wanted to own a television set for the news or entertainment. The radio news broadcasts kept him contented and well informed.

Cardinal Wright was not a sports lover. More, he particularly disliked football. He had once seen a teenage boy playing football without protective clothing killed in a sand-lot game. And that, as he told me, turned him off. Yet he could understand—if not always approve of—people (such as his first chancellor) who loved football.

In those days and to this very day I usually managed to attend the annual Holy Cross–Boston College game. I was graduated from Holy Cross College. If Holy Cross lost that New England Catholic Football Classic—which unfortunately it did much too often in the years the Cardinal lived in Worcester—I could, without fail, expect upon my return to the bishop's house the following reception. Be it early or late in the evening, on the main door of the bishop's house, black crepe was hung. Inside in the hallway and in the main parlor, the lights were dim and the Hi-Fi record player, turned up to full power, was playing Verdi's *Requiem*.

There was however one sport, baseball, which did attract his attention. Although I cannot recall him attending any major league games, he did know the game and the players—and was willing to make, now and again, a small wager on the outcome. I learned the hard way—after twice losing in what I thought was a sure thing—that he was no one to bet against without some previous and careful study of the odds.

Yes, the Cardinal knew that athletics have a part in the complete education of youth. In Worcester, whether it was the annual Saint Peter–Saint John High School Thanksgiving Day game, or (during the winter months) an important basketball game (be it a high school, or the Holy Cross–Assumption College contest) the Cardinal had to be there. And when he could not attend, a diocesan official was asked to substitute for him. The promotion of a healthy athletic program in the Worcester diocesan secondary schools was a permanent feature in any curriculum approved by him.

Cardinal Wright was always a loquacious person. He loved to be with people and to talk with people. His mind was ever active and conversation on many topics came easily to him. Italy, and the city of Rome, was a favorite topic between us. My own acquaintance with and affection for that country and city could not be compared to his, yet it was a bond between us until his death.

121

If ever a person loved Italy and the city of the Popes and Caesars of the world, it was Cardinal Wright. I am always happy for him that his active life, in the Church he loved and served so well, ended in Rome and that he died in office as the American-born prefect of a Roman Congregation, in the Roman Curia. The often quoted line of Robert Browning, in the *De Gustibus II*, truly can be applied to John Wright:

> Open my heart and you will see
> Carved inside of it 'Italy'.

I must also say that Cardinal John Wright was a very human person. In his busy career he never forgot that life is made up of human saints and those many others who, to overcome their faults, need saints and their examples. In this regard, read *The Church of the Saints*, an address he delivered on June 6, 1952. The Cardinal loved perfection and being a very thorough person himself, he rejoiced when he found it in others. More, he was quick to praise excellent performance in the lives of others regardless of their vocation in life.

His zeal for souls was never harnessed by religious, ethnic, or intellectual bonds and for this reason he will long be remembered by those who knew him. Monsignor Francis Manning—a fellow diocesan priest, friend of many years and a former co-worker in the Worcester chancery—speaking about Cardinal Wright once said to me: "You either liked him and therefore admired him or you did not like him. You, and most of us who worked for him, liked him."

In the lobby of Saint Vincent's Hospital, Worcester, there is a fairly large portrait of John Wright, who was the bishop of Worcester when this present hospital was built to supplement the first and earlier hospital. He had worked hard with the Sisters of Providence, the administration, the surgical and medical staffs, the hospital personnel and many, many interested citizens of Worcester City and Worcester County—Catholic and non-Catholic alike—in order to provide the best of medical care in the new hospital. Indeed his interest in helping the sick—see *A Clergyman Views Medicine* (1951) and *The Nurse's Vocation* (1953)—welded together, from that time on, the trustees, administration, physicians, and the entire hospital personnel to function in harmony for the spiritual and physical well-being of all who came to the hospital for aid.

The last public service I was able to render the Cardinal was in June 1969. This time, as a Plenipotentiary Apostolic, he asked me to read the document from the Vatican naming him the titular of a lovely new church in the Monte Mario section—a new development of residential buildings—in Rome. The Church is named: *Gesù Divino Maestro*—"Jesus the Divine Teacher". Almost twenty years had passed since I had read a similar document, from the Vatican, in Saint Paul's Cathedral, Worcester, for the installation of the then first bishop of the newly formed diocese of Worcester.

Cardinal Wright because he was so human never thought, or presumed to think, that he was even a little omnipotent. In fact, he always prayed for God's help in his work as a priest, bishop, or cardinal. In spite of the very many good things he accomplished in Worcester and wherever God called him, in spite of the high office he held in the Church, in spite of the confidence he enjoyed from several Popes and many acknowledged civil leaders in Europe and these United States, Cardinal Wright was always a Christian gentleman with the sincere trust and humility to be worthy of the Creator he served so well.

Otherwise, how can I explain his "Pray for me" request—a request made so often to the people and even to those closest to him? I remember he made it to me, in particular, on the day he was ordained a bishop, in Boston. I remember he made it to me many times afterward when I would meet him during his active years. I remember he made it to me during the last visit I had with him, in Boston, just a few days before his death.

He was dying and his vision was gone. He could not see me,

123

but he recognized my voice. He told me how he had received the Sacrament of the Anointing of the Sick again that day and that he was ready to die. He asked for my blessing. And finally, for the last time in this life, I heard his voice . . . and he said to me: "Pray for me."

John F. Gannon

IX

Monsignor Walter S. Carroll, 1908–1950

It is my sad privilege to speak this morning a few words of fraternal tribute to Monsignor Walter Carroll and of Christian comfort to his loved ones.[1]

I speak as the representative of Monsignor's classmates and of his priest friends. However, if I may intrude a personal note, there is a slight reason why I might appropriately serve to interpret the sympathy of us all to Monsignor's family.

In the first days after our ordination to the priesthood Father Walter and I offered our Masses simultaneously one morning in Saint Ignatius' great Roman Church.[2] Father Walter's mother was present at those Masses, and afterwards, out in the sunshine of a Roman square, we had a reunion which she will remember as having been made lighthearted by the joy of new priests, by genial Roman customs and by the happiness of *First Masses*.

The Mass this morning is one of Requiem—but it is the same Mass as rejoiced us that day. The same Christ is offered. The same priesthood is His instrument. The same Roman Faith is expressed. The same God is pleased. The same persons are present for this moment of passing sorrow as were present then on that morning of springtime priesthood.

The Mass which Father Walter then offered himself is not less efficacious now that it is offered for him by the representative of Christ's Vicar in our land.[3] The same Christ with Whom Father Walter was then united at the altar is even more intimately his life and being now that he is united to Him in eternity. Roman Faith has been transmuted for him into a yet more perfect form of knowledge in the vision of that

This eulogy was preached at the Saint Matthew Cathedral, Washington, D. C., on February 27, 1950.

Divinity of which we saw only the broken reflections when we were students those years in Holy Rome.

The God Who gave joy to our youth and to Walter's mother on that morning fifteen years ago is with us yet, to give us and her joy, one more subtle, more profound, spiritual, the joy of resignation to God's will, of confidence in Christ's promise that: ". . . he who believes in me, though he die, yet shall he live, and whoever lives and believes in me shall never die."[4]

It is easy to see in false perspective the dignities and distinctions which came so early in his life, but perhaps so fatally for the health of Monsignor Carroll. It is easy to misunderstand these things. One might be tempted to say: "How wonderful that one so young should have honors so great, be entrusted with responsibilities so serious!" Yet such a speaker would reveal no understanding of the crushing weight of some honors, the toll that such responsibilities take of those who bear them. On the other hand, another might be tempted to say: "How sad that one so young should die, should be broken in the very maturity of his priesthood!" Such a speaker would reveal no understanding of what a privilege it is to be worn out in the service of Christ's Vicar and Christ's Church, to be quickly, eagerly spent in the service of Christ Himself.

The time of a good priest's death is always in the hands of God and we would be rash indeed to speak of it as *premature*, however young, however gifted, the priest might be. When Giosuè Borsi wrote his spiritual testament in the very springtime of his life, yet the eve of his death, he set forth sentiments which spring even more spontaneously to the lips of the good priest, such as Monsignor Carroll most certainly was. "A better end could not have crowned my life, and I feel the pleasure to have made a good and generous use of it. . . . Do not weep, mother, for it was written in Heaven that I should die. Do not mourn, or else you would regret my happiness. I am not to be mourned but envied. My daily death shall have come to an end, and I shall be face to face with the Judge

Whom I have greatly feared, to the Lord Whom I have greatly loved."[5]

If the devout Italian soldier so wrote, surely this devoted priest would have spoken in no less patient and joyous resignation to God's Holy Will. Think of how many things, much more difficult than dying, he did out of love and loyalty for Christ and for His Church!

Two years ago, in a London bookstore, I was fingering through the war memoirs of a British Army officer in Africa and Italy. I was suddenly startled to find in the index the name of my classmate, Walter Carroll. The references were few, but significant. Reading around them and between the lines one could imagine the firmness and fortitude with which Monsignor Carroll, like so many of the representatives of the Holy See and Christ, was obliged to resist political maneuvers when these would do violence to the Law of God or the true welfare of men—to state, simply yet strongly, the position of the Church and therefore of God when this might otherwise have been forgotten or neglected or despised.

Reflecting on the priestly life that Monsignor Carroll was destined to live, especially during the recent War, I thought of the words in which Saint Paul proclaimed the glory—the hard-earned glory—of his apostolate: ". . . on frequent journeys, in danger from rivers, danger from robbers, danger from my own people, danger from Gentiles, danger in the city, danger in the wilderness. . . ."[6]

Surely the parallel is clear. What journeys Monsignor Carroll undertook on errands for the Holy See and in the service of the Church and therefore of Christ! Journeys under wartime conditions and with all the hazards of war. In danger, in a sense, from his own people whenever, as must frequently have been the case, it was necessary in the name of religion and of the Church to resist plans or policies conceived in considerations of mere political or military convenience, or shortsighted reasons of State, not to say sometimes of prejudice, irreligion, or ignorance. In danger from other nations constantly. In danger in cities as an agent for Christ in the midst of intrigue. In danger in the wilderness as an envoy of Christ to soldiers far from home and from normal spiritual controls as they did the brutal work of Caesar.[7]

So, Monsignor Carroll can also say with Saint Paul, as early exhausted he lays down his arms from strenuous service: "I have fought the good fight. I have finished the course. . . . Bonum certamen certavi. Cursum consummavi. Fidem servavi."[8]

So we come back to the thought of his journeys, the journeys from Rome to Africa, to Paris, to New York, to other places which were to be the threads out of which was woven his apostolate, an apostolate unique among the priestly careers of our classmates. On each of these journeys friends would see him off as the boat sailed or the plane left the ground. And each time that friends would see him off, they thought the thoughts which people have always thought, from the beginning of time, when loved ones go forth on a journey. We stand on the pier, or on the ramps above the airfield, or on the railroad platform. The ship moves slowly away from us; it gains the great ocean. The train slides from its terminal, gently at first, then it gathers speed and rolls rapidly on its way. The plane vibrates, eager to leave the earth; it skims along the field, it is lifted skyward, it recedes further and further into the blue. At length we no longer see the loved ones who have ventured forth on their journey. First they, then the ship, the train, the airplane, become mere specks and disappear beyond the horizon where earth and sea and sky all meet and merge with one another.

Then someone always says: "There! He's gone."

Gone where? Gone on his journey—out of our sight, that's all. And even as we say: "He's gone!" we think to ourselves and we remind one another of those who shall be awaiting at the other end, waiting to meet him, to welcome him, to learn of him the details of the journey.

The ship, the train, the plane, though now they seem mere specks, remain areas large in dimension, as strong in force, as able to bear their load of living freight as they were when they stood by our sides. Their diminished size as they fade from view is in us, not them. And just at that moment when we say: "He's gone!" other voices, beyond the limit of our sight, are ready to say: "Lo! He comes!"

So it was with the wartime journeys which constituted so great a part of Monsignor Carroll's apostolate. So must it be with this journey by which his journeys end.

We stand by the side of death and, in language like that of the traveler's friends as they see him off, we cry: "There! He's gone!" Gone where? Gone from our sight, that's all.

Gone on the journey which ends where all journeys must: in God, in Eternity, with Christ. Gone to be welcomed by all those who before him made the same journey—but especially, we cannot doubt, by those who prepared for eternity by doing work like to the work that he did, the unique work of special service to the Holy See.

Surely Christ must have some special welcome for those who collaborated with His Vicar at the heart's core of His Church. Surely, the Holy Apostles, Peter and Paul, must receive with special warmth one who labored so long, so hard, in the City that is theirs. Surely they must acknowledge the right of our priest to echo the words of one of them: "I have fought the good fight. I have finished the course. I have kept the faith."

Eternal rest grant unto him, O Lord! May he rest in peace! May his soul and all the souls of the faithful departed through the mercy of God rest in peace.[9] Amen!

X

A Clergyman Views Medicine

It is a refreshing sign of the times that you invite a clergyman to offer his contribution to the deliberations of today's medical conference.

As the Chairman has said, the priest and the doctor, the clergyman and the physician, have many points of contact and of mutual interest. When moral guidance breaks down, when I fail to make my teaching effective, then my wayward sheep turn to you for sedatives, for shots, and for relief from the allergies to their own wild oats.

Conversely, and as a kind of professional courtesy, I maintain a discreet silence as I stand by the graves of your incomplete diagnoses.

On the other hand, you and I have inevitable and friendly tensions between us. A doctor sweats for days on end; he keeps vigils for long waking nights. Finally the patient pulls through. He becomes conscious, and the hospital chaplain tells him—"Thank God."

Yet, the Italians have a proverb: "God cures you and the doctor sends the bill."

The occasional tensions between the priest and the doctor, the prophet and the scientist, have other and more deep roots, however.

The technician, the scientist, the research man, the doctor—these are the masters of *know-how*. The prophet, the poet, the priest—these are the exponents of *know-why*. One group is concerned with proximates; the other is concerned with

This address was delivered at the Traymore Hotel, Atlantic City, New Jersey, on June 10, 1951, before the Conference of Presidents and other officers of the State Medical Association.

purposes. Each is indispensable ultimately to the other; both are sensitive to each other, sometimes even allergic.

Civilization depends on the happy blending of the two. In some moments of civilization, *know-why* predominates. Such periods are times of great dreams, great mystics, great cathedral builders, great contemplatives, great peace.

The late Dr. James J. Walsh used to point out, in connection with the thirteenth century, something which was confirmed by an investigation at Harvard, of all places. In 1937 the Harvard Department of Sociology announced it as a fact that the average man of the thirteenth century had six thousand, five hundred more chances to die peacefully in bed and of natural causes than has any member of the twentieth century. This is worth thinking about, particularly if you have any hopes of dying in bed. The average man of the thirteenth century, the period when the ideas of the mystic, the poet, and the priest tended to dominate culture and civilization, the average man had six thousand five hundred more chances to die peacefully in bed than has his descendant in the twentieth century. That was a *know-why* period of civilization.[1]

Other periods of civilization are periods of *know-how*. The first half of the present century, for example, has been largely a *know-how* period of civilization, a time of extraordinary mechanical, technological, scientific, and material advances, reaching their absurd development in the age of the *gadget*.

I hope it is not unfair to hope that *know-how* has presumably reached its peak in the A-bomb, or unjust to suggest that it has gone to seed in the *gadget* civilization which is now upon us, a civilization which produces in its citizens the pathological condition Dr. John Fallon, of Worcester, describes as *gadgettarrhea*: "A disease characterized by the inordinate desire to make something useful, preferably from junk."

In more dignified terms, this instinct sometimes passes for the scientific spirit—an excess of which, even in medicine, is unhealthy.

131

So, the thirteenth century belonged to the mystics. The first half of this century has belonged to the scientists. Perhaps there is a good chance that the last half (please God, all the future) will belong to both—to mystics with their feet on the ground and to scientists with their eyes on Heaven.

The reaction against scientism, against mere technology, against mere *know-how*, has not been limited to the friendly or the critical laymen. It has been manifest in the medical profession itself.

For instance, I find in the *New England Journal of Medicine* for November 2nd, 1950, some exceedingly healthy remarks under the heading *Medicine, Science, and Humanism*, from which permit me to quote:

> Sir Henry Cohen, professor of medicine at the University of Liverpool, delivered the presidential address before the British Medical Association this year on *Medicine, Science, and Humanism*. These subjects and the homilies that can be based on their reactions to each other are hardly new, but they are of recurring value; like the characteristic signals of a lighthouse they must be repeated at regular intervals if the purpose for which they are intended is to be served.
>
> Looking back, as it is the fashion of the year to do, on the gains and losses of a half-century, Sir Henry Cohen finds that the changing order of medical training, research, and practice has been the result of two main influences—the rapid expansion of knowledge and technical skills in the sciences, and the evolution of the profession's ideas of social responsibility. At the beginning of the period, he notes, man was still regarded as a member of a family and of society, "greater than the sum of his parts".
>
> The advance of science to the point where a scientific age might be labeled as such placed this attitude in jeopardy. It made the physician too often forget not only "the essential humanity", but that science is not an end in itself. Scientific achievements had not been lacking since the Renaissance began—but now science became all-important and tended to crowd out that humanism without which the most perfect mind and body seem yet to lack a soul.[2]

But it is not enough to focus our attention on the priest and the doctor, the prophet and the technician in society. There is yet another gentleman with whom both must sooner or later come to terms. That third party is the king—whether he wears a crown or a straw hat. And so, whether we talk of the thirteenth century, or of scientific civilizations such as that of the early part of the twentieth century, all civilization works itself out within the framework of a political order, of the political State. The problems of each civilization tend to be political problems. In the age of the mystic, the thirteenth century, it was the conflict of Church and State, the conflict between the emperor and the Pope.

In our age it is more often than not the problem of the conflict between the king and the professional man, and the increasing effort of the former to regiment the latter. In the age of the mystic, it was the fight over the right of investiture, the struggle between the bishops and the temporal princes. In this age, it has become the fight between the politicians and the doctors, the politicians and the press, the politicians and business.

So, the proximate problems of every period of civilization are political, although as General MacArthur remarked once upon a time when it was more easy for him to make remarks, that the *ultimate* problems of our age are theological. So it always is: The *ultimate* difficulties of every generation are theological. The proximate difficulties are *political*. That is true no matter what the form of the political order.

In each political system, the poets, priests, professional men, and scientists have to come to working terms with the realities of the existing political order. There is always the danger that they may forfeit too much in this process. We could apply to doctors, for example, the point that is applied so frequently to laborers, to workers.

Four workers were sailing in a boat when suddenly a gust of wind tipped it over. It quickly sank. The four men were respectively a Fascist, a Communist, a Capitalist and a

133

Socialist Trade Unionist. The Capitalist drowned first; he tried to hold on to too many of his belongings and couldn't make more than a few yards. The next to drown was the Fascist; he kept raising his arm in a stiff salute and so impeded his swimming. The third to drown was the Communist; he was so busy shouting propaganda that his face filled with water. Last was the Socialist Trade Unionist; he was swimming along very well until he heard a whistle blow. Then he quit swimming and sank.

So each tends to come to terms with the political system of his age and sooner or later the political system tends to prove his undoing.

In an age of socialism and collectivism, such as ours has become, there is need for great vigilance if you are to keep the profession free. Medicine is in particularly grave danger of enslavement by absorption into the bureaucratic machinery of the socialist State because your profession is susceptible to the fallacies of the eugenic State. The eugenic State is simply another aspect of the socialist State, as socialism is simply one form of the collectivist or totalitarian State.

You see, the names used in politics are largely a question of salesmanship. The totalitarian chooses his vocabulary according to the prejudices and the preoccupations of the group that he is attempting to *sell*. If he is talking to trade unionists, he speaks in the *economic* terms of socialism. If he is talking to doctors, he uses the medical jargon of the eugenic State. In both cases, he is *selling* the despotism of the slave State.

Your particular danger stems from the fact that in the fallacies of the eugenic State, as in all fallacies, there is a certain show of truth.

Health is a concern of the State. Health is an aspect of the common good. The State has for its object the protection of that good. And so, medicine does serve the State, very definitely. Hence the eugenicist and the Socialist are able

134

to weave a highly plausible case for the political control of medicine.

Samuel Butler, in his book *Erewhon*, describes the very great importance of health to the State. He described it in the exaggerated terms of satire, but his argument has that show of truth which is in all pleas for the eugenic or socialist State.[3]

This is what I gathered (says Samuel Butler):

> that in that country, if a man falls into ill health or catches any disorder, or fails bodily before he is seventy years old, he is tried before a jury of his countrymen, and if convicted is held up to public scorn and sentenced to jail. . . . But if a man forges a check or sets a house on fire, or does any other such things as are criminal in our country, he is either taken to a hospital and most carefully tended at the public expense, or if he is in good circumstances, he lets it be known to all his friends that he is suffering from a severe fit of immorality, just as we do when we are ill; and they come and visit him with great solicitude and inquire with interest how it all came about, what symptoms first showed themselves, etc.—questions which he will answer with perfect unreserve.[4]

Butler says he visited a court in Erewhon, and saw prisoners being sentenced for eating improperly and otherwise injuring their health. To one hardened criminal the judge said:

> Prisoner at the bar, you have been accused of the great crime of laboring under pulmonary consumption, and, after an impartial trial before a jury of your countrymen, you have been found guilty. . . . This is not your first offense: you have had a long career of crime. You were convicted of aggravated bronchitis last year; and I find that, although you are now only twenty-three years old, you have been imprisoned no less than fourteen times for illnesses of a more or less hateful character.[5]

And so, in Erewhon, in the eugenic State, the man who lets his health go to pieces is counted a greater criminal than the man who burns down a barn or forges a check. His health is a part of the State's assets. By ruining it, he defrauds the State. For one thing, he complicates the life of a draft board, which is very much a part of the socialist State. He makes himself liable to punishment, which is perfectly good sense in Erewhon or in the eugenic State.

Now, medicine does serve the State, and, as a consequence, the State has very real claims on the profession. However, the nature, or rather, the manner, of those claims must be gauged from the manner of the service. The profession serves the State by indirection; it promotes the common good indirectly, save in the case of specialized problems of a specific kind. The direct service of the profession is to the *individual*, to the person, and in the scheme of things still ours by lip service at least, the individual person is accounted a free man.

Civilization has always accorded the doctor, like the priest, a wholesome maximum immunity from civil and political controls in his service of the free man. Even the ancient Greeks drew a sharp distinction between the service of the free man and the service of the slave.

The Greek writer Lucian, for example, who lived in the second century, makes a physician say in one of his dialogues: "In the case of the medical profession, the more distinguished it is and the more serviceable to the world, the more unrestricted it should be for those who practice it. It is only just that the art of healing should carry with it some privilege in respect to the liberty of practicing it, and that it should not be subject to enslavement by the law."

In a word, the art of healing serves directly and principally the *person*, not the State, and thus indirectly it builds up, as do all other arts, that common good which is the State's legitimate concern—a common good which the State itself destroys, however, the more it depersonalizes it, the more that good becomes *collectivized*.

The *common good* is not the same as a *collective good*. It is one thing for me to hold certain benefits in common with you. It is quite another for you and me to be the beneficiaries of a *collective benefit* which is neither yours nor mine.

The idea of "everything in the State, nothing outside the State", Mussolini's blunt but honest definition of Fascism, is by no means dead. The rose by any other name retains its special fragrance; but the same is true of the stinkweed. Fascism frankly talks of the mystical exaltation of the State; State Socialism sometimes talks a loud anti-Fascist *line*—but it remains nonetheless "everything in the State, nothing outside the State."

When we hear talk of increased socialization of services to the *person* in order to increase economic democracy; when increased socialization of the professions is argued in terms of alleged *liberalism* and of resistance to Fascism, then it is time to meditate the cynical, but shrewd, quip of Huey Long. Someone once asked Huey if Fascism would ever come to America. "Sure it will," said the Kingfish, "but when it does, we'll call it anti-Fascism!"

In an age of socialism and collectivism, such as ours tends to be, there is need, I repeat, for great vigilance if you are to keep the profession free.

But if it be true—and it is true—that the political freedom of the profession derives from its privileged relation to the free person, then it is pertinent and important to point out *why* the person *is* free—by what title the person eludes the pretension of the State and retains his freedom, his right to service and consideration independent of the State.

If medicine serves the person and owes its own dignity and freedom to the intimacy of that service, then the doctor should possess an appreciation of the spiritual nature of the complete personality, an appreciation hardly less than that of the priest.

Such an appreciation will include a recognition of the *moral* climate as well as the *material* environment in which personality achieves its healthy development; it will include an acknowledgment of the *spiritual* as well as *physical* elements of the total human person.

There are grounds for complaint that this well-rounded appreciation is not always as present or as honest as it might be, with respect to either the *moral* or the *spiritual* order.

It is here, of course, that the priest is in danger of degenerating into the common scold—but it is also here that his responsibility begins, a responsibility in the conscientious discharge of which he well serves both the medical profession and the democratic community.

The treatment of social disease offers the most obvious, but by no means the only, example of the truth that medical treatment on the material level alone, scientific techniques without reference to moral considerations, are far from sufficient for the adequate protection or improvement of persons. Obviously here, less obviously but no less truly elsewhere, the problem is not purely scientific—and neither can the solution be.

In *Social Medicine*, a publication of the New York Academy of Medicine, I read this significant report:

> Not long ago health administrators thought that if only some excellent curative agent were available to treat venereal disease cases, the problem could be solved fairly promptly. Now penicillin is providing more satisfactory treatment than the most sanguine might have dared hope, and yet we find that instead of diminishing, the venereal disease rate is rising. Recently the venereal disease director of one of our best state health departments said that he is convinced that the problem is much broader than that of treatment alone. There must be a concerted assault on all aspects of the situation if effective control is to be secured. Treatment must be pushed as completely and carefully as possible. There must also be an attack by all community agencies which can help to remove conditions leading to promiscuity. Sex education must be improved and decent recreational opportunities made available. Home ties

will have to be strengthened, prostitution repressed, and intensive efforts made to rehabilitate socially those now engaged in prostitution.[6]

Now what a priest finds discouraging, what, as a matter of candid fact, he finds downright dishonest in this paragraph, as in the whole report, is the studious avoidance of the use of the word *moral*. There is talk of *family relations*, *prostitution*, numerous other notions all involving *morality*, *moral codes*, *moral judgments*, *moral relations*, *moral questions*—but a careful omission of the word *moral*. The omission is significant, and it is also fatal, fatal not merely to morality, but, in final terms, to the work, prestige, and interests of the medical profession itself.

An even more grievous discouragement to the priest and disservice to the profession is had when preoccupation with the physical becomes exclusive, so that an insensibility to spiritual values and to the immoral factors of personality appears to paralyze certain members of the profession. Sometimes the insensibility reveals itself in a crude and vulgar fashion, the crudeness and vulgarity not being diminished by the eminence of the doctor who suffers from it.

For instance, here is an astonishing piece of vulgarity, the crudest kind of absolutist materialism, of Hitlerism transferred from politics to medicine, as displayed by a Director General of the World Health Organization in a talk on psychiatry in the William Alanson White Memorial Lectures, as quoted with approval in *Social Medicine*:

> Let us be our own authority. We know far more than any of our ancestors. Scientists of this generation have no obligation to admit superiority of knowledge or of wisdom in any body of traditional belief or authority. There is no room for authoritarian dogma in the field of human relations. Let us discard the bromides which have kept us drugged, obedient to old people and afraid of their displeasure.[7]

This might be brave and brilliant talk on the lips of a college sophomore leading a march on the dean's office for more generous late permissions or increased smoking facilities in the lunch room; but it is windy stuff indeed as a statement of the relationship of medical practice to the great tradition of human experience, of moral wisdom, and of wider values than those of any single generation, profession, or field of interest.

The reaction against such crudeness as that displayed in the Director General's harangue is sound and strong in the profession, but it is more articulate outside the ranks. Sometimes the reaction is surprising in its strength.

I have been reading to other audiences a letter that a soldier sent home to his girlfriend during the recent war. I beg leave to read it to you as a summary of the points I am striving to make. He was with the Medical Corps during the war, which explains the somewhat technical terms in which these two wrote to one another.

He wrote: "This afternoon I attended a medical staff meeting directed by Major M., an eminent pathologist, rather a good person when you get him alone. He performed an autopsy for us. Lieutenant So-and-so, of the Medical Corps, who had treated the case, read the background and the clinical history. I remember that he had discussed at table two weeks previously the question of there being a pons lesion or a disseminated sclerosis—and had correctly diagnosed it then.

"He commented on the various turns for better and for worse that disease might have taken had the young man lived. He spoke of the partial paralyses that would come and go, the effect upon his face and jaw bone. He painted a beguiling picture of life in the postwar world"—That, by the way, is the world you and I *now* live in! Anyway: "He painted a beguiling picture of life in the postwar world, the world in which you and I will have our children if you still feel the same way about it.

"He told us the wonders that research had accomplished, the

new techniques which were coming out of the science made necessary by war. He told us that by then a young man who contracted this same disease need not die of it. There would be means to anticipate it, control it, arrest it in its first beginnings. The young man now dead could, in that period, have an indefinite life expectancy of health and of service.

"It was a seductive picture, this picture of the scientific world in the making, until, when he completed its history, Major M. took over again. In a blackboard diagrammatic explanation, he traced the course of the tumor and accounted in detail the varying phases of the patient's clinical history. After concluding his discussion of the cause, the factors, and the effects upon the brain, he discussed the other organs, one by one.

"This is what he said: 'Spleen—markedly diseased—not unusual in case of brain tumor, but here is a tissue very largely invaded. Stomach—characterized by softening of some tissue, with accompanying self-digestion. This phenomenon scholarly discussed in an article in *Medicine* for October, 1940. Liver condition—heathy. Lungs—exhibiting marked pulmonary edema . . . resultant disorganized function of other nerve centers. Heart indications—negative. Are there any questions, gentlemen? That's all there is to these fellows!' "

Then this boy continued: "My God! In a single instant—in a careless phrase, the implications of which I am sure he would have denied had I pointed them out, this medical man articulated fears which have been in my heart ever since I joined the outfit, dreads for which I couldn't find the words. But he found them: there it was—'heart indications—negative. Are there any questions, gentlemen? That's all there is to these fellows.'

"All there was to him! All that went into his birth and being—the tears that were shed to conceive him, the hours spent watching for him; all of childhood's frets and frustrations; his young school days; his books, his brooks, fields, and fireside; the sights and sounds of home; all the angers of his adolescence that purified him; the joys of young manhood that made him sweet; friendships, loves—love of sweetheart, love of family, love of country—all the treasure of heart and hearth and home that breathed into him goodness, courage, faith, and value—six short hours before!

"All these now became 'heart indications, negative. Are there any questions, gentlemen? That's all there is to these fellows!' "

And the lad concludes: "Yes, Major M. I have some questions, but I am very much afraid that with all your learning and wisdom, your slides and microscopes, your research, your federal subsidies, and your laboratories—you can't answer my questions. And I'm even more afraid that if you and those who share your spirit have the full say in the writing of the curricula of the future and the planning of society, then a half century hence there won't be any who can answer my questions, and very few who will think them worth asking. But while there are some who live in the tradition of spiritual and humane values which produced me and those I love, I pose my question in a letter to a girl who came from the same tradition.

"This is it: What of that boy's loves, Major? What of his dreams? What of his courage? What of the idealism that made him volunteer for the service in which he died, Major? Did they show up under your microscope? In your examination of the tear ducts of his dead eyes you found the cheap chemistry that enabled him to weep, but did you find the causes, the motives, of his tears? Did you find the things that made him bow his head at the name of Jesus—that made him genuflect before my eyes a few weeks ago in a French church—that made him step back with beautiful courtesy to let the aged and the less privileged go before him into buses? Into what slides do you peer, Major, when you are looking for goodness—for sorrow—for repentance—for fidelity—for generosity—all these things which have little to do with the condition of his spleen or his lungs, but which made him so much more valuable to us in life than he is interesting to you on your dissecting table? Truly, in the face of these heart-hidden, eternal things, the medical scientist and every scientist will do as you have just done, Major, unless he goes beyond his laboratory. If he refuses to go beyond it, then he can only laugh it off, saying, 'heart indications, negative. Any questions, gentlemen? That's all there is to these fellows.' "

Doctors—*it can't be laughed off, either on religious or on professional grounds*. We have said that in an age of statism—of socialism and collectivism—we must keep our eyes constantly on the notion of the *person*, the person medicine serves, if the profession is to remain free. And that is true. But we may also say, we must also say, that in an age of materialism, secularism, and scientism, we need to keep a clear vision of the truth by which men are made the sons of God—or they cease to be free. They become slaves, and they drag down to servitude, all those who serve them; first, and worst of all, their priests and their doctors.

You doctors should be the first to defend religious faith and to insist upon scrupulous observance of the moral law, for once the moral law is eclipsed your profession will sink fatally into the slavery which was the condition of physicians and teachers in the pre-Christian days of a moral totalitarianism.

If you doubt me, read the front pages of the daily papers.

XI

The Law of God

I am deeply conscious of the kindness behind the invitation which brings me here this noon and I want you to know that I received and accepted your invitation with sincere gratitude and respect.

We all suffer from inevitable illusions with regard to ourselves and our friends, but I like to think that despite occasional tensions, most of them, please God, remediable, the constant spirit among us here in the community is one of sympathetic interest and friendly forbearance wherever interest is possible and forbearance may be needed.

In November each year the Catholic hierarchy in the United States meets for a three-day session in Washington to weigh the moral trends of the times and to issue a statement which summarizes the preoccupations of our bishops, priests, and people, together with commentary on them. There was such a meeting two months ago and during the past week I have been studying the statement issued from it.[1]

Last week I phoned your Mr. Shoemaker to ask his advice as to topics we might discuss today. He jotted down a list of questions which, in his opinion, express the most prevalent and most basic preoccupations of his associates in the ministry, and I found that his list comprised some eight or nine topics, most of which reflected preoccupations identical with those of the Catholic hierarchy.

The coincidence is not at all strange. Many of the moral preoccupations of the hour disturb all those who believe in the sovereignty of God, the supremacy of the moral law, the

This address was delivered in Worcester, Massachusetts, on January 15, 1952, at the luncheon meeting of the Worcester Ministers' Association.

primacy of the spiritual—and who acknowledge that without the universal acceptance of at least three moral postulates, the land we love and the world of which it forms a part are doomed to something rather worse than mere physical extinction.

For these reasons I venture this afternoon to present for our reflection together some of the principles, observations, and conclusions set forth in the recent statement of my brother bishops and the archbishops of the Catholic Church here in America. I do this with the greater sense of fitness because there has been gratifying evidence that, whatever the occasional more obvious and even painful differences of position between us, the most recent collective pastoral of the Catholic Bishops and the voice of Protestant witness concur with one another and both with the dictates of enlightened conscience. I say this because of the large number of Protestant leaders who took the time and the trouble to express their agreement with this particular pastoral.

For instance, Dr. Fred E. Reissig, Executive Secretary of the Washington Federation of Churches, referred to the section dealing with morality in politics as treating of one matter on which the churches speak with one voice. Dr. Edward B. Willingham, Chairman of the Baptist Joint Committee on Public Affairs, was prompt to make the same point. With one voice, he said, we can now call for moral indoctrination which will transform the political corruption about us, and he declared that the statement of the Bishops would be welcome as a strong stand upon an essential principle.

A spokesman for the Society of Friends spoke with the particular feeling we would all expect from a group bearing such a name, of the way in which the denunciation by the bishops of political name-calling and of defamation of character when resorted to by men in political life was tremendously heartening to his people.

Dr. Eugene Carson Blake, an executive of the Presbyterian

Church in the United States, made it clear that his co-religionists, whatever their positions on other matters, would stand together with us in the common fight against the inroads of humanistic secularism and the attacks of atheistic Communism which seek to undermine the spiritual foundations upon which our freedoms, civilization, and culture rest. He described as timely and valuable the statement on moral conditions in the United States issued by the Catholic Bishops on November 18.

While confining myself to these particular quotations, I dwell on them a bit because they are refreshing indications that we share a common fear, a fear which may prove very healthy and constructive, the fear of the disastrous operation in our community, even among people who profess religious convictions, of a double standard of morality, a situation against which our common conscience must speedily and strongly protest.

There are not two standards of morality. There is only one. It is the norm of rectitude, righteousness, the state of justice. That single standard covers all man's relations to God, to himself and to the world about him. It applies in every conceivable situation in life—in the home, in business, in the school, in the political field, or in the field of entertainment. The thoughts of men are many; the Will of God is one—and so by its very nature, God's standard precludes that duplicity which not only tempts man to live his life on two levels but beguiles him into thinking that this can be done without any compromise of moral principles.

Such a two-faced way of living explains the scandalous anomaly evident at times in our national life of paying lip service to God while failing to honor His claims in daily life. Of such a way of life, the God is neither Jehovah nor Jesus Christ; it is Janus, and I pray that we will always be at one in repudiating the two-faced god of the pagans.

The bishops in their statement pointed out what would, I know, have been emphasized no less by all here present: that one and the same standard covers stealing from the cash

146

register and dishonest gain derived from public office. They insisted, and all here present would insist no less, that it will not do to say, by way of extenuation, that the latter can be excused or condoned because it occurs in the political order. One and the same standard, God's standard, prohibits false statements about private individuals, and false statements about members of minority groups and races. By the same token, it also prohibits false statements about majority groups—or any other kind of group. It will not do, by way of excuse, to say that false statements concerning groups are diminished in their guilt because of a background of longstanding prejudice, or to say that defamation of character becomes something more understandable or less offensive when it is done on the group rather than the individual level.

This single standard of morality, God's standard, sets a clear, positive, and complete pattern of right living. It gives an integrity of outlook and an integrity of action in daily life. By adhering to this standard, man's life becomes all of a piece, characterized by a sincere singleness of purpose. Such a life will not have its *Sunday side* in which we dress up in *Sunday go-to-meeting* clothes and acknowledge God's claims for a day or an hour, and then its *weekday side* in which we put on our work or play clothes and completely ignore God's claims for the other six days of the week.

Rather, all aspects of life will be so integrated that the standard to which a man subscribes in his private life will be extended logically and without qualification to his life in the community. Then, if faithful to moral principles as an individual, he will be faithful to the same moral principles as a citizen, as a voter, and in all his actions as a member of society.

That God's standard has disappeared more and more from our national life is due, as the Catholic bishops and the Presbyterian moderator both bear witness, to that utter secularism, practical atheism, or complete and mere humanism, which rule out all idea of the sovereignty of God.

Against such lamentable pretensions we must bear, in season

and out, uncompromising witness to God's dominion over all the works of His hands, ourselves and our societies included. Where there is denial of God's place in human affairs, we must be as one in our anxiety to offset the effects of the denial. For instance, it should be a source of common concern to all who believe in the Providence of God over history and in the intervention of God in human affairs—through His prophets and His saints but above all through His Christ—when the story of mankind is to be written in a standard set of history books, enjoying the prestige of patronage by the UNESCO, under the direction of a committee seemingly dominated by men notorious for anti-Bible, anti-Christian, and anti-religious prejudices.

What place is the age-old spiritual witness of Israel likely to have in a history written under such auspices? Or the person and the teaching of Jesus, around Whose coming the very years have for centuries been numbered? What hint will history so written have of the sovereignty of God?

The undermining of God's standard in community affairs has been further hastened by the denial or neglect of the primacy of the spiritual, with a consequent debasing of human personality and degradation of human society. Ours is a technical civilization, a *know-how* rather than a *know-why* civilization, and therefore one in which material and mechanical values tend to dominate thought and action. Excessive emphasis on *know-how* and impatience with *know-why* have produced the cult of the body, the predominance of the material, the worship of the gadget, an indifference to the spiritual and a repudiation of the moral.

We may note this in professional discussions, especially those pertaining to sociology, medicine, and politics. Take, for example, the question of social disease. It offers an obvious example of how medical treatment on the material level alone, scientific techniques of *know-how* without reference to moral considerations of *know-why* are woefully inadequate as means

148

to the protection or the perfection of persons. Obviously in the case of the treatment of social disease, the problem is never purely scientific—and neither can the solution be. The old taunt used to be: Religion is the opiate of the people. The new unfortunate fact is that, in disturbing degree, opiates have become the religion of the people.

In *Social Medicine*, a publication of the New York Academy of Medicine, I read this significant report:

> Not long ago health administrators thought that if only some excellent curative agent were available to treat venereal disease cases, the problem could be solved fairly promptly. Now penicillin is providing more satisfactory treatment than the most sanguine might have dared hope, and yet we find that instead of diminishing, the venereal disease rate is rising. Recently the venereal disease director of one of our best State health departments said that he is convinced that the problem is much broader than that of treatment alone. There must be a concerted assault on all aspects of the situation if effective control is to be secured. Treatment must be pushed as completely and carefully as possible. There must also be an attack by all community agencies which can help to remove conditions leading to promiscuity. Sex education must be improved and decent recreational opportunities made available. Home ties will have to be strengthened, prostitution repressed, and intensive efforts made to rehabilitate socially those now engaged in prostitution.[2]

Now what all of us, you and I, should find discouraging, what, as a matter of candid fact, we should find downright *dishonest* in this paragraph, as in the whole report, is the studious avoidance of the use of the word *moral*. There is talk of *family relations*, *prostitution*, numerous other notions all involving *morality*, *moral codes*, *moral judgment*, *moral relations*, *moral questions*—but a careful omission of the word *moral*. The omission is significant and I am afraid it is symptomatic. It is also fatal, fatal not merely to morality, but, in final terms, to the work, prestige, and interests of both medicine and sociology. It exemplifies that repudiation of the primacy of the spiritual which is the unhappy byproduct of a *know-how* without a *know-why* civilization.

In the practical order, from the repudiation of the sovereignty of God and the denial of the primacy of the spiritual, comes the refusal, born, as it were, out of the blend of the two, to acknowledge the necessary relation which must exist between all human positive law worthy of the name and the moral law that God has writ in nature, that He causes to echo in the healthy conscience and that He has clarified through Revelation.

Before the appeal to conscience can recover its ancient power to change men, to renew the very face of the earth, there must be universal all-out witness to the sovereignty of God, the spiritual responsibility of man and the all-inclusive application of His law. God's law, God's standard as we have been calling it, once preached with all the energy at our command, will prove the central force alone capable of unifying the carefully departmentalized elements of so many lives.

Against the idea of God's Law there are a host of rival norms of conduct which plague our generation. Expressions such as *my life is my own affair* or *I may do as I please* or *who cares?* or *in politics, anything goes* or *all's fair in love and war*—all betray a gross misunderstanding of the moral order of those interlinking relations among men and nations of which God's standard is the only correct measure. All human rights and duties have their source in God's law; otherwise they are meaningless.

Morality, concerned with bringing human activity into conformity with God's will, has therefore a bearing on everything that touches human rights and duties. It has a definite place in the educational life of a nation. The forming of character is part of the educational process; and character cannot be formed unless children are given a clear indication of what is right and what is wrong. This cannot be done without reference to the ultimate standard which determines right and wrong, namely, God's law.

Morality has its place in business and industry because the conditions under which men work, the wages they get, the kind of work they do, all are subject to the jurisdiction of the moral law. When economic conditions are such that the raising of a family by working people is made dishearteningly difficult and at times impossible, then those responsible for this deplorable situation are guilty of breaking God's law and they are also accomplices in the sins resulting from their injustice.

In politics, the principle that *anything goes* simply because people are thought not to expect any high degree of honor in politicians is grossly wrong. We have to recover that sense of personal obligation on the part of the voter and that sense of public trust on the part of the elected official which give meaning and dignity to political life. Those who are selected for office by their fellow men are entrusted with grave responsibilities. They have been selected not for self-enrichment but for conscientious public service. In their speech and in their actions they are bound by the same laws of justice and charity which bind private individuals in every other sphere of human activity. Dishonesty, slander, detraction, and defamation of character are as truly transgressions of God's commandments when resorted to by men in political life as they are for all other men.

In this connection, I think all who preach have an urgent obligation to be far more constructive than is perhaps our wont in the matter of the dignity of public office, the sanctity of public authority, and the legitimate title to special respect of those who wield it. You and I do not believe in the Divine Right of Kings as did the absolutists, but there is still a divinity that hangs about a king because he holds authority which comes from God. And we pay no tribute to democracy when we strip the wielders of civil authority of a dignity and even a divinity which surrounds them so long as they hold, as our designees, an authority which still comes from God—as we too easily forget simply because they sometimes forget it, too.

Perhaps our public officials will be more mindful of the truly sacred character of their trust when those who elect them have been taught the roots of its sanctity by us, and have thus become a little more reverent about public authority and wary about those to whom they commit it.

In any case, God's standard requires that, even in a democracy, we think twice and twice again before we threaten public order by pot-shooting at the persons or the policies of those who duly hold public office. It is sound democracy to point out that the President or the Chief Justice is no better a man than any one of us; it is bad morality to forget what the Presidency is—and the magistracy and the office of the judge. Even democracy punishes contempt of court—no matter what the private merits of the man who is the judge.

Fresh emphasis on the reality and supremacy of the moral law will give direction and cogency to our several and joint efforts to curb such evils as gambling rackets, to inculcate temperance and purity and to eliminate public incitements to sin against these, to control juvenile and not-so-juvenile delinquency, to arrest the disintegration of the home under the impact of infidelity, to promote the public welfare by work for international peace and national stability, to resist the inroads of militarism, the divisive demands of racism, the violation of civil rights by unfair economic, political, and social discrimination.

Here is a vast field which challenges our common concern and that of our people. And in this area of social action, who would not welcome cooperation within the community, above all within the local community, among all men of good will in pressing for that recognition of the sovereignty of God, the supremacy of the moral law and the primacy of the spiritual?

Cooperation to these urgent ends among religious groups might easily be established through committees or authorized representatives who would engage in *joint conference*, even when they might be bound to pursue *independent action*.

Moreover, cooperation for such civic and social ends by means even of joint action should be greatly strengthened in communities like ours by encouraging upright men and women to enter generously, honorably, and wholeheartedly into those civic and social programs which bring together the best minds, hearts, and hands of our respective groups.

Joint cooperation of various religious committees under the auspices of civil or social groups is certainly to be sought, above all for purposes of cordial exchange alike of information and opinion on public matters which affect that common good which all our people gladly share.

Representatives of our respective groups already meet for USO, for Community Fund, for housing, and for many more economic, civic, and social problems than we sometimes remember to note. The areas of social action where we should consult and cooperate for the increased stability of the community still remain much larger and it is earnestly to be desired that we seek common counsel in these areas.

True, in the domain of the discussion of dogma and above all in the realm of worship there are many and supremely important *fences*. Such *fences* for conscience's sake will remain so long as God's Kingdom on earth lacks the all-embracing unity which Christ intended. These *fences* are familiar; they should be stated fearlessly and fairly.

Some of your people are unable to understand the *fence* which prevents us and our children from participating in formal religious services of public worship in churches which are not our own. (I might note that many of your people appear to have like *fences* of their own when there is a question of prayer, as witness the militant protests of certain Jewish and Protestant spokesmen against even the very brief common prayer suggested recently by the New York Board of Regents for use in the public schools of that state. Some people find that protest difficult to understand.)

That there are such *fences*, it is pointless and unworthy to deny. But it should be acknowledged that such *fences* erected

153

by conscience are built upon basic religious principles which are supremely important, too close to conscience and to the soul's relationship to God for any one to dismiss them cynically or impatiently.

Among refined and religious people such *fences* do not create enemies. There is wisdom worth our meditation in the shrewd observation of the New England Yankee poet that sometimes "good fences make good neighbors."[3] Certainly, honest *fences* around the things which protect deep, religious principle and the relationship between conscience and the final Judge of conscience are not inconsistent with the ideal of "malice toward none and charity toward all;"[4] nor do they prevent social action in behalf of at least one common concern: the improved moral tone of the community which we all so sincerely desire.

XII

The Church of the Saints

It is a great pleasure to come to Pittsburgh and find the Retreat Movement making such progress in its work.

Since I am prevented by a Commencement Program from being here Sunday for the concluding dinner, I beg leave at this time to pay my tribute of warm admiration to our president, Alfred Berghoff, for the wholehearted leadership he has given during his term of office. It brings back wonderful memories of our convention in Los Angeles to see him here; that convention was made unforgettable by the generosity and extraordinary thoughtfulness with which he did his work. The spirit he brought to the Movement has been with us constantly. We are forever grateful to him.

Permit me also to say a word in the name of the National Board to Bishop Dearden for the apostolic hospitality he has extended to us and for the openhearted encouragement he has given every aspect of the preparations for this convention. We are deeply grateful to his lieutenants, priests and laymen, and particularly to Father Lackner and to Dan Hamill for the time and talent they have devoted to the convention plans.

The theme of our deliberations this week-end will be *The Man of God*. Cardinal Newman once spoke of the contrast between the Man of God and the Man of the World. He did so in terms of another contrast, that between the religion of the world and the religion of Christ. The Cardinal said that in every age the world produces a counterfeit of the true religion. This counterfeit usually emphasizes some points of complete Christianity, appropriating them to its own purposes and

This address was delivered at the William Penn Hotel, Pittsburgh, Pennsylvania, on June 6, 1952, on the occasion of the fourteenth National Catholic Laymen's Retreat Conference.

weaving them into a spurious *religion* so perfectly imitating the religion of Christ as even to deceive the unstable and unwary.

Newman pointed out that the world does not oppose religion as such. Quite the contrary, it appears to insist that religion is a good thing, even necessary. But the world prefers to pick and choose those elements of religion most consistent with its own aspirations; it tones down or quietly repudiates those further elements which might hamper its own self-expression. The world fastens on one or two points of the Gospel of Christ and says, in effect, that it admires these very much; that these constitute *real religion*.

And thus the world destroys even that portion of the Gospel which it pretends to practice, for he who cultivates only one precept of the Gospel does not really accept even that single precept on the grounds consistent with the Gospel. The religion of Christ is too integral to admit of such selectivity, choosiness, and opportunism. There may be a counterfeit of the religion of Christ, but there is no counterpart. Either you take the whole Gospel or you practice no part of it, even if you imitate a section of its code.

Just as the world has selected some points of the Christian code and tried to spin these into a religion of its own, so the world attempts to counterfeit the man of God by selecting one or another of his characteristics, isolating these from the integral pattern of Christian manhood, and announcing the result as *God's man*. The synthetic figure thus idolized by the world presents a different feature in each generation. It is always some point taken from the total picture of the true man of God, but it is always a characteristic emphasized to the exclusion of all the other qualities which should characterize God's true man.

In a civilization like ours, increasingly secular and strictly political in its values, the world's ideal man is apt to be hailed as a *good citizen*. Nothing more is asked of a man than that he be a good citizen. Before the rise of emphasis on democracy, the same world hailed the man who could call himself *the king's good servant*, and the world's ideal man was then characterized by those loyalties which were consistent with the good order of the king's realm.

It was carefully pointed out then, as it is now, that in being a good citizen one is fulfilling a Christian duty, acting as the man of God should act. It is not so carefully noted, however, that he may be fulfilling only one of the duties of a Christian, that he may be imitating only one side of the man of God. A man may be the best of citizens in a purely secular sense and still be no Christian at all, as he may have been the king's best servant and God's least loyal subject in all things else but civic loyalty.

In other words, just as the religion of the world caricatures Christianity in attempting to imitate it, so the world's ideal man tends to be a caricature of the man of God. He counterfeits the virtues of the man of God but even the counterfeit, as always, is only partial. The world's good man is kind in certain of his practices, where the man of God is kind on principle. The world's good man is tolerant, which is easy enough for him since he has no fixed principles disagreement with which could disturb him. The man of God is also tolerant, but his tolerance is given substance and value because it is part of an integral outlook based on a firm creed and a binding code.

The world's good man is described in phrases which reflect the fads and fashions in goodness. The man of God can only be described in terms of goodness which are as objective and as permanent as God Himself.[1]

These terms will be our points of meditation during this convention and our pattern of progress in the next two years of the retreat work here in America. They are the terms in which Saint Paul sketched the Church's understanding of the man of God when he wrote:

But thou, O man of God, fly these things: and pursue justice, godliness, faith, charity, patience, mildness. Fight the good fight of faith. Lay hold on eternal life, whereunto thou art called and hast confessed a good confession before many witnesses. I charged thee before God who quickeneth all things, and before Christ Jesus who gave testimony under Pontius Pilate, a good confession: That thou keep the commandment without spot, blameless, unto the coming of our Lord Jesus Christ, which in His times He shall show, Who is the Blessed and only Mighty, the King of kings and Lord of lords: Who only hath immortality and inhabiteth light inaccessible: Whom no man hath seen, nor can see: to Whom be honor and empire everlasting.[2]

This, then, is the portrait of the man of God as opposed to the man of the world. This is *God's man*, *a good citizen* to be sure, but very much more than that; the *king's good servant*, to be sure, but *God's servant first*.

In a single word, the man of God is a saint. He wishes he were a saint in fact, but he is at least one in intention—*saltem in voto*, as the theologians say of the relationship to His Church of the truly sincere seekers after God.

The man of God is a member of the Church. The Church is not a society of the perfect, but it is a school of perfection, and the man of God is one who desires to be perfect. He belongs to the Church not because he believes that he is perfect but because he is seeking perfection. He understands that it is the sole business of the Church to produce saints, to mold men of God.

The Holy Catholic Church exists for this purpose; it has no other work, at least none which ultimately matters. Everything else which it strives to do is strictly subordinated to this supreme objective. We build hospitals. We build schools. We organize programs of every species. If we had all these as admirable as they now are and ten thousand times more so, yet lacked saints and failed to produce men of God, then we would have totally missed the point of our existence.

Our institutions would be so many millstones around our necks. They would cry out in judgment against us.

Conversely, if all our institutions were taken from us, as from time to time they are taken by the ruthless and the evil, if every last brick of our buildings were reduced to rubble but we still produced saints, then we would be doing God's work and could take leave of all else with light hearts.

The work of the Church is the production of saints, men of God. She has no other purpose, save of an incidental kind. The primary objectives of the Catholic Church are not political, economic, social, or cultural. There may be political or economic corollaries to the moral teaching by which the Church produces men of God, but these are by-products of the main work. There may be social or cultural overtones to her preaching, but the purpose of that teaching is to produce the spiritual personality of the man of God.

The Laymen's Retreat Movement is one of the means which the Church employs to achieve her holy purposes. In my own prejudiced opinion, it is a principal means at this particular moment of history. The aspiration of this movement is the production of saints, the making of men of God. The success of the Retreat Movement is itself a proof of the power of the Church to produce saints; it is a proof that she is exercising that power as fully in our day as she did in days gone by. The Lay Retreat Movement exists to intensify in our times the truth of Saint Paul's contention that ours is the Church of the Saints.

Writing to the Ephesians, Paul pointed out how the Church, being one with Christ, shares His holiness. It is holy in its Founder, holy in its doctrine, holy in its sacraments, and holy in its work. But Paul also insisted that it is holy in its members. He was neither so naive nor so uninformed as to suppose that those whom he called *saints* because they were members of the Church were on that account confirmed in grace, incapable of sin. As a matter of fact, Paul makes it perfectly clear throughout his Epistles that the members of the Church which he founded were very far from being confirmed in grace; such salvation as they had achieved they still bore in fragile vessels. Nonetheless, they were members of the Church, striving to be men of God—and so he hailed them as *saints*.

With all our faults and even our grave sins, we are the fellow-citizens of the saints so long as we strive with the help of God's grace to make good our salvation, to preserve unity with the saints in the living temple of God which is the Holy Catholic Church.

That is precisely what we are doing in the Lay Retreat Movement. Saint Paul would find himself, I think, perfectly at home with the men of this Movement. He would recognize them, as they recognize themselves, as sinners; frail vessels of election. But he would recognize them no less unmistakably for what they also are: serious seekers after salvation, saints by intention, convinced members of the Church, and eager to achieve in themselves her principal work: the formation of the man of God.

If he stood before you tonight Saint Paul would speak to you as he did to typical gatherings of Christian men in the infant Church. They were from all races and classes; so are you. They represented every state in life; so do you. Theirs were great differences in temperament and title; so are the differences among you. And yet to you in the Lay Retreat Movement can be applied with perfect truth the word of the Apostle: "You are now no longer strangers and foreigners, but you are citizens with the saints and members of God's household: you are built upon the foundation of the apostles and prophets with Christ Jesus Himself as the chief cornerstone. In Him the whole structure is closely fitted together and grows into a temple holy in the Lord; in Him you too are being built together into a dwelling place of God in the Spirit."[3]

Ours, then, is the Church of the saints and we are their brothers. The Lay Retreat Movement seeks to deepen the bonds of that kinship. It is most important that we emphasize this particularly at a moment in history when the criticisms against the Church are so often political and social. So many, in their prejudice, have risen up in these latter days to berate the Church for the political theories, the economic schemes, or the social programs of some of her members that it is important for the Lay Retreat Movement to make itself better known both in the Church and in the general community.

It is extremely important that the Retreat Movement never forget that, while the Church may include social reformers, political economists, military experts, candidates for public office, or technicians of every other kind, the purpose of the Church does not exist to produce politicians, scientists, or professional men; it should not be judged by the competence of these. The Church exists to produce saints. The Church is edified when she finds her saints among these temporal categories, but she is not unduly amazed when she fails to find them there. In any case, she is not discouraged by political or social reversals, for these pertain to a city which is not hers. Her city is the City of God, the company of the saints.

Even we Catholics are sometimes too preoccupied with the impact of the Church on the world; our critics seem preoccupied with little else. The important thing about the Church cannot be stated in directly political or economic terms; it reveals itself in the spiritual terms of the sanctity of which we have been speaking.

The true nature of the Church, the sources and the purposes of her power, are all understood when we think of her in terms of Christ. More than once we have been reminded by preachers and spiritual writers of the parallel between Christ and the Church.

When Jesus was dragged before His judges, His accusers cried, "We have found this man perverting our nation . . . and saying that He is Christ a King." But Jesus said: "My Kingdom is not of this world. My Kingdom is not from here.

161

(But) I am a King. That is why I was born, and why I have come into the world, to bear witness to the Truth. Everyone who is of the truth hears My voice."[4]

Jesus had already said to His disciples: "You shall know the truth and the truth shall make you free."[5] He delighted to speak of the freedom of the sons of God, who are the saints, and of the truth by which the saints are made.

Jesus in His Mystical Body, His Church, periodically repeats the mysteries of His betrayal, the Passion, and even the death by which the world was sanctified. In every generation He is dragged again before new judges, and in our age as in all ages, the cry is still heard: "We have found this man perverting our nation and claiming to be a king. The Church acts counter to the interests of our way of life. The Church is hostile to our democracy. The Church seeks political power. American freedom is threatened by Catholic power. We shall have no king but Caesar. Ours is a strictly secular state. The Church perverts our political ideal."

And still the Church answers, as two thousand years ago her Founder, her very self, first answered these same false charges. The Church replies: "My work is in this world, but not of it. I have power, but it is not of this world. For this was I brought into being, that I might bear witness to the truth, the truth by which men are made spiritually free with a freedom so contagious that, though it is not of the world nor itself political, it nonetheless spreads throughout the world and produces those conditions in which alone other freedoms, including political freedom, become possible. The freedom which I give is the freedom of the sons of God, who are the saints, and it is my work, my holy destiny, to raise up, in all times and places, a race of saints for the glory of God and the redemption of men."

During His life on earth, above all in the hour of His suffering and death, they taunted Jesus saying: "You boasted that you could save others; save now yourself and save us!"[6]

162

Jesus had indeed come to bring salvation. He had come to seek out and to save the lost tribes of Israel, and to be the salvation of the Gentiles. What His enemies did not understand was that precisely by His suffering He fulfilled His redemptive, saving mission; precisely by His death He made possible the life of the saints.

Jesus in the Church is still taunted with the same reproof as that with which His enemies mocked His dying hours. In the face of the Church's claim to give saints to the world, we hear her critics' scornful words: "The Church is dead, or at least is dying. The fire of Pentecost no longer burns in and around her. The spirit of Jesus seems to have abandoned her. She has become vitiated by the infidelities of her members, paralyzed by politics, feeble with infection from the spirit of the world. She has no longer the power to produce saints."

And so her enemies fall upon her. Sometimes they betray her with a kiss, as working from within through new Judases they salute her as *friends* in order to take her captive. Sometimes they seek to overwhelm her from without; they scourge her, crown her with thorns, and lead her forth to die.

And behold, even as she walks to Calvary new women of Jerusalem seek to console her; new Simons from a thousand Cyrenes step forth to help her bear the cross; new Dismases hail her as their salvation and die together with her; new centurions are converted to faith in her and in her Christ; new saints are raised up by her power, even when that power seems to be broken and gone.

What Origen said in times past is still true today: "False witnesses unceasingly rise up against Jesus, and as long as evil dwells in the heart of man, accusations will rise against Him. As for Him, He holds His peace, today as formerly: He does not reply by words, but defends Himself far more by the life of His true disciples, which speaks in an unmistakable language of its own."

That language is sanctity and the true disciples are the saints.

Christ is still at work in the world through His saints: the Church is still the Church of the Saints. She produces her saints all about us, before our very eyes. A wise confessor once remarked: "People lament that there are no more saints. As for me, I find them wherever I go!" This is certainly true in the Lay Retreat Movement.

Not only does the number of saints remain undiminished in our day, but never has the power of the Church to produce saints been more tested or more fruitful. In every walk of life, in every corner of the world, under every sky and every condition, millions are daily growing in deep, active identity with the Communion of Saints, living the Catholic life on levels of heroism which even the faithful among their neighbors frequently fail to perceive.

Any priest in the work of the Lay Retreat Movement knows that these things which I have just said are demonstrably true. If it can be said, as unfortunately it can, that we live in evil days, days of treason, disbelief, hatred, and lust, then it must also be said that such days are days which call for saints.

That means they are days which call for God's grace and God's grace has not been lacking. It is poured forth abundantly, nowhere more so than in the Retreat Movement.

When a guilty society is threatened with punishment even by fire, the remembrance of Scripture should prompt us to watch for saints, to estimate how many just persons there may be in our midst. We were told of old that ten such would weigh more than a thousand others in the balances of God.[7] The worth of any country or of any civilization depends in God's scheme of things on the number of saints that it produces. This is so true that the day on which the earth no longer sends saints to Heaven will assuredly be the day marked for its destruction.

Someone has said that "the saints consecrate the world", and this is true. But they do more than this, as Raoul plus points out: It is the saints who preserve the world. They are the true, the only conservatives, in the sense that the world

164

owes its preservation to them. They are also the true, the only, liberals in the best sense of that abused word, the magnanimous, great-souled people whose minds are big enough to include Heaven and whose hearts are large enough to hold all the world—plus God.

Retreat houses are schools where these qualities of the saints are taught. They are seminaries for the training of the priesthood of the laity. They are citadels of the Church's true strength. They are the best hope America has of a genuine spiritual revival. They are households of the man of God.

XIII

Pastoral Letter on Sacred Scripture

This month the world of scholarship and that of religion concur in the observance of an anniversary great with significance for both. It is the five-hundredth anniversary of the first printing of a book, the Gutenberg Bible. This noteworthy event suggests that I address you a letter concerning the Sacred Scriptures.

The making of books and the art of printing have become so commonplace in our day that it may be difficult to appreciate what an extraordinary work of human ingenuity was the achievement of John Gutenberg in perfecting movable type and producing the first printed book. Printing by means of seals, stamps, or wooden blocks had been known to antiquity almost two thousand years before Gutenberg achieved his scientific triumph. But it remained for this master of the printer's art successfully to combine four factors which had never been effectively brought together prior to him: paper on which to print inexpensively; ink that could be applied by type to paper; a press that would bring perfect contact between paper and type; and, finally, type in an alloy which would be capable of holding up under repeated use and heavy pressure.

It is the great distinction of John Gutenberg that he coordinated these four factors so perfectly that even today his ink and type-metal formulae have not been basically changed despite the astounding technical advances of the past five centuries.

As a result of Gutenberg's work the wisdom of ages past

This Pastoral Letter, written on September 21, 1952, was addressed to the clergy, religious, and laity of the Diocese of Worcester, Massachusetts, as part of the observance of Catholic Book Week, September 28 to October 5, 1952.

is now preserved for ages to come. The recorded thought of the past and that of the present is made readily available to every man, woman, and child who can read. Following upon Gutenberg's invention of printing with movable type, craftsmen in the art of printing have been able to reproduce words, illustrations, charts, and graphs in almost unlimited quantity and with superb clarity for dissemination throughout the world and across the ages.

It is often said, especially in our confused and controversial times, that printing, like most inventions, has brought with it numerous possibilities of evil as well as power for good. Sometimes people lament the large number of false notions which have been as successfully disseminated as have sound teachings, perhaps even more so. It is undoubtedly true that destructive propaganda is as readily printed and communicated through books and newspapers as is constructive thought, and that the despoilers of mankind can just as easily exploit the press as humanity's benefactors can utilize it for high or holy purposes.

All this has been true in each of the five centuries since printing began, but the thoughtful will agree that the gains have so far outweighed any evil done through printing that Gutenberg's work must be accounted one of the greatest natural blessings with which mankind has been favored. It has also proved a principal channel of supernatural graces to the civilized world.

Only the captious will question the conviction that the invention of Gutenberg must be classed with the greatest events in the history of the world. It caused a revolution in the development of culture greater than almost any other in the history of the Western World, particularly by popularizing treasures of the mind hitherto almost inevitably reserved to privileged classes. If it be true (as it doubtless is) that the rapid spread of knowledge made possible by typography outstripped the inward refinement which might have prevented vulgarity and helped balanced intellectual discrimination, still Gutenberg's art was necessary for the otherwise so largely beneficial development of the sciences in modern times and for the eventual wider spiritual and scientific education of the general public.

It was a happy omen that the first book to be printed by the inventor of movable type should have been the Bible. This is not surprising when we reflect upon the mentality of the man who produced this book and upon the spirit of the age which produced him.

John Gutenberg was a devout Catholic craftsman. Even as Columbus was motivated in his work of exploration by the desire to extend the Holy Catholic Faith, so Gutenberg made of his printing an apostolate for the spread of the Faith. Despite discouraging lawsuits and the burden of debts incurred in his efforts to perfect his printing, Gutenberg doggedly kept to his work in a shop equipped with borrowed capital, patiently printing the monumental works of the great philosophers and theologians of Catholic Christendom, notably Saint Thomas Aquinas, as well as popular calendars and manuals of the Catholic Faith.

The times in which he lived were avid for the preaching and exposition of the Word of God. The widespread passion to read the Scriptures had prompted the Church to make ever more broad provision for bringing the Bible, open and complete, within reach of the multitudes. Prior to the invention of printing this was an exceedingly costly and difficult task. The many books of the Scriptures had to be copied diligently by hand, and manuscript Bibles, thus lovingly but laboriously produced, immediately became priceless possessions beyond the reach of almost any but princes. Each Bible was a separate work involving months of patient, persistent toil by devoted monks whose reverence for the sacred text impelled them to illuminate and embellish their manuscripts with those exquisite decorations which make even single pages of the Medieval Bibles museum pieces and coveted objects of art.

The value of such hand-copied Bibles as well as their restricted numbers made it necessary that they be kept carefully guarded in libraries and that they be protected from mutilation theft, or careless handling when they were placed at the disposition of the people. Thus the custom arose, in the days before the invention of printing, of *chaining* Bibles in public places much as we now chain cumbersome directories or great reference books which are too expensive to reproduce in quantity, even in our age of easy printing, but in which great numbers of people are interested.

Sometimes uninformed people have pretended that the *chained Bible* of the Middle Ages typified some reluctance on the part of the Church toward the general reading of the Sacred Scriptures by the common people. Quite the contrary is the truth: the *chained Bible*, magnificent in its reproduction of the sacred text and yet exhibited for all to admire and to read, was a symbol both of the veneration of the Church for the written word of God and of the desire of the Church that all her children have access to that word under circumstances consistent with the possibilities of an age which had not yet discovered printing by movable type.

Then came John Gutenberg. He was inspired by the Church's ancient eagerness that the Word of God be reproduced with exquisite beauty and maximum clarity. Accordingly, his immediate aim, technically and artistically so difficult, was to reproduce mechanically the characters used in the traditional manuscripts without losing any of the elegance or legibility which dedicated copyists had by then perfected in their hand printing.

Gutenberg's ultimate aims were spiritual and apostolic. He shared the Church's desire that the Scriptures be diffused as widely as possible and this aspiration must have powerfully motivated his choice of the Bible to be the first book reproduced in its entirety by his newly discovered art of printing.

There is no book which had been more studied than the Bible. No Bible has been more studied than John Gutenberg's.

Every copy, page, column, line, and letter has been the object of careful and critical scrutiny. Its historical significance could not be greater. The Gutenberg Bible, as has been remarked, is not a unique book; there are forty-five known copies. It is by no means the rarest of books, though a complete copy is so costly to acquire that only an exceedingly wealthy person or an endowed corporation would consider its purchase. Neither is it the finest book in existence either from the point of view of printing or from that of other artistic considerations; it has hundreds of rivals in beauty and in technical perfection. But it holds an incomparable place in the world of science and learning because it is the first of all books to be printed and particularly because it is the first complete printing of the Book of Books, the Bible.

In the history of Catholicism the Gutenberg Bible holds a place no less important than its place in the history of printing. Behind John Gutenberg's work there lay, as we have said, the Catholic instinct to reproduce the Inspired Word of God with all the artistic beauty and technical perfection that human ingenuity could devise. This instinct had found earlier expression in such monuments of human culture and sacred study as the Book of Kells and like masterpieces of lettering.

Moreover, behind John Gutenberg's Bible there lay, as we have also said, the Catholic desire to bring the Word of God in all its forms intimately close to the lives of all peoples in all times and places. Thus in an age that depended on gesture or pageant, the Church reduced the content of the Sacred Scriptures to drama through the medium of the mystery plays which were the sacred beginnings of the modern secular theater. Another generation had depended chiefly on pictorial arts for its instruction in sacred history, and so stained glass, as at Chartres conspicuously but by no means exclusively, became the medium by which the histories, maxims, and revelations of the Bible were interpreted to the millions under the patronage of the Church. Painting, illumination, sculpture, eloquence, and music have all been instruments by which the Church has sought to expound and to popularize the Word of God in one age or another.

Printing became a further and even more effective instrument in the hands of the Church as she strove to spread knowledge and love of the sacred writings.

The invention of printing coincided, as it happened, with the rise of nationalism and the consequent spread of enthusiastic attachment to the vernacular languages of the suddenly self-conscious nations into which Europe became sharply divided once the social, cultural, and spiritual unities of Catholic Christendom began to be loosened under the impact of politics and the spirit of division.

Hence began, shortly after the discovery of printing, a sudden flood of vernacular translations of the Bible, at first under the patronage of the Church and in expression of her perennial desire to accommodate the channels of her unchanging teaching to the expanding needs and changing interests of her children. However, John Gutenberg's Bible, the first printed book, was an edition of the great Latin Bible, Saint Jerome's Vulgate, which had been for much more than a thousand years the standard Scriptural text of the Western World and which remains to this day preeminent in dignity, influence, and authority among all the versions of the books of Sacred Scripture from their original languages.

Since John Gutenberg's Bible there is no nation nor tongue in which printed versions of the Bible have not appeared, usually in many editions. The English-speaking world, as we know, fell early and almost completely under non-Catholic leadership, cultural and political, after the Protestant Revolt, the spread of which was in great degree facilitated both by the insurgent nationalism of the sixteenth century and by the unwonted rapidity with which ideas of every kind, true and false, were spread after the invention of printing. Thus it came to pass that early English editions of the Bible, though not the first, many of them milestones in the history of printing and powerful influences in the shaping of our language, were published under Protestant auspices and reflected Protestant concepts in their editing and phrasing.

The piety of traditional Protestantism has always centered strongly about the Sacred Scriptures. The devotion of Protestant Christians to the Bible, however we must regret its negations, has resulted on the positive side in the survival of a strong heritage of Scriptural moral idealism among good people descended from those who broke from the integral Catholic tradition in unhappy days gone by. We can scarcely exaggerate, moreover, the beneficent influence on the secular culture of our part of the world exercised directly or indirectly by the literary excellence of certain of their historic editions of the English Bible, editions which proved unacceptable to Catholic people for theological and canonical reasons but which rank high in the history of the English language.

Considering the fewness of their numbers and the hardpressed circumstances of their lot in the areas of the world dominated by post–Reformation English power, Catholics have a re- markable record of scholarship in translation and zeal in the loving use of the Sacred Scriptures. The catalogue of the British Museum lists three hundred and thirteen publications by Catholics of editions of the Bible in whole or in part between 1505 and 1950. It is interesting to note that the first biblical text ever to be printed in English was a translation of the Penitential Psalms by Saint John Fisher, the Catholic bishop who died a martyr in his resistance to the spiritual pretensions of the English king.

In America alone Catholics have published two hundred and sixty-four editions of the Scriptures in English, of which more than fifty have appeared in the last ten years. This number of editions is the more remarkable when we consider that until after the middle of the nineteenth century the number of English-speaking Catholics in our country was not at all great, and that during this time the Middle West was frontier country and the Far West hardly settled at all.

Some of our Catholic English translations of the Bible are probably not to be compared to the great Catholic versions of the Bible in the European languages, French for example. But generations of godly people have derived from them that unique consolation and holy wisdom which the written Word of God has at all times brought to the devout, even from those days at the dawn of Christian history when readings from the Scripture first became part of the liturgical life and the private devotion of Catholics.

In these latter years Catholic scientific research and popular interest have combined to give us new translations, wider distribution, and increased study of the Old and New Testaments both in their entireties and in selected parts. Faithfully accurate yet beautifully written texts of the Psalms, the Canticle of Canticles, the Book of Job, the Epistles, and above all, the Holy Gospels have notably multiplied; these are available in editions of the widest variety both of bookstyle and of price.

So, too, modern Catholic translations of the whole Bible in our day and tongue are numerous and excellent. Catholic Americans are justly proud of the editions of the Sacred Scripture published under the auspices of the Confraternity of Christian Doctrine here in the United States. All the English-speaking world is indebted to the scholarship and literary genius of Monsignor Ronald Knox for the authentic English and authoritative skill of his modern translation of the Bible.

Convenient manuals introductory to the Sacred Scripture and attractive handbooks of selected Bible passages arranged for daily reading or occasional meditation have recently increased in Catholic bookstores, inheriting the popular response so long given by our priests and people to standard Scriptural anthologies like Kenelm Vaughan's *Divine Armory of Sacred Scripture*, well-thumbed copies of which are still

173

found in the libraries of an older generation of priests and people.

This revival of interest in the Bible and in books pertaining to Sacred Scripture is doubtless due to the simultaneous operation within the Church of two powerful forces, both in turn impelled by the Holy Spirit of God Himself. First, the authoritative voice of the Teaching Church has been clear and consistent in pointing out the special utility in our day of the lessons the Bible teaches, the relevance to our worries of the consolations, directives, and aids which Sacred Scripture provides.

Then, too, great numbers of the faithful, clearly urged by God's grace, have turned anew to the Word of God to find a sanity and sanctity which are not to be found in the conflicting words of men, at best so imperfect and at worst so often misleading or even malicious.

The guidance of the Church has been given us on every level of her authoritative organization. Pope Leo XIII, Pope Benedict XV, and our present Holy Father have made extended expositions of the reasons why modern Catholics should recapture the ancient, earnest devotion of their forefathers to the Scriptures.[1] The many editions of the Bible in our own country constitute striking proofs of the effort of the Catholic bishops of America to interest their flocks in the reading and study of the Word of God. Not a few of these editions appeared under the patronage of individual bishops, some were the work of scholars in the hierarchy. The recent monumental edition of the Holy Bible, translated from the original languages by members of the Catholic Biblical Association of America, is sponsored by the Bishops' Committee of the Confraternity of Christian Doctrine. Assuredly there has been no lack of leadership from the Shepherds of the Scriptures to salvation.

How lamentable it would be if with all this encouragement and opportunity to profit from the Sacred Scriptures our people were to fall behind their neighbors in loving knowledge and grateful use of the Holy Bible. It is fear of this unfortunate possibility which in great part prompts my present letter.

Catholics should find in the reading and love of the Sacred Scriptures a source of spiritual refreshment second only to that which is theirs in the Blessed Sacrament Itself. Not a few of our saints or writers on Christian perfection have drawn a parallel between the Incarnate Word of God wonderfully present in the Sacrament of the Altar and the Inspired Word of God given us in the Holy Bible.

Such writers have found it fitting that our forefathers in the early Church should have kept, as they did, both the Eucharist and the Gospels in special tabernacles. To this day the liturgy of the Church reveals the Catholic understanding of the uniquely sacred character of the Bible. The Gospel book is incensed in Solemn Mass, even as is the Sacred Cross, Tree of our Salvation, and the Adorable Host which hides the very Presence of the Son of God. No other book is incensed because no other book could be of comparable sanctity.

In the Mass there is another striking parallel between the way in which God comes to us through the Word of Scripture and the way in which He comes through the Word made Flesh. The first part of the Mass, the Mass of the catechumens, centers about the Sacred Scripture. It is composed almost entirely of Biblical texts; the Psalm at the foot of the altar, the Versicles and Responses after the Confiteor, the Introit, many phrases of the Gloria, the Epistle, the Gradual and finally the Gospel: All these are straight from Scripture.

When the Mass is solemnly sung, the Gospel is borne in devout procession before it is chanted; it is surrounded with burning tapers and its pages are venerated with a reverential kiss. Thus the rubrics surrounding the use of the Scriptures in the liturgy are not unlike those by which we pay homage to the Sacrament.

In the later parts of the Mass Christ is really present in our midst, but in these opening stages of the Divine Liturgy He is also somehow present in the Scripture phrases which foretell His coming or proclaim His words and works. And finally the marvel of the Consecration brings Jesus as truly to our altars as ever the consent of Mary brought Him to her bosom or the rejoicing throngs led Him to Jerusalem, the words of the Mass become strongly Scriptural in their tone and message. Where could the Church have found accents more worthy to welcome the Word made Flesh than in the written pages of the Inspired Word which is Scripture?

Saint Jerome, who adored the Blessed Sacrament and loved the Sacred Scriptures, delighted to parallel the two. He declared that Christians must be nourished by both the living flesh and the living phrases of Jesus; the first is given us in the Eucharist, the second in the Bible.

The author of the *Imitation of Christ* sketches the same sublime parallel between the Holy Eucharist and the Holy Bible when he writes, "For two things do I feel to be exceedingly necessary to me in this life, without which this miserable life would be intolerable to me; being detained in the prison of this body, I confess that I need two things, even food and light. Thou hast therefor given to me who am so weak, Thy sacred Body and Blood, for the refreshing of my soul and body, and has set Thy Word for a lantern to my feet. Without these two I could not properly live; for the word of God is the light of my soul, and Thy Sacrament the bread of life. These may also be called the two tables, placed on this side and on that, in the treasury of Thy holy Church. One table is that of the Sacred Altar, being the holy bread, that is the precious Body and Blood of Christ; the other is the table of the Divine Law, containing holy doctrine, teaching the true faith, and leading steadfastly onwards even to that which is within the veil, where the Holy of Holies is."[2]

The Bible is so rich a source of spiritual refreshment because Christ, the source of all grace, is found in its every chapter.

The Old Testament is the record of humanity's longing for Him and of Israel's vocation to produce Him, the New Testament is the account of His coming and of the first beginnings of the Church's mandate to spread His Kingdom. Jesus is somehow present in every verse of Sacred Scripture. His person dominates every page.

In the opening lines of Genesis the promise of the Redeemer restores joyful hope to the melancholy hearts of our sinful parents. Abraham is made strong in his courage and sure in his faith by the knowledge that out of his seed shall come the Messias, the Holy One in whom shall all the nations of the earth be blessed. Jacob raised his dying arms toward the star that shall rise out of him, the star which heralds the coming of Jesus. The tears of the Psalmist are shed partly for himself, partly for Christ; the prophets and kings desire to see Him and pour out their hearts in impatient words descriptive of the day of His birth, His death, and His victory. In the exile of Egypt His People hunger for Him, the Hero of their race; even in their stubborn isolation from the Gentiles they dimly understand that He is the Desired One of all the nations, the Prince of Peace and King of Kings in a spiritual sense which is obscured whenever they look forward toward Him.

And then the song of angels suddenly is blended with Israel's expectant psalms; John the Baptist sums up the prophetic hopes of the Old Law and points to the saving realities of the New; holy Simeon uses the hallowed words of the Hebrew Scriptures to announce the advent of the Christian Gospel—and thenceforth the Bible explicitly speaks of nothing but Jesus. The Gospels follow His every step, strive to save for us His every word. The Epistles seek to initiate us in the imitation of His perfection. The Acts of the Apostles relate how His Church first began to perpetuate His influence and His teaching. The Apocalypse predicts the splendor of His unending glory in the New Jerusalem where He shall reign forever. The last lines of the Scripture are preoccupied with His second coming as our Judge and our Reward, just as the first chapters of Genesis awaited His coming as our Savior. "Come, Lord Jesus. The grace of our Lord Jesus Christ be with you all. Amen!"[3]

There is no place in Scripture, from Adam below the eastern wall of Paradise to John in ecstasy on Patmos, from which is absent the echo of that prayer: "Come, Lord Jesus!"

To those, then, who read the Bible as the Church offers and understands its inspired pages, there is given that wisdom which comes from God and which is God, the wisdom which is the Word of God. To them Christ Himself becomes a familiar friend, their Redeemer and intimate Guide to God. How pale and lifeless, as contrasted with the living truth of the Gospel history, are those recent romantic fantasies which seek to tell the life of Jesus in fictional form!

It is when we think of the Bible in terms of Christ that we best understand what it is and what it is not. Back in the days when some students, exuberant in their new-found and heady knowledge, used to speak of the conflict between Reason and Scripture, the devout were frequently scandalized because they could not reconcile Genesis and the popular science of the Sunday supplements or the sophisticated lecture halls. Then wise men pointed out to them that the Bible was not written to teach us how the heavens go, but to teach us how to go to Heaven.

The preoccupations of the moment are more often with economics than with evolution; they are political and sociological rather than concerned with material science as they were a generation or two ago. However, a like warning against a misunderstanding of the nature, purpose, and use of the Sacred Scriptures is sometimes needed. The Bible was not written to teach us how to grow rich, nor to provide technical advice on how to administer secular affairs. The Scriptures were given us to teach the rich moderation, responsibility, and mercy; to tell them how they might pass through the needle's eye which is the Gate of Heaven despite the encumbrances of their possessions. The Bible was written to give the poor hope and patient wisdom; to teach princes God-fearing righteousness and people noble virtue.

The Bible is not a scientific treatise on economics, a book of quotations for the convenience of propagandists, or a political textbook for diplomats. It is a guide book to the spiritual perfection of persons, which, when we have it, contributes mightily to the right order of earthly society but which is primarily a matter of eternal and supernatural considerations rather than of technical questions of a temporal kind.

Why, then, do Catholics love the Bible and rejoice in the commemoration of the discovery of the scientific arts which have made it so readily available to us? Catholics love the Bible because it is one of the greatest treasures of their dearly cherished Mother, the Church, a source of some of her greatest spiritual riches. The missal beloved by her children as they gather for Mass, the Divine Office chanted by her monks and holy religious, the breviary read by her priests, the rituals and symbols of her sacramental life are almost entirely fashioned from it. Our Catholic prayers are woven around scenes recalled from the Scriptures and their phrases repeat the hallowed words of the poetry and prose of Holy Writ. To the Bible we are indebted for the Our Father, the Hail Mary, the articles of the Apostles' Creed, the Magnificat, the Mysteries of the Rosary, the Stations of the Cross, the De Profundis and numerous other of the public and private devotions which are the heart and soul of Catholic spiritual life.

Catholics love the Bible because it is the history of all their spiritual kinsmen, of all who are pilgrims and strangers on the face of the earth, seekers after God, from the beginning of time until time shall be no more. They love the Bible because it is a promise and a prophecy, a constant reminder that the walls of this world are destined to dissolve and that our true fatherland,

179

the Promised Land of our souls, will assuredly be ours if we walk in the ways of our fathers and follow in the footsteps of Jesus.

Catholics love the Bible because it is the Word of God, lifegiving and availing to salvation. They love it because it tells us of Christ and there is no one of us, however imperfect and even base his other loves, who does not live out his days eager to be found with Christ at the end, to die worthy of Christ's love and returning it in some measure.

For Catholics, in a word, as Christ is the King of kings and Lord of lords, so the Bible is the Book of books. They understand what Sir Walter Scott meant when he was dying and asked a friend to read to him out of "The Book". The friend wondered which book the great novelist meant, and Scott answered, "There is only one book, *The Book*, the Bible!"

It has always been thus in Christendom; thus it is today. There are almost ten million books catalogued in the Library of Congress in Washington. Twelve thousand titles are added each year from among books published in America alone. But the Book of Books, the Book of the Ages, as opposed to the Book of the Month or the Book of the Year, remains the book which Saint Jerome translated from so many languages into Latin; which the Church protected through all the Dark Ages, guarding it even as she did the Sacraments and the Apostolic Traditions; the book which John Gutenberg chose when first he found it possible to print: the Holy Bible.

Wherefore I exhort you, my brother priests and beloved people, to grow in the knowledge and love of the Sacred Scriptures. Let each be mindful of the bidding of our Holy Father, Pope Pius XII, that we scan the pages of Scripture to find there Christ, exemplar of justice, charity, and mercy, divine solution of every difficulty. Let us heed the reminder of the Chief Shepherd of Christendom that it is the serious duty of the faithful to make free and holy use of this treasure, taking up the Scriptures as we would a letter from Heaven addressed to each of us individually to bring inspiration, instruction, correction, and courage.

I ask families to develop anew that love for the Sacred Scriptures which used to characterize devout households. The Holy Bible should have first place in the spiritual reading of each home, as the Rosary, with its meditations on mysteries drawn from the pages of the Bible, has come to have first place among family prayers.

Each home should cherish a family Bible, jealously guarded as the repository of those records of births, baptisms, marriages, vocations, and deaths which are the mementos of the joyful, sorrowful, and glorious mysteries of life in a Christian household.

I beg our priests to preach the Scriptures, mindful of the warning of Saint Jerome that to be ignorant of the Scriptures is to be ignorant of Christ.[4] Drawing the themes of our sermons from the Bible we shall profit from the matchless example of Jesus Himself and may more frequently merit the consolation of having our people say, as the disciples at Emmaus said of Jesus, "Were not our hearts burning within us when He spoke to us on the road, and when He made the Scriptures plain to us?"[5]

I counsel one and all to discover the many indulgences with which our Holy Mother the Church encourages the prayerful reading of the Bible and I recommend that those in every state of life who aspire to be saints imitate the devotion of the saints to the Sacred Scriptures. Of this devotion the Blessed Mother, Queen of All Saints, may be the exemplar, for surely we hear echoes of her attentive listening to the Old Testament in the song of her Magnificat even as we detect the influence of her holy reminiscences in parts of the New Testament, especially in the early chapters of Saint Luke's Gospel.

Thus through the reading of the words which John Gutenberg first printed five hundred years ago we may come to the understanding of the Word Eternal which God alone, in Whom there is neither first nor last, could utter.

I beg you to join in my prayer that we who have loved the Inspired Word of God here below may hereafter be forever united in the possession of the Infinite Word, the Word which is God.

I ask His blessing on each of you and I beg your prayers for me.

XIV

Education for an Age of Fear

This season of centenary finds our part of the world—the part that calls itself free and that publicly professes religious faith—in a strange mood. It is a mood to which we of the New World and the younger nations are unused, a mood of defeatism and fear.

It is the more strange and the more pathetic, this almost universal sense of panic, because it follows so closely on a brief period of the precisely opposite attitudes of optimism and enthusiasm which followed World War II.

It is less than a decade ago that men were talking of a *brave new world*, a world of four universal freedoms (among them *freedom from fear*), not a world divided into those possessed of these blessings and those deprived of them, but rather *one world*, a world of nations united and peoples at peace in a reign of concord and prosperity within a global new Arcady.

Such a Pollyanna outlook, so woefully mistaken in the event, was born of a blend of naiveté, untimely optimism and sheer weariness with the rude by-products of the age of nationalism. Its Messianic touch—sometimes it seemed to seek a Messianic Age without the Messiah!—was described by one astute critic in the early 1940s as *Dawnism*, the ingenuous expectation that the millenium was at hand, at the very most a political conference or two away.

It is easy now, with the bland wisdom of hindsight, to make fun of those who placed too sanguine credit in the political hopes kindled by *Dawnism*, but at the same time, even ten years ago, if there were many who did not share *the general*

This sermon was preached at Saint Francis Xavier University, Antigonish, Nova Scotia, on September 2, 1953.

mistaken sense of well-being and whispering hope, they maintained a discreet silence which certainly no longer serves to identify them.

Moreover, if we may choose among follies, the comfortable excesses of *Dawnism* were somehow preferable, at least for the moment, to the opposite extremes to which we have more recently gone. For now naive optimism has yielded to nervous fears and *Dawnism* has melted into *Defeatism*, or, to keep the figure, turned into *Twilightism* in which there hang about us, our minds, our lives, and our societies, the pessimistic despair, the brooding fears, and the trepidation of *Götterdammerung*.

It is no longer necessary, I take it, to rebuke the sunny follies of the *Dawnists*. They are a sad company by now, and any Jack-in-the-Pulpit lacking a better text or village Hampden intent upon election can give a hundred prompt and wondrous reasons to stoke with warmer fagots the sorry pyres of the *one world* dreamers, the visionaries, and the Utopia-seekers of less than a decade ago.

What now calls for diagnosis and for cure is the contagious mood of universal discouragement spread on every side by a host of Giants of Despair. These have turned Doubting Castle into a mighty convention headquarters for panic-stricken editors, lecturers, candidates for public office, and even clergy who, disenchanted with prospects for the millenium, bid us now prepare as best we may for the approaching dissolution of every hope and help.

There was a kind of political Pelagianism in the pretensions of the *Dawnists*, a foolish trust that mankind could be lifted by its own bootstraps to that peace which the world cannot of itself give nor attain; accordingly, Christians should have been on their guard against the too arrogant hopes of the *Dawnists*. But the *Defeatists*, the unduly sad of mind and too sick of heart, the current prophets of inevitable and general doom, have their heretical taint, too. Perhaps we may call it political Jansenism, particularly in its implications that the world suffers from total depravity, mankind from complete corruption of his will to achieve or improve, and God Himself from the paralyzing restrictions of a limited atonement.

If Pelagius, headstrong and vain, is the patron of the *Dawnists*, the *Defeatists* find their spiritual kinsmen (whether they like it or not) in the bleak shades of Calvin, Jansenius, Quesnel, and Schopenhauer.

In any case, it is their pessimism and spirit of fear which threaten to overwhelm us at the moment. Some of the Defeatists preach the refuge of Christians in a false mysticism, a pseudo-spiritual flight from the realities of the world in which God has placed us to work out our salvation. Others in their fear urge recourse to the outmoded and false securities of a reborn nationalism, political isolationism, or pagan militarism. Most of them are frankly cynical, but a few are romantics in their reactionary retreat from whatever is unfamiliar or tentative or untried. All have in common a fundamental pessimism and a paralyzing fear. Even when they speak (as certain of them do) of Christian values and their defense, they repeat the letter of Christian phrases with little if any of the spirit of Christian hope, confidence, and divine courage which is, as rarely before, the supremest need of mankind.

Much of the dispirited and fearful defeatism is perhaps a form of *battle-fatigue* in the age-old struggle of mankind to wrest some measure of order and security from the chaos about it, but much is also due to loss of perspective. People always tend to see their times out of focus and each generation is tempted to believe that nobody before has known the troubles it must endure or been so menaced by outrageous fortune as it has been.

The centenary jubilee of an historic Christian university provides welcome occasion for the reminder that our schools and colleges have for a principal function continually to correct this false perspective which so dangerously limits vision to prospects of doom. A university which emphasizes the liberal arts tradition and particularly one which integrates the humane disciplines with the divine sciences, has a momentous work to do in an age of fear. It must raise up Christian intellectuals with that historical perspective and vigorous faith which enables them to accept all times as God's times, profiting from seasons of prosperity without effrontery or softness and meeting times of disaster without despair or undisciplined lamentation.

Here in Nova Scotia Saint Francis Xavier University has valiantly done such a work; on its centenary it serves as a symbol of the saving spirit and constructive activity which must characterize every Christian university worthy of either name. Saint Francis Xavier is old enough to have a sense of history and the conservatism which such a sense engenders; every Catholic university, moreover, has roots deeper than its particular origin and is therefore always older than its own years. To the conservatism of the liberal arts college Saint Francis has added the progressive, venturesome spirit of a campus close to the life of the general community and has therefore sought to apply opportunely the principles of unchanging wisdom to the problems of changing society.

Accordingly Saint Francis University bears witness to certain intellectual and moral virtues of which our timid, impatient generation, even of believers, stands in grave need if we are to meet, as Christians must, the disturbing challenge of revolutionary times and the sickening impact of so much undeniable evil.

Take, for example, one of the most outrageous of the typical problems which so disturbs us and accounts for our fears. It is shocking that the Primate of Croatia should be in the toils of Comrade Tito; that the Primate of Hungary should have been broken and degraded by Citizen Rakosi, that the Cardinal of China should be in exile; that the Primate of Bohemia and the spiritual princes of the people of Poland and a score of other

186

nations should be in peril of their lives, prevented by violence from the public preaching of the Gospel.[1] All this is shocking and sacrilegious, and that some should condone such crimes is also iniquitous and unworthy.

These things scandalize but they should not depress to hopelessness or throw into panic those who, as Christians, are privileged to see and to hear with better faculties than the eyes and ears of sense.

The devout should know that God is still at work and that perhaps the hallowed chains of His modern servants, like those of Peter and Paul of old, will, in His strange Providence, prove stronger bonds of His Church, restored and renewed, than ever would the happier freedom which only yesterday permitted us to mingle in joyful fraternity and visible fellowship with our brethren of the present Church of Silence.

The devout intellectual not only perceives this, as do the simplest of the faithful, but he remembers that it was ever thus. He does not react to the skyrocketing headlines of the hour with disorganized dismay and vehement rage as if he had never seen or heard the like. Rather, recalling the small print of his history books, he watches with serenity as once again the tyrants who would tame God's men like Cardinal Fisher or Blessed Plunkett, are in fact slowly but surely tamed by them, if not in themselves, at least in their descendancy.

It steadies his faith (as well as his nerves) and clarifies for him the immediate as well as the ultimate issues in the great tensions between the City of God and the City of this world, when, seeing the plight of Beran or Mindszenty or Stepanic, he remembers Becket and Hildebrand and that blood of the martyrs which was once and is still the seed of the Church.[2] He reflects that the torches kindled along the villa drives of Nero are black and cold, but God's stars still shine; that Attila is dust, and no man can point out the grave where rots the threefold coffin of gold, silver, and iron in which they buried him—but

God's Son still speaks through new Leos to the converted sons of the soldiers of Attila, the earlier Scourge of God.

Malice and brutality, the Christian intellectual understands, are of men; they disintegrate and die. True wisdom is of God, Who endureth forever; it comes to us through Jesus Christ, yesterday, today, forever the same.[3] It partakes of His unchanging permanence. Religion teaches this and history confirms it.

It therefore becomes the duty of the Christian intellectual to intensify in himself and communicate to the rest of us this balanced, serene perspective which sees all things in their proper relation to one another and, above all, to God, evaluating them in the light of eternity as well as of history. Such calm detachment may be more than we usually expect from partisan politicians, though we have a right to ask it of any who aspire to be true servants of the common good or genuine statesmen. A sense of history and of eternity may not be present in pamphleteers and their radio equivalents, though we may properly expect it of responsible journalists and of others who presume to shape that greatest of powers for good or evil, which is public opinion. But, however others may fret and frenzy, our intellectuals—professors, writers, preachers, and editors—are called to maintain something of the equanimity of the saints, thus preserving us from the extremes of giddy complacency or vituperative despair to which the foolish and the uninformed are alternately driven by the shifting fortunes of history.

This is the perennial vocation of the Christian intellectual: to resist the intemperate talk alike of the brash innovators and the nervous traditionalist; to remain spiritually confident and intellectually calm in the face of change or challenge, the threat of evil or the seduction of novelty. It is to recapture the spirit of Gamaliel in the face of new directions and challenging changes which do not touch on the great dogmas of Faith or basic precepts of the Christian moral code, but which startle those attached (understandably but, please God, not excessively) to certain secondary corollaries of a social, economic, or personal kind.

Sometimes as we read our press or listen to our speakers on these questions we wonder what has become of the sober moderation, both of balanced judgment and of controlled emotion, which made Gamaliel a Christian intellectual before his time. How sobering the memory of him should be to our hotspurs, so ready in wrath, so fearful in reactions, so upset in judgment!

How sanely Gamaliel summed up the lessons which religion and reason, Christian hope and human history should teach us in times of disturbing new ideas and far-reaching changes. Faced with ideas which alarmed the traditional concepts of his contemporaries, he said in effect, "If these things be of man, they will run their course and have their end; if they be of God, you will have no power to overthrow them and had best come to understand them, seeking to discern how much may be good in what at first jars; how much true in what seems novel, how much beautiful in what is unfamiliar; how much, in a word, is divine plan, though it seem at first to be no more than human striving."[4]

How does the Christian university, the institution like Saint Francis Xavier, hold forth the promise of new Gamaliels to help us achieve the resolute calm and imperturbable equanimity sometimes so painfully absent from the reactions of even Christians to the events of our times, and always so needed in an age of great fears?

We have mentioned the liberal arts and their refining discipline, plus the divine sciences of philosophy and theology. Perhaps the relevance of these in our generation needs new emphasis.

Cardinal Newman, in his Oxford University sermon on Wisdom, describes for us the *majestic calm* which the study of philosophy gives to the intellect of a man of right reason. The very phrases of the English Cardinal suggest the need of such studies in which our own day stands. "In the mind of a philosopher," he writes,

> the elements of the physical and moral world, sciences, arts, pursuits, ranks, offices, events, opinions, individualities, are all viewed, not in themselves, but as relative terms, suggesting a multitude of correlatives, and gradually, by successive combinations, converging one and all to their true centre. Men, whose minds are possessed by some one object, take exaggerated views of its importance, are feverish in their pursuit of it, and are startled or downcast on finding obstacles in the way of it; they are ever in alarm or in transport. And they, on the contrary, who have no firm grasp of principles, are perplexed and lose their way every fresh step they take; they do not know what to think or say of new phenomena which meet them, of whatever kind; they have no view, as it may be called, concerning persons, or occurrences, or facts, which come upon them suddenly; they cannot form a judgment, or determine on a course of action; . . . But Philosophy cannot be partial, cannot be exclusive, cannot be impetuous, cannot be surprised, cannot fear, cannot lose its balance, cannot be at a loss, cannot but be patient, collected, and majestically calm, because it discerns the whole in each part, the end in each beginning, the worth of each interruption, the measure of each delay, because it always knows where it is, and how its path lies from one point to another.[5]

Next after philosophy among the natural arts and sciences which impose intellectual and disciplined moderation of judgment, one may well place historical studies, sacred and secular. Perhaps of especial help to our generation, so fearful in its faith and so preoccupied with the power of evil, would be a new approach to hagiography, the luminous history of the saints.

This neglected field of historical studies prepares the serene Christian intellectual to keep before our eyes, so often frightened by maps which show political frontiers overrun by violence, another map, ultimately more accurate and certainly more reassuring. We might call this other map *An Atlas of the City of God on Earth*, and it might well be accompanied by *A Gazetteer of Human History in the Light of the Saints*. These would remind us that not all places under heaven are battlefields where evil triumphs, or cities of confusion where justice is mocked and malice, treachery, and violence hold their evil courts. Such an *atlas* and *gazetteer* of the saints, continually correcting our perspective, would not forget the treachery of Eden and the courtyard of Peter's betrayal, but they would feature for our times the Mount of the Transfiguration and the Garden of the Resurrection.

They would record the places of our shame and humiliation, but highlight the many and magnificent scenes of God's intervention in our behalf, the places where His provident power has more than once revealed itself: the Road to Damascus would be there with its reminder that our most violent foes, touched by God's grace, have times beyond counting become ardent apostles and defenders of the Faith; the Milvian Bridge would be there, too, and the legendary cross above it with its promise of victory through that sacred sign; Monte Cassino, not as a scene of destruction and fratricide, but as a high point it once marked in the history of human self-knowledge and self-discipline; Constantinople and Canterbury to tell us of days when Christendom was building its compact yet varied commonwealth of sanctity, a commonwealth crippled by schism and sad history, but still vigorous with the energy of God Himself; Bobbio, Iona, Cluny, Clairvaux, Paris, and Oxford, with their reminders that as once the words of human wisdom were channels of the Word Divine, so they can be again; Canossa, perhaps, and Lepanto, and even Runnymede, serving as tokens that the ambitions of tyrants and kings do not forever override the Providence of God and contravene the progress of His people. Also would be some sad associations: the scenes of dungeons, prison towers, and racks, the places of exile—but, above all, it would display the birthplaces of the saints, the corners of the world where the leaven of the Gospel revealed, if only for a lifetime or a century, that power to change the whole face of the earth of which we should ever be mindful in times like these: Tarsus which gave us Paul; Rome which gave us Gregory the Great and the great Saint Leo; Dalmatia for Jerome, Antioch for Chrysostom, Alexandria for Cyril, Glastonbury for fifteen centuries of saints, North Africa for Augustine, Roccasecca for Thomas Aquinas, Dijon for Bernard, Domrémy for Joan, Avila for Teresa, and hosts of others. Their source and fountainhead of the supernatural quickening of all others: "Thou Bethlehem the land of Judah . . . for out of thee has come forth the captain that shall rule my people Israel."[6]

These are the places that would shine for our enheartening on the *atlas* of the Christian intellectual; their memories would make us bold as we scan the *gazetteer* of God's world and ours.

The moderating power of history, properly studied, its capacity to teach temperate patience and to restore balanced perspective, makes the more regrettable the decline, not to say the disappearance of ancient history courses in our schools and colleges. Men are less likely to despair in the face of the physical destruction of their cities when they remember the topless towers of Ilium and yet the poetry and heroic vision that the human spirit salvaged from them. They will still resent treacherous fifth columns, but will be better able to cope with them, reasonably and resolutely, if they are spared alarm and given mature wisdom by the memory of the Trojan Horse and the recognition that the ingenuity of evil has not shown much progress in all these many centuries.

Men who have once reflected, through long evenings of study, on how titanic a task it was to found the Roman state will be reassured rather than exasperated as they read of the intricate, painstaking trouble needed to organize a whole world in peace and prosperity. They are less likely to rail at the failures of the United Nations and the meager progress of world courts and Leagues of Nations who remember the fortunes of the Amphictyonic Leagues twenty-five centuries ago in Greece and who have diligently traced from that day to our own the patient efforts to organize tribes, then towns, cities, and states, then continents and hemispheres into something like a collaborative human community.

Few books will better equip our generation to evaluate objectively and dispassionately their chieftains and the names that make the news than Plutarch, writing not of those whose names provoke modern partisan passion and excite the fears of current-events classes in our day, but of the perennial types of the good and the evil in public life as these were exemplified in the lives of the noble Grecians and Romans.

This is particularly true, perhaps, of the characters in the last years of the Roman Republic; they have so many lessons for those who understand that history may not repeat itself, but historical situations recur and the natural man changes not at all.

The terrifying impact of the daily newspapers is bound to be diminished on the mind which has learned that, just as there were many brave men before Agamemnon's time, so there were many traitors, schemers, and villains before the evil individuals whose crimes cause so strident a voice and startling a style in our contemporary radio, press, and platform alarmists. The typical procedures and inevitable fates of all these were spelled out, faithfully and finally, far away and long ago; it is the vocation of the Christian intellectual in our day to recall them to us whenever the living objects of our unhealthy fears (or, for that matter, our excessive hopes) unduly disturb our perspective.

Not only ancient history, but more recent, too, will help the Christian intellectual imitate the patience of the saints and share the perspective of the Church. Wise students of modern English history, for example, will recall how often leaders before our times have despaired of civilization and have been prepared to throw in the sponge too soon.

They will reflect how William Pitt, speaking in 1790, reached the melancholy conclusion that his people had come to the end of their rope. There is scarcely anything around us, he said, but ruin and despair!

They will remember that the Duke of Wellington, dying in 1851, at about the time when plans were being made for the foundation of this institution a hundred years ago, thanked God that by his death he would be spared from the total ruin that he felt sure was close at hand for his people. That was a century ago and since then his people have survived a dozen fatal crises to see the rejoicings of this year's Coronation.

In 1849, just over a hundred years ago, Disraeli was on the verge of utter despair. He said, "In industry, commerce, and agriculture, there is no hope whatsoever!" But in the century since, industry has reached peaks which he could never have imagined; commerce has outstripped anything that he knew in his most prosperous days and, with all its worries, the world is hardly worse than the world Disraeli knew.

Such examples from English history could be duplicated from our own. And if the natural society of mankind, the realms of secular civilization, reveal this hardihood which continually cheats the prophets of despair, even more remarkable is the resilience of the Christian Commonwealth, strengthened and made supple as it is by the enduring energies it receives through the Church from the unconquerable Christ and the Eternal God Himself.

Let me illustrate this, too, from the history of that same period which has included the story of this institution, the hundred years since Saint Francis Xavier was established. What are the worries, the grounds for fear, in the hearts today of those who love the Church? We are told by certain popular lecturers and by typical spokesmen of the Left that now at last the Church is doomed, and we, losing perspective and therefore weakened in hope, almost believe them. They tell us that conditions in Europe make the final collapse of

Christendom imminent and inevitable. If we have the courage left to ask for a bill of particulars, it is promptly provided in clippings from this month's newspapers and this year's liberal reviews. Look at Italy, we are told. Within the month I read the grim prophecy of a political commentator that Italy may soon prove renegade to her ancient faith by voting against Christian Democracy. He suggested that what clearly seemed to him an entirely novel and extraordinary situation would then confront the Holy See if *this* percentage of the voters, or *that* or *another* veered by this degree, or *that* or *another* to the Left or the Right. Look at France, we are warned. Public opinion polls reveal that on ever so many issues even the Catholics are divided among themselves and the Church, it is said, herself admits that France has become a missionary country in disturbing degree. Think of Germany: revolutionary ideas are taking root there and new errors and evils are loose; God only knows what future faith or freedom may have in a land so vexed! Consider Britain: we hear rumors that ancient moral codes are being further relaxed; we know full well that others have been. And Spain: What need we say of the situation there, as it affords themes for the current pretense that the Church can hardly survive a situation so precarious and, it is loudly cried, so compromised?

And so on our own shores a cry is raised which strikes terror in the hearts of the timid flock. The Church has had her day, it is asserted. She may have been pertinent in a feudal order, but she is obsolete in the age of democracy. Her power may have been tolerable or intelligible to the sacral civilization of the thirteenth century, but it is alien and not to be borne in the free atmosphere of twentieth-century secularism. Challenge, then, her affectations; expose her irrelevancy; undermine her efforts and annul her influence. The time has come at last to end this dated farce.

Such things are said, they are written and widely read, in my own country by Mr. [Paul] Blanshard, for example. Their

195

essential point, if not always the same spirit, is accepted by millions. They are said and written elsewhere as well: Mr. Wells' *Crux Ansata* still sells in England, and it is tame, of course, to what rolls from the anti-religious presses of the Continent and the East. It presents an appalling prospect to the unsteady in faith or the unread in history.

The devout student of history, on the other hand, takes down his history books as he hears these things, and, going no further back than the nineteenth century, he finds a single paragraph from a history of the Church in the United States which restores his sane perspective. It tells of the very decade in which your forefathers began this college a hundred years ago, and from the chapter entitled "Growth Amid Bigotry (1850–1860)" he reads phrases which might have been written last evening to arouse the apprehension of today's faithful concerning their own worries of the 1950s.[7]

Describing this decade a hundred years ago Roemer tells how the self-styled *Know-Nothings* were joined in their attacks by some militant anti-Catholics who then thought they could discern the total collapse of the Catholic Church in the near future. To their way of thinking, conditions in Europe once again presaged this collapse. Then he specifies that Italy had in part risen up against the Pope. French Catholics were not in agreement among themselves. Germany was breeding a gang of intellectual malcontents, who were endangering the Church in the home country and could be used to influence the Catholics in our country. England was vehemently protesting the restoration of the hierarchy and was causing upheavals. Spain could not drag herself out of her dynastic revolutions and was sadly influencing the Church. Consequently these Protestants thought it should not be difficult to persuade the Catholics in this country that their Church was nothing more than an antiquated *medieval fossil* for which there was no future.

Meanwhile they judged that some prodding, with the aid of

the nativists, would help hasten the end. The prodding was bitter and the results frequently violent as may be seen in the incendiary crimes committed in my own native city, or the indignities suffered by Archbishop Bedini and the madcap mischief let loose in America by the visit of Louis Kossuth or the blood-curdling harangues of Alessandro Gavazzi. But this, too, all passed—and few recall the burning of the Ursulines or the beating of Father Bapst as they visit the hundreds of New England convent schools and witness the enlightened descendants of the Know-Nothings joined now in friendly action for the general good with priests whose fathers helped scrape the tar and feathers from John Bapst's bleeding flesh.[8]

The lesson, then, that the patient Catholic intellectual learns from all this (a lesson, I repeat, which his untutored peasant cousin has intuitively understood for centuries) is not that we should be Pollyannas but that we should be Christian, men of a confidence rooted in the recognition that men and events pass, God and His work endure. It is the lesson, too, that the tensions which plague us are not new, either in form, or in substance, or in the remedies for them, and that what made our fathers strong should not find us timid. Nothing can happen in our day, or in the days to come, so calculated to appal but what the Christian scholar, glancing at his *Roman Martyrology*, or Challoner's *Memories of the Missionary Priests*, or any standard church history manual, will say with greater right than Virgil's hero: *"O passi graviora, dabit deus his quoque finem."*—"O you who have borne even heavier things, God will grant an end to these too."[9]

That is why we reserve the right to question the spiritual soundness as well as the intellectual acumen of those whose editorials or lectures (or, for that matter, sermons) perpetually cry havoc or proclaim the bankruptcy of hope and the early end of all. The authentic, sober yet radiant spirit of the Church is more perfectly echoed in the manful words pronounced last month in the ruins of Cologne by Cardinal Feltin of Paris. "We believe in the future of humanity", the French cardinal declared. We Christians are more optimistic than all others, even though we recognize the vast errors of which human nature is capable. We are not Utopians, but we know that grace is stronger than sin.

That same spirit of Christian optimism animated the valiant Pope Pius XI (a *librarian*, by the way) when he thanked God that he lived in times of such trouble and testing that it was no longer possible for a Christian to be mediocre.[10]

And if philosophy and history thus steady the sights and compose the soul of the Christian intellectual, what shall we not expect of Religion, the faith by which the scholar is made one with the living, indestructible Church and, through the Church, with Christ, predestined for victory. The words of Saint Bernard will prompt the Christian intellectual so to perfect his own spiritual life that he may finally come to see history itself through the eyes of Christ and thus achieve, sinner though he be, some share in the majestic dignity, the spiritual liberty and unafraid poise, of the Son of God.

Hence the new urgency of courses in theology for the laity, in strictly theological departments in all Christian universities, that reasoned faith may reinforce the devout reason of our Christian intellectuals in preparation for their apostolate in an age of fear.

Again it is Cardinal Newman who suggests at once the contemporary problem of fear and its needed remedy in soundly instructed faith when, in his *Idea of a University*, he sketches the unreasonable fears of the devout a century ago and describes the Christian calm which most effectively dispels them. In the Cardinal's day, the period which saw the beginnings of this university, the occasion of alarm was an alleged threat of new physical sciences to the old faith; today it is more often the menace of new political philosophies to the same old faith.

Newman's placid statement of the agitated scientific concern in his day offers a pattern for adaptation to certain of the political and social fears of today.

He wrote:

> I say, then, he who believes Revelation with that absolute faith which is the prerogative of a Catholic, is not the nervous creature who startles at every sudden sound, and is fluttered by every strange or novel appearance which meets his eyes. He has no sort of apprehension, he laughs at the idea, that anything can be discovered by any other scientific method, which can contradict any one of the dogmas of his religion. He knows full well there is no science whatever, but, in the course of its extension, runs the risk of infringing, without any meaning of offence on its own part, the path of other sciences: and he knows also that, if there be any one science which, from its sovereign and unassailable position can calmly bear such unintentional collisions on the part of the children of earth, it is theology. . . . And if, at the moment, [there] appears to be something contradictory, then he is content to wait, knowing that error is like other delinquents; give it rope enough, and it will be found to have a strong suicidal propensity. I do not mean to say he will not take his part in encouraging, in helping forward the prospective suicide; he will not only give the error rope enough, but show it how to handle and adjust the rope—he will commit the matter to reason, reflection, sober judgment, common sense; to time, the great interpreter of so many secrets. Instead of being irritated at the momentary triumph of the foes of Revelation . . . he will recollect that, in the order of Providence, our seeming dangers are often our greatest gains; that in the words of the Protestant poet,

> The clouds you so much dread
> Are big with mercy, and shall break
> In blessings on your head.[11]

In such an attitude as Newman's the Christian intellectual is not, of course, condoning evil; neither is he minimizing it nor forgetting that it is evil. Quite the contrary; he is simply robbing it of that victory over himself which would be Satan's real triumph if once even evil could make the good man mad, depriving him of the spiritual equilibrium by which he is able to pass unruffled and unscathed through the scandal of the world. And how much better, even as a tactic but certainly as an evidence of Christian conviction, is the self-possessed urbanity of Newman's approach to the tension between the Christian's faith and the pretensions of the world, as contrasted with the asperity, the air of personal indignation, and the frequent bad temper of those who sometimes bring to the defense of Christian values a zeal not proportionately matched by prudence, wisdom, or patience.

An intellectual pattern such as we have tried to sketch would produce Christian champions in the great war between truth and error now being waged for the conquest of the empires of the mind, champions more given to reason than to wrath; more conspicuous for their share in the patience of God Himself than for the explosive resentments and petty irritations of men who, because they are unreasonable, are really less than men.

Saint Paul asked that the Christian Gospel be defended "in season and out of season". But he admonished his disciples to rebuke, when rebuke they must, "in all patience and doctrine", two phrases which sum up succinctly the qualities of will and intellect which most become the Christian intellectual.[12]

A generation of genuine Christian intellectuals, mighty in patience and powerful in doctrine, would have neither time nor taste for ill-tempered denunciations, cheap verbal victories, and frenzied argument; they would prefer the persevering long-suffering work of leavening, quietly and calmly, the world's resistance to the truth; of building with confident determination and Godlike magnanimity the enduring walls of the Kingdom of God among the tribes of men.

Thus they would work and speak with the genial tolerance

of Gamaliel, the disciplined patience of Paul, the sweet forebearance of John, the long-range vision of Augustine, the cheerful optimism of Francis of Assisi, the painstaking, meticulous accuracy of Aquinas, the magnificent equanimity of Thomas More, the gentle moderation of Francis de Sales, the detachment and good-humored common sense of Philip Neri, the sensitive sobriety and scholarly insight of Newman, the fearless criticisms yet transcendent calm of the great encyclicals of the modern Popes.

These are the marks of the Christian intellectual, the true expositors of the Catholic faith and defenders of the Christian heritage—these, and not the embarrassing impatience and half-truths of nervous guerilla warriors on the Christian front, men full of fears unworthy of the kinsmen of the saints and so often given to tactics unbecoming those who claim to love God and to hate only error.

Such truly Christian intellectuals could lead our generation out of the dismal forests of its fears. They would be men responsive to the prophetic witness of Isaiah, made good by Christ and His Church: "Take courage and fear not. . . . The land that was desolate and impassable shall be glad, and the wilderness shall rejoice. . . . Strengthen ye the feeble hands, and confirm the weak knees. Say to the fainthearted: Take courage, and fear not: behold your God will bring the revenge of recompense: God Himself will come and will save you. . . . In the dens where dragons dwelt before, shall rise up the verdure of the reed and bulrush. And a path and a way shall be there, and it shall be called the holy way. . . ."[13]

The Catholic universities and colleges of the free world have, therefore, a unique contribution to make to education in an age of fear. Our colleges lack great endowments and material resources; it is a perpetual miracle how much they accomplish with so little in the way of this world's goods. As contrasted with their wealthier State or privately endowed contemporaries (I shall not say competitors) they operate on a shoestring, usually a shoestring on shoes for which full payment has not yet been made. In an era of costly equipment, high salaries, prohibitive construction costs, and overwhelming maintenance expenses, our colleges and universities cannot aspire, generally speaking, to establish great laboratories or research centers for the physical sciences and like costly areas of study. So be it; there will be no lack of these, however little we may contribute.

Nor are these any longer the great need. The earth is cracking under the weight of technical institutes and scientific laboratories; men are stoop-shouldered from bending over microscopes and test-tubes, and increasingly fearful of what they find and produce in their own laboratories. The need is of another kind now, and to it our religious universities have an unparalleled contribution to make. The word of God which inspires and ennobles is needed to counteract the divisive, crippling words of material-minded men.

So the material poverty of our universities is of minor moment if our campuses are spiritually alive, alert to the needs of the hour and robust in responding to them. We have apostolic example of what is at once the plight and yet the glorious power of religious colleges in a generation crippled with fear and paralyzed by pessimism. "Silver and gold I have none; but what I have, I give thee: In the name of Jesus Christ of Nazareth, arise and walk!"[14]

This is the constructive, courageous witness Saint Francis Xavier has borne in Nova Scotia these full hundred years. It is the prophetic witness every religious campus must bear to a fearful, bewildered generation. God grant that none will fail this apostolic mission!

XV

The Nurse's Vocation

Despite the age of *miracle drugs*, of medical progress and new methods of therapy of every kind, it is noteworthy that greater hospitals must still be built and that newspapers continue to print death columns.

The average span of life has been somewhat increased, but life remains (and always shall) a hazardous process of temporary resistance to, but eventual conquest by, those forces of disintegration which fatally lead to eventual death. There is nothing morbid about this process, since it is a provident part of God's merciful plan. Neither should it seem tragic, at least to one who believes, as Christians do, that every human adventure, death included, is a prelude to that eternal life before which the longest and most healthy earthly sojourn is but a fleeting spark in the face of the undying sun.

What is tragic, however, is that since sickness is so permanent a part of the physical lot of mankind, so much of its potential spiritual value should be lost. Even more sad than the suffering in the world, more sad than the most cruel sickness, is the fact that much of it is heedlessly wasted and fails to find the place in the total scheme of things which God, Who required suffering of His own Incarnate Son, intended it should have.

If we lived in a purely natural order, in a world limited to what the eye can see, the hand can touch, and the clock can time, sickness and suffering would be largely without point or profit of any kind. Much of it would seem staggering in its injustice, if it were possible to speak of either justice or

This sermon was preached at the Cathedral of Saints Peter and Paul, Providence, Rhode Island, on November 21, 1953, on the occasion of the Mass for Nurses sponsored by the New England Regional Conference.

injustice in a blind world without God above it or any human destiny beyond it.

But in point of fact we do not live in such an order of things. By the mercy of God and the grace of His Christ, there has been opened up to us a supernatural destiny in the light of which no human suffering need be wasted and no physical evil may be looked upon as final.

The worst of physical evils, the most distressing of all diseases, can be the occasion of enormous moral and spiritual good in terms of our eternal destiny. Sickness, as a physical evil, can take on an immortal significance and supernatural value which would be unintelligible to a race without faith or without knowledge of God's love for man and man's divine destiny.

Physical evils on the level of sick and bruised nature can produce incalculable merit on the level of the spirit and of God's grace. The real tragedy is that all too often they are not made thus spiritually profitable, but become doubly unfortunate by reason of their moral waste.

Devout nurses can help tremendously in correcting this unfortunate condition. They can accomplish great good by opening up the eyes of the sick to the precious spiritual treasures which pain and physical evil of every kind make possible to the person of faith.

It goes without saying that Christianity is at one with secular civilization in seeking that our nurses be skilled in all the arts of healing, that they master each new method of effective therapy and that devout nurses be second to none in modern professional competence. But Christianity expects more of the devout nurse than the wisdom of this world can even dream, let alone demand. It asks that together with their grasp of modern technical sciences, they possess themselves and share with others a mellow understanding of the ancient Christian philosophy concerning sickness as a physical evil which may have its providential place in the spiritual perfection of God's child.

We must not call indifference to the spiritual values of physical sickness a *modern* trait or fault. Impatience with the evils of our human condition and blindness to their place in God's plan and God's mercy, have always characterized the spiritually immature and the infirm of faith. We preachers too often pretend that our generation is less enlightened in its understanding of God's purposes and more pagan in its flight from pain and in its hunger after comfort than were generations gone by. Such pretense is neither fair nor factual; there is nothing particularly *modern* about pagan philosophies concerning comfort, pain, or the problem of sickness and of physical evil. Such philosophies are as old as Job; they are, in fact, as old as sin, as sickness, and as human error.

Impatience with pain and blindness to the spiritual uses of sickness, *naturalism* in our understanding of the problem of physical evil, are pagan, but they are *not* specifically modern. So, too, holy resignation under testing of every kind, including sickness, and patient, persevering faith that God's love is equally at work when He sends sorrow and when He sends joy, are found not merely in the saints of old but in millions of heroic sufferers under physical evils, including sickness in our own day.

And so it is not to decry an exclusively *modern* error but to bear witness against a perennial danger that I ask you, as devout Catholic nurses, to help prevent the waste of pain and to do all you can to teach the sick how they may profit in spiritual and eternal terms from the temporal and physical trials which sickness inevitably involves, yesterday, today, and forever.

The fact that science can do new and wonderful things in the way of therapy leaves unchanged, and always shall, the need for a philosophy concerning sickness, a practical part of the general Christian philosophy concerning physical evil in a world created by a benevolent God.

Let me remind you this morning of some of the providential aspects of most sickness, so that meditating on these old, familiar spiritual truths, you may perhaps be inspired to communicate the understanding of them to the troubled souls of those whose bodies you seek to heal.

One of the obvious spiritual advantages of sickness is that it withdraws us momentarily from the world and its unrelenting demands on our souls, thus warning us to turn our thoughts, momentarily at least, to that life which is our eternal destiny as opposed to the passing life which so dominates us that it threatens to destroy us.

Many things tend to dissuade us from thinking of eternity and even of our need of God, but nothing is more likely to do so than the heady, false sense of security that comes from habitual, untroubled physical well-being. Saint John, most gentle and tolerant of the Apostles, warns us against that "pride of life" which is the special peril of the strong, the energetic, and the healthy—that proud awareness of their own vitality and strength which so often leads the healthy, dazzled in their own conceit, to the very doors of eternity before it occurs to them that the soul has its health, as well as the body, and that the life of the world to come is more to be desired than the life of the world that passes.[1]

Everyone remembers the bitter verses that Belloc wrote about the health-faddist who strove to keep his arteries whole, but died of hardening of the soul. This is the temptation and the spiritual peril of all the healthy—and against this background of it one begins to understand how providential sickness can sometimes be.

Think of the manner in which our days are usually spent when we have no worry about our health. We rise in the morning refreshed for the day's work; letters, newspapers, visitors, all furnish us with absorbing topics of interest; eating is a diversion and a source of further strength; business is an outlet for our energies and enthusiasms; we glide triumphantly down the stream of life. If we grow tired it is a healthy fatigue, and we seek relief from it in recreation, amusement, or the untroubled slumber of the physically strong.

A little reflection on this carefree round of the healthy reveals how easy it is for those thus superficially blessed with strength to be carried along by the river of life far beyond points of spiritual importance, the desirability of which is frequently not recognized until it is all too late. How many a person, riding triumphantly the river of healthy existence, arrives at the ocean of eternity physically intact but spiritually completely unprepared to enter upon that life without which all life will have been futile, pathetic, and tragic. How such a healthy one would have profited from an occasional pause along the way to study the maps and learn the disciplines which prepare the spiritually robust for their immortal destiny!

Sickness sometimes provides such fortunate enforced pauses along the journey to eternity, the spiritual fruits of which can be incalculable.

Even pious people are not free from the dangerous delusions which can come from undisturbed good health. The devout have the constant teachings of the Church concerning that mortality to which we are all subject; they have the warnings of Sacred Scripture and of their spiritual directors about how death comes as a thief in the night and about how we must prepare for the dread day when we can prepare ourselves no longer; they have the sobering words of the Penny Catechism to remind them that we know neither the place, the time, nor the manner of our death, but that he who dies in a state of sin, forgetful of God, is forever lost.

But to the healthy, even the devout, these great truths frequently seem remote and even irrelevant so far as they are themselves concerned. Eternity is a distant place and Heaven a far country when times are happy, the day is sunny, and the body rejoices in its strength. The question of death seems even morbid to those who are conscious of bodily health and present strength. It is an exceptionally recollected and spiritual person whose prayers will not become perfunctory and whose devotions do not become routine when all is well and life is one grand, sweet song, untroubled by sickness and unthreatened by physical evil.

Moreover, the pious, as well as the impious, when they are healthy and happy, are easy victims to the complacent illusion of those who consider that, while *others* fall from grace through sin or fall from the skies in airplane disasters, *these things never happen to me*.

As a matter of fact, one of the spiritually most dangerous of all the illusions of the physically healthy is this idea that they themselves will always be around to send notes of sympathy or reassuring gifts of flowers to the bereaved relatives of their deceased friends, or to comfort their acquaintances afflicted by those physical evils which appear to befall the rest of mankind but *never happen to me*.

For human nature thus so easily and willingly deluded, it is surely a manifest mercy, the kindest and most paternal of warnings, when God's Providence permits sickness to withdraw one for a time from the torrent of sheer activity, diversion, and distraction which rushes the untroubled and the strong to the perilous brink of spiritual disaster. The sick should be reminded of what a privilege it frequently is when a man is stricken down, as was Saul on the road to Damascus, so that he may discover God's Will for him rather than forever pursue his own pleasure and purposes. They must sometimes be reminded that frequently the only chance the soul has to grow strong comes when the body grows weak, and that often suffering is the only force powerful enough to turn the body toward the soul and the soul toward God.

Let us be honest about this supposed *blessing* of untroubled good health. Must we not confess, those of us who are well and strong, that it takes a real effort to turn aside from the business of the world long enough to reflect on the business of Heaven? Do we not usually need superhuman strength, a literally supernatural determination, to resist the bewitchery of temporal trifles long enough to contemplate the substantial values of eternal life? How much planning, budgeting of our time, even scrimping of the fragments of our attention must we do before we save an hour for meditation, a day for recollection, or a few moments for prayer in the midst of our healthy rushing about and our complacent vitality!

But when sickness comes it brings a chance to draw near to God, an opportunity to grow in that beauty of soul which we pretend, even the worst of us, we would forfeit every physical advantage to acquire. Perhaps we would never have heard His voice had we remained strong enough to frequent forever the crowded ways of the world. Perhaps it was only through the enforced silence of the sickroom that we would ever have a chance to hear the word of direction, of vocation, or even of salvation itself which God has been waiting to speak to us.

It should be disturbing to those of us who boast that we never know a sick day, to reflect on the extraordinary number of the saints who first turned to God on their sickbeds, or who found their way to perfection along trails of bodily disease and natural infirmity which somehow left their minds more open to the vision of God, their wills more generous in His love, and their spirits more robust in divine grace than the souls of the physically strong sometimes seem to be!

Every age needs to be reminded of these simple truths. Our age has its particular need to recall them. We are sometimes so strong in our own conceit, so drunk with our own power, that we forget the seeds of inevitable disintegration which we carry hidden within us. We frequently need to be reminded of the power of God in the midst of our preoccupation with our own great gifts.

To help you understand the Christian philosophy of the

place of physical evil, including sickness, in God's scheme of things, I commend to your meditation the passage from Saint John's Gospel in which Christ, the Divine Physician, paused in His work of healing to drive home the basic spiritual point concerning sickness: "And Jesus passing by, saw a man, who was blind from his birth. And his disciples asked him, 'Rabbi, who hath sinned, this man or his parents, that he should be born blind?' Jesus answered, 'Neither hath this man sinned, nor his parents; but that the works of God should be made manifest in him.' "[2]

That the works of God should be manifest in him! That the power of God should be revealed in him! That the glory of God might be served by him! These are the purposes of sickness.

But sickness also comes so that the *mercy* of God may be demonstrated, together with God's power and wisdom, in and through and *by* those who serve His sick, afflicted, and tormented—as do you, devout Catholic nurses, instruments of the Almighty, healers of physical evil and teachers of spiritual truth!

XVI

A Good Boy

The invitation to speak at these ceremonies of tribute to Mayor O'Brien emphasized that the occasion has been planned on a strictly non-partisan basis and by way of a community salute to our newly elected Mayor.

I rejoice that such is the spirit behind the gathering. It permits me to speak in the capacity of one of the Mayor's neighbors and, in a proper sense, as the spokesman of them all.

The Mayor has already given us wholesome and refreshing evidence that he proposes to maintain just such a spirit in his concept and conduct of the high office to which he has been elected by his fellow-councilors, the office of Mayor of all the people of Worcester.

There were two statements which Mayor O'Brien made at the time of his inaugural which appealed strongly to that sense of pride in our prevailing traditions which is the soul of the city which sustains us through those occasional moments of civic embarrassment when the unfortunate spirit of division and contention reveals itself.[1]

The first of the statements that all of us liked was the new Mayor's reference to his predecessor, whose previous term as Mayor and whose presence now in the post of Vice-Mayor, offer proof of the community spirit in which Mayor Holmstrom does his work.[2]

We were all, I repeat, proud and happy when Mayor O'Brien paid tribute to that spirit and assured us that it would be his

This address was delivered at the Municipal Auditorium, Worcester, Massachusetts, on February 14, 1954, on the occasion of the dinner honoring Mayor James D. O'Brien.

own. We were all glad to say "Amen" to the prayer which the newly elected Mayor expressed in these words:

"I earnestly hope I shall earn and merit the wholehearted support, admiration, and respect of my fellow councilors that Mayor Holmstrom so deservedly enjoyed throughout his entire administration."[3]

Such a generous statement on the part of Mayor O'Brien justifies a word of appreciation of ex-Mayor Holmstrom even at an affair honoring his successor. Right-minded people of the entire Worcester community will see in Mayor O'Brien's tribute to his predecessor no mere conventional phrases of political wisdom, but the expression both of the sincere personal affection and honest gratitude which we all feel for the former Mayor and of a spirit of mutual respect which we must never cease to pray will always animate the citizens of this city.

We welcomed Mayor O'Brien's cordial references to ex-Mayor Holmstrom because they showed that the new Mayor appreciated and shared the general community attitude toward his predecessor. As a result, his tribute to Mr. Holmstrom was also a tribute to Mayor O'Brien himself.

He told us, in effect, that whatever partisan or kindred secondary differences there might be between the old mayor and the new, Worcester may expect the same kind of emphasis on essential, basic and primary moral values of a personal and public kind such as that to which we have become used. He also suggested that he knew the reasons why Mr. Holmstrom so deservedly enjoyed the admiration and respect of the general community—and that he trusted, in all humility, that during his own time as Mayor, Worcester would have like reasons for satisfaction.

I cannot emphasize too much how good that initial statement of Mayor O'Brien made us all feel. It was probably more unique than many have realized. I read more than my share of newspapers from many cities throughout the country and

I think it is important to point out that one rarely finds sentiments of that sort expressed elsewhere after municipal election, or at least expressed with the simplicity, straightforwardness, and sincerity which one felt in the local situation. It is a tribute to ex-Mayor Holmstrom, to Mayor O'Brien, and, please God, to all Worcester that such a spirit now exists here.

Having thus ventured onto the dangerous ground of the friendly spirit between two leaders in their respective parties within our community, I think I shall take the even greater risk of lingering for a moment or two on the delicate question of the reasons why I believe this friendly spirit found expression and why these two men receive such substantial support from our voters.

Fortunately, I think the pertinent reasons are not so much political as they are popular. If they were strictly political, I would not feel free to discuss them. To the extent that they are popular, they shed light on certain moral preferences and spiritual values which the larger and saner element in our community commonly cherish—and on such points it is my duty to speak and my privilege to be heard.

I think that Mayor O'Brien was revealing something about himself and about the example he aspires to give us when he recalled the respect in which Mr. Holmstrom was held as Mayor. I think he was paying the homage that we all expected of him to these moral and spiritual considerations which our people like to find reflected in the personalities of their political leaders. He was telling us, in a way which won instant approval from us members of the general public, that he understood why people liked Andy Holmstrom—and he was also telling us that Jimmy O'Brien would like to be liked for the same reasons.

Permit me to suggest some of the reasons. We like our city to be represented by Mayors who do not yell at us with demagoguery and bombast. The various religious, fraternal, and civic groups in Worcester like to bring conventions here and when they do, they like to have the certainty that when he stands up to speak the Mayor will have something pleasant, friendly, and pertinent to say. If the affair to which he comes is in the evening, they are doubly pleased to know that he will be *able* to stand up and to speak *soberly* in every sense of the word.

Because so many of our organizations are preoccupied with ancient religious values, like the dignity of women, the valor of men, and the supreme value of children, we like our city to be represented by Mayors who speak of their mothers with manly devotion, without affectation, political rhetoric, or artificiality of any kind. We pride ourselves that we can tell the difference between the politicians who ring the changes of *mother love* for campaign purposes and those who are bearing witness, man-fashion, to certain human spiritual and civilizing forces of which mothers are or should be symbols. We always felt good when Mr. Holmstrom mentioned his mother; nothing makes us feel better than the things we know about Mr. O'Brien and his mother.

We like Mayors whose wives like them, whose public careers may interfere somewhat with their family lives but who, when they are married, are unmistakably, unashamedly, and unqualifiedly *family* men. We like men in public life whose wives are the *same* wives that they had when they started out and before they became *big shots*. We like Mayors who do not push their attractive daughters or their lovely children into the limelight during the campaign—but are frequently seen with them on the way to their churches, who take pleasure in talking about them when we meet them socially and are obviously loved by them with the eloquent affection which tells us that a city is in good hands because its public affairs are presided over by a man whose private life merits such tender devotion from those who know him better than possibly could a State Committee, the City Hall reporters or the rank and file of the voters.

Further than this I shall not go. Suffice it to say, I think these were the thoughts in Mayor O'Brien's mind, rather than any nice points of mere political philosophy, when he spoke of the respect he was glad our people gave Mr. Holmstrom and had every reason to hope they would gladly give him.

The second statement which the Mayor made, and which also made us proud and confident, was that concerning the type of government we have tried to attain and still hope to perfect here in Worcester. This question, too, has certain technical and political angles; these are none of my affair. But it is also associated with real popular preferences of a moral and spiritual kind. These are very much the affair of all of us in Worcester who are bound by office to speak to the people on the things which appertain to God and to godliness, personal and public.

Mayor O'Brien gave us unmistakable witness that he understands and welcomes this when he called upon the new council to "preserve and protect with zealous devotion" the accomplishments of the council-manager form of government that has been worked out here in Worcester.[4] Then he went on to say: "The people of Worcester know what kind of government they want. They want good government dedicated to the best interests of all."[5] The little phrase "of all" comes at the end of the sentence, of course, but it is obviously at the beginning of the thought—and we are grateful to Mayor O'Brien that, as the official representative and authoritative spokesman of our city, he has placed it first thus early in his career as Mayor.

Mayor O'Brien's phrase: "The best interests of all" suggests a distinction which I am sure everyone who shares with him the love for our city and the desire to see it prosperous, united, and proud would wish me to emphasize this evening.

Here, too, there are political questions involved; but these political angles are enormously less important than those moral and spiritual considerations which animate the popular preferences and the common will of our general community.

Local government "in the best interests of all" necessarily

presupposes the maximum subordination of the partisan spirit. As a matter of fact, of course, that subordination is equally desirable on every level and in every area of civil life, but the Worcester community is the primary and pertinent object of our moral concern.

Enlightened communities are beginning to understand a little better the distinction between *politics* and *public administration*. It is probably nobody's fault that the word *politics* is hard to define. The fact that we find several definitions of *politics* in *Webster's New International Dictionary* shows in itself that public understanding of this word is badly confused.

Father James Keller has written a remarkable little book called *Government Is Your Business*, a copy of which would be distributed to every registered voter by one of these great foundations we read about if the foundations were interested in the future of freedom.[6] In it he discusses this whole question of the present-day meaning of *politics* and the present-day demands of *public administration*.

He points out that in its primary definition *politics* is: "The science and art of government; the science dealing with the organization, regulation, and administration of a state, in both its internal and external affairs."[7] But its secondary definition has become this: "In a bad sense, the artful or dishonest management to secure the success of political candidates or parties."[8]

Politics, as now generally accepted, often means *party politics*, with party loyalty as its guiding principle, rather than the common good

It is essential to understand the difference between *public administration* and politics if we are to eliminate the confusion and embarrassment which so often exists in the field of public affairs.

Public administration is an essential part of American life; politics may be an occasional practical necessity or a diverting by-product of life in a republic, but it is most certainly less essential than public administration and, like cheese in the spaghetti, while excellent up to a point, can badly gum up the main course when overdone.

Public administration, such as the council-manager plan seeks, means the art of government conducted for the common good, rather than for partisan advantage. It is only fair to insist that many who are leaders in political circles, even partisan, are also excellent public administrators and appoint people who are fully qualified, but it is as *administrators* and not as *partisans* that they contribute to the common good.

It is wise to understand that a good politician can be not only a good public administrator but even the best, if he consistently places the public good above party interests. Public administration employs the skills and techniques based on loyalty and honesty needed for government, without the artfulness sometimes found in purely partisan activity.

The best favor any political party can do a community is to produce office-holders who are public administrators more than they are party representatives. To the extent that both parties have failed to accomplish so lofty a function, the party system has suffered a certain discredit.

However, such failure is far from as great as people sometimes pretend. We are grateful to the Mayor for the prompt, clear assurance he has given that our municipal government is committed to *public administration* rather than partisan advantage.

Colleges and universities now offer courses in Public Administration. It is by no means demonstrated, however, that such specialized training, largely theoretical and sometimes highly doctrinaire, necessarily produces a better public administrator than does practical experience in the College of Political Hard Knocks. As a matter of fact there is sometimes much unintended evidence in the surveys made by experts on municipal departments, such as schools, firefighters, police, or recreation, that the professors have not too much to teach the conscientious politician. Professors of public administration

217

may scoff at the doorbell pulling and the baby-kissing of the politicians, but there is something to be said even for these. It is good for the city, as well as himself, when the public administrator knows where the people live; how much they get paid; what baby food costs; where the babies *are*—other intensely practical items of a similar kind on which experts can sometimes be sadly uninformed, but which a good city cannot forget. The experts frequently create ten times as much of a mess in political affairs as would a seasoned politician who is street-wise and has a grain of common sense. Public administration requires a pattern of ideas and a code of conscientious controls, but it is not the same as political philosophy. It frequently happens that good professors of medicine lack an equally good bedside manner and are therefore better in the classroom than in the sickroom. Sometimes excellent teachers of theology are very mediocre preachers of the practical word. Conversely, politics can be an excellent introduction to and preparation for public administration.

But the two ideas remain distinct—and we are deeply grateful that the Mayor proposes to dedicate his political experience to helping our municipal government achieve distinction for proud, prosperous, and impartial public administration.

I should like to cite a third occasion since his inaugural when the Mayor has made us proud. We all very much liked the dignity, the calm assurance, and soft-spoken firmness with which he presided at the recent public hearings on a project which touches on so many personal and community interests, with inevitable emotional, economic, and other highly inflammable implications. The many of us who listened to the broadcast of those proceedings were both impressed by and grateful for the manner of the Mayor, not merely in parliamentary skills but also in the wholesome personal patience which he revealed. We thought of the lines of Kipling: "If you can keep your head while all about you are losing theirs and blaming it on you"—and we prayed that he will not allow the heat of future battles or the tensions of the job ahead so to fray his nerves or impair his sense of humor that he will ever speak for us less graciously or effectively than he did that particular night.

I have spoken with a little daring this evening because I have touched on delicate matters involving personalities and remotely political considerations, though always from the moral premise proper to my position and consistent with what you would wish of me. In concluding, let me speak in the vein which primarily and at all times becomes the priest. That is, of course, the formulation of the collective prayer of the people for our Mayor, the guest of honor this evening.

What is the essential prayer that we always make for our leaders, whether they be elected or appointed? The posts we hold on the various levels of community life are widely different and their responsibilities, their opportunities and pitfalls vary greatly. But the prayer of those who truly love us is the same for each and every man who holds a post of leadership.

When I was ordained a priest or consecrated a bishop, my mother did not immediately pray that I would convert every sinner, though undoubtedly she hoped I might. When some of you were named judge, your mothers did not pray that you would make the Supreme Court or solve all the thorny issues which plague the professors of jurisprudence. When you councilors were elected to the various posts of trust which you hold, trusts so sacred that you properly rate the title of *Honorable*, your mothers did not pray that you would please everybody and win unanimous reelection. They knew you can't. They knew you couldn't be truly *honorable* and always popular.

The prayer that good mothers offer for their sons when they become bishops, judges, bank presidents, councilors, or mayors is no different from the prayer they offered for them the day they were born. It is the essential prayer of all who love them. When we were first given back into our mothers' arms as infants, not one of those mothers prayed that we would be bright or handsome or rich or strong. Each prayed that her son would be a *good boy*—and that is what each prays still. If people must concede that their sons were *good boys*, our mothers do not care whether the crowd agrees with us, votes for us, or even likes us.

And so as I formulate the prayers of the community for the new Mayor tonight, I give no care about whether the Honorable James D. O'Brien lives up to the hopes of the Democrats or the fears of the Republicans so long as Jimmy O'Brien fulfills the prayers of his mother, who asked God to make him a good boy when he was the most recent baby born in Worcester—and who prays the same for him now that he is the First Citizen of his native city.

XVII

Channing and Cheverus

It is always pleasant and sometimes profitable to dip into past history and recall the examples of our fathers. Frequently the preoccupations of the present and the occasional tensions which they produce are eased by the recollection of a story or two out of the past.

G. K. Chesterton may have had something of the sort in mind when he remarked that whenever a new book came out, he made it a point to read an old one.

And so, I turn back this evening to an earlier chapter of New England history to find there a story which I think to be of mutual interest; meeting, as we are, as neighbors and under circumstances so friendly. It is a story which, it seems to me, has lessons worth our respective meditation nowadays, and it is perhaps more timely, even more urgent, that we recall it than has been the case for years.

The memory I would like to bring back this evening is that of the first Catholic bishop in New England, Bishop John Cheverus of Boston. His story is interesting if only as a too little known chapter of New England history, but it is significant as an altogether too much neglected page from the common history of your people and mine.

Bishop Cheverus was in his last years as Bishop of Boston when the renowned Boston Unitarian preacher, William E. Channing, was still a young man, and we Catholics in New England remember Channing because, in an entirely unique set of circumstances, he became the most eloquent eulogist, in the English tongue at least, of our first bishop.[1]

This address was delivered in Worcester, Massachusetts, on March 16, 1954, before the Unitarian Laymen's League.

It is to this extraordinary circumstance of the mutual spirit which prevailed between so many members of Channing's flock and Bishop Cheverus, a spirit which found generous expression in Channing's famed tribute to Cheverus, that I appeal in response to your neighborly gesture in inviting me to speak this evening.

I think it is important, perhaps particularly so at the moment, for some of us to remember the attitude of Channing and so many of his flock back in the days when we were negligible in numbers and almost entirely without material resources in New England. I also think it important that your people should remember Cheverus and the things about him which made him so beloved by your fathers, kindred souls to the saintly bishop themselves or they could not possibly have felt toward him as in fact they did.

I think the best way to begin the story of Cheverus and your people is by quoting from one of your great laymen of yesteryear, Josiah Phillips Quincy.

Perhaps the most delightful memoirs of his generation left by any New Englander are those which Josiah Quincy wrote under the title *Figures of the Past*, and in which he gave later generations such unforgettable sketches of early nineteenth-century Boston, its people and its life.[2] As Walter Whitehill points out in a recent publication: "even in this vivid book there are few recollections more striking than that" of the friendship between "the author's father, Josiah Quincy—later Mayor of Boston, President of the Boston Athenaeum, and President of Harvard College", and Bishop Cheverus.[3] Quincy writes:

> Cheverus was greatly esteemed by my father, who was fond of relating the manner in which their acquaintance commenced. One day, near the beginning of the century, he was driving from Quincy to Boston in a pelting storm. When about five miles from his destination, he overtook a forlorn foot-passenger,

who, drenched and draggled, was plodding along the miry road. My father drew up his horse and called to the stranger to get in and ride with him. "That would be scarcely fair", was the man's reply. "My clothes are soaked with water and would spoil the cushions of your chaise, to say nothing of the wetting I could not avoid giving you." These objections were made light of, and with some difficulty the wayfarer was persuaded to take the offered seat. During the ride my father learned that his companion was a priest, named Cheverus, who was walking from Hingham, whither he had been to perform some offices connected with his profession; and thus commenced the acquaintance, which afterwards ripened into friendship, between men whose beliefs and ways of life were outwardly so different. . . . I have a distinct recollection of hearing Cheverus preach in the Franklin Street Cathedral. His style was very direct, and I remember how startling to my ears was the sentence with which he opened his discourse: "I am now addressing a congregation which has more thieves in it than any other assembled in this town." Owing to the social position and peculiar temptations of his people, the fact may have been as the Bishop stated it; but only a strong man would have ventured upon an opening so little conciliatory to his audience. But besides the great Christian virtues, Cheverus had those gifts of tact and humor which are not without value to an ecclesiastic. He had a sly way of reminding his Protestant friends that their forefathers had fled to this country, not to escape the persecution of Popery, but that of a Protestant Prelacy.[4]

It was entirely characteristic that the Reverend Jean Louis Anne Magdeleine Lefebvre de Cheverus should have been trudging along a Massachusetts road in the rain pursuing his calling in New England with apostolic simplicity, in journeyings often, taking neither slaves nor scrip, neither bread nor money.[5] It was equally characteristic that he should have been reluctant to wet the cushions of the chaise, but that when persuaded to enter he should have formed a lasting friendship with a man so different from him in all worldly aspects.

Three decades later, as Archbishop of Bordeaux and a Peer of France, Cheverus was to send affectionate congratulations when his old friend, Josiah Quincy, was elected to the presidency of Harvard College.

Born at Mayenne, France, on January 28, 1768, Cheverus was ordained to the priesthood on December 18, 1790, in the last public ordination held in Paris before the French Revolution.

Returning to his native city of Mayenne, Father Cheverus at first assisted his aged uncle, the parish priest of the place, and then for a time served as Vicar General of the diocese of Le Mans. Soon after assuming his duties, he was called upon to take the oath of loyalty to the revolutionary constitution. Of course, he refused to do so and therefore was deprived of his office. With the increasing violence of the revolutionary spirit it soon became evident that he could no longer exercise his ministry to any useful purpose, and so, in the autumn of 1792, Father Cheverus fled to England.

There, for four years, he lived as best he could. Arriving without any resources, and with little knowledge of English, Cheverus found work as a teacher in a boarding school presided over by an Anglican clergyman; and there, while studying English, he gave lessons in French and mathematics. At the end of the year, with enough English to speak intelligibly and correctly, he sought an interview with the Roman Catholic Bishop of London, and after proving that he possessed a sufficient knowledge of English to perform his ministry acceptably, he obtained permission to officiate in the diocese, and Cheverus devoted himself to missionary work. At first he preached in private houses to Catholic families lacking a regular place of worship, but as his influence grew, a chapel was procured for his use, and so, having acquired both a congregation and a chapel for services, Father Cheverus left the boarding school and devoted himself entirely to parochial duties.

While thus occupied in England, Father Cheverus received a letter from an old associate at the Sorbonne, Father François Matignon, who in 1792, after fleeing France, had come to Boston.[6] When Father Matignon came to Boston, the Catholic Church was in no way welcome. But Father Matignon soon made a place for himself. The pastoral care of the various French groups, of the increasing Irish population, as well as that of the Indians in Maine—all these were Father Matignon's responsibility, and a nearly impossible task alone. Therefore, he sought the assistance of his former pupil, Cheverus, who in fact landed in Boston on October 3, 1796.

Though the prospects in Boston were dismal enough, the difficulties of the Maine Mission to the Indians were even greater. Penobscots and Passamaquoddys had long since been converted by French missionaries from Canada, and they had remained devoted to the Faith despite the absence of priests. Soon after Father Cheverus' arrival a good opportunity for work among them occurred, for in the summer of 1796 a Massachusetts commission had successfully negotiated a final land settlement with the Penobscot Indians and had promised to assist in obtaining a priest for them. In June 1797 several chiefs of both the Penobscot and Passamaquoddy tribes visited Boston to request a priest, and Father Cheverus set off for Maine.

His earliest biographer, the Abbé Hamon, tells a dramatic story of Cheverus' journey through the Maine woods on foot. Hamon relates that one Sunday morning, when approaching Oldtown, the priest heard voices singing in the distance. They were singing a portion of the *Messe Royale* by Dumont— frequently used on festivals in the great churches of France. Upon reaching the source of the music, the missionary was greeted with joy by an Indian congregation and treated to a meal that gave him little pleasure. Of his arrival at Pleasant Point, in the Passamaquoddy settlement, Cheverus wrote to Matignon:

225

As soon as I put my foot on the ground, the Indians fired their guns and gave me altogether an hearty and moving welcome. We walked together to the church, and after having given thanks to God, I begged Him to bless my mission and addressed them in a few words. I was then introduced into the parsonage house. It is next to the church. Both are built upon a hill above the Indian wigwams. . . . My house is about ten feet square and eight feet high; the church as large again but not a great deal higher. In both of them no other materials but bark and a few logs of wood and sticks set crossways to support the bark; no windows, of course, the only opening is the door. This makes the church very dark and I can hardly read at the altar. The only piece of furniture in the house is a large table made of rough boards, no seats, etc. I put my mattress on the table and slept tolerably well. . . . I have just said Mass for the Dead and spoke to them about drinking. I have told them I would not admit anybody to Communion, except they had not gotten drunk since a very considerable time, about a year. I think I shall have very few communicants, but I cannot expose the Sacraments to an almost certain profanation. . . . They sang this morning the Mass for the Dead exactly upon the same tune as we do. In the Kyrie they have preserved the same words and they answer the Preface in Latin, etc. What courage and patience in the first missionaries![7]

After learning something of the Indian language, Father Cheverus was in a better position to deal with his flock. Hearing the Indians' confessions proved extremely trying, for it was in this close contact that he acquired the insects that he afterwards claimed, humorously, were the only perquisite that he had derived from his ministry in Maine!

Although Father Cheverus' work among the Indians had proved helpful, Father Matignon soon concluded that he would be of greater value to the church as a curate in Boston than as a missionary in Maine. But this did not put an end to Cheverus' journeys, for when he received the appointment from Bishop Carroll of Baltimore, as Father Matignon's assistant, one of his duties was to maintain the missions at Newburyport and Plymouth.

As the lease of the hired chapel on School Street was about to expire, the project for the construction of a suitable Catholic church in Boston began on March 31, 1799, the Sunday after Easter. A subscription was opened and by Christmas the purchase of a piece of land on Franklin Street had been accomplished; and Charles Bulfinch—architect of the new State House and of the nearby Federal Street Theatre—generously gave plans for the projected church of the Holy Cross. After the land was purchased only six hundred were left from the monies collected.

Further contributions came slowly, and in August 1800 a subscription was circulated outside the parish among "the inhabitants of the town of Boston and other gentlemen." That the list was headed by John Adams, President of the United States, with a gift of one hundred dollars, is evidence of the place that Matignon and Cheverus had made for themselves in the community.

Although it was uphill work, the church was finally completed and consecrated by Bishop Carroll on September 29, 1803. Of the nearly seventeen thousand dollars that it had cost, the credible sum of $10,771.69 was raised by the local Catholics; $1,948.83 came from Catholics elsewhere in the country, while $3,433.00—about one-fifth of the total—came from local Protestants. John Quincy Adams, James and Thomas Handasyd Perkins, John Lowell, Harrison Gary Otis, Joseph Coolidge, David Sears, Theodore Lyman, and other Bostonians added to the subscription begun by President Adams. In Salem, a Unitarian clergyman, William Bentley, secured contributions from such hard-headed merchants and seamen as Joseph Peabody, William Gray, Nathaniel West, and George Crowninshield. In graceful recognition of his services in designing the church, the Catholics of Boston on January 1, 1806, presented Charles Bulfinch with a handsome silver tea-urn which is now in the Museum of Fine Arts, in Boston.

In 1801, while Holy Cross Church was still under construction, Cheverus had been urged by his former parishioners in Mayenne to return to France now that Catholic worship was being restored, but he chose to remain in Boston. And when Pius VII, in 1808, expanded the organization of the American Church by elevating Baltimore to an archdiocese and establishing four new dioceses—of which Boston was one—Father Cheverus was appointed Bishop of Boston.

Monsignor Lord has well observed of Bishop Cheverus that "a deep, solid and ardent piety was the core of his character and the mainspring of all his actions. It was a piety of a specifically French flavor, the joyous smiling piety of a Fénelon, a Saint Francis de Sales, a Saint Vincent de Paul."[8] When a load of firewood that he had sent to a poor, sick woman in Water Street remained unsawed by her neighbors, the Bishop quite simply got up before daybreak, shouldered his own sawhorse, walked to the woman's house, and did the job himself.[9] Similarly, when fortifications were being built at South Boston during the War of 1812, Bishop Cheverus came out, pushing a wheelbarrow.

Charles B. Fairbanks, one-time Assistant Librarian of the Boston Athenaeum, remembered that the Bishop's calm, wise, benign face always had a smile for the children and that his pockets were never without sugarplums. Yet this was the same Bishop Cheverus who, in Josiah Quincy's hearing, began a sermon in his cathedral, one day, with the words: "I am now addressing a congregation which has more thieves in it than any other assembled in this town."[10] However, even thieves who did not frequent the cathedral were not exempt from Cheverus' pastoral concern; for a certain John Martin, whom the Bishop had attended in Lechmere Point Jail shortly before he was hanged for highway robbery on December 20, 1821, stated that had he "been blessed with the directions of such a man when he was young, he should never have ended his days on a gallows."[11]

Cheverus never was the victim of personal persecution, but he had, of course, to face the annoyances which were destined to remain common for some time in these parts. For marrying two of his people in Maine—although he had sent them to a justice for the civil ceremony acceptable as an alternative to marriage by the established clergy—Cheverus was tried in a criminal action, but found not guilty. With the help of two Irish merchants from Newcastle, Maine, he built a small chapel for the Catholics there. But the Superior Court made support of the church very difficult by ruling that Catholic parishioners were still obliged to pay Congregationalist tithes.[12] In 1820, when Bishop Cheverus brought the Ursuline sisters to Boston, there was a violent outburst which he silenced by a letter to the press. A few years later, however—after Cheverus had left Boston for France—his successor witnessed perhaps the most disgraceful outrage in New England history: the burning of the convent of the Ursulines by a fanatic mob. The instigators of this shameful deed had, of course, their partisans while Cheverus worked in New England, but he clearly recognized how unrepresentative they were and how they, too, would eventually be tamed by the spirit of the New World, for in later years he praised American toleration to King Charles X of France.

The excellence of his own relations with his neighbors sprang both from their magnanimity and from Cheverus' moral character, as well as from the dignified simplicity with which he exemplified the tenets of the Roman Catholic Faith. His cordial relations with the Boston Athenaeum are a case in point. These cordial relations, as Walter Whitehill notes, appear "to have developed from his skillful handling of a trying situation that might, with a lesser man, have degenerated into acrimony. The February 1807 issue of *The Monthly Anthology*,

229

edited by the band of friends who in the same year founded the Athenaeum, published a letter from John Lowell—described only as 'an American Traveler in Europe'—that contained, after preliminary lofty denials of prejudice and professions of charity, an 'exposure' of 'superstitious opinions and observances, and pious frauds, existing in Italy at the present moment.' In particular, indulgences were denounced as 'permissions, either general or more limited, to commit offenses.' Cheverus could not condone by silence the misunderstandings of Catholic doctrine contained in the piece, so on April 7, 1807, he addressed a reply to the 'American Traveler' " . . . which *The Monthly Anthology* described as being written in "a liberal and gentlemanly style" and which stated the Church's position on the misrepresented dogmatic and political points clearly and calmly.[13]

I find no evidence that Bishop Cheverus won over Mr. Lowell from his mistaken point of view, but I find abundant evidence that the friendliest spirit was not only maintained but greatly increased by the personal contacts established.

"The subject was not raised again", but Bishop Cheverus significantly "became one of the most constant and generous donors of books to the Boston Athenaeum, which had been founded by the Anthology Society. Although a man of slender resources, living in the most modest way, he gave more books to the library than any single man except the same John Lowell"—so that a rivalry in good deeds took the place of one in argument, to the great good of the library, at any rate![14] During the next thirteen years the Bishop presented the varied classical and literary texts, dictionaries, historical and theological works that are listed in the catalogue published by Walter Whitehill three years ago as the appendix to a masterful essay on Cheverus to which my own notes are largely indebted.[15]

By the autumn of 1822, Cheverus' health was so poor that he had half-contemplated resigning his service in Boston and retiring to France. A French baron—convinced that Cheverus could no longer survive the rigors of our winters and anxious that his services should be utilized by the French Church—convinced King Louis XVIII to nominate Cheverus as Bishop of Montauban.

When word of Cheverus' departure became known, there occurred the completely unparalleled incident of two hundred and twenty six non-Catholic citizens of Boston—public officials, merchants, lawyers, clergymen—dispatching a petition to the French government begging that Cheverus be left in Boston!

These two hundred and twenty six non-Catholic citizens of Boston, from Daniel Webster and Harrison Otis down, wrote to the French government: "We hold him to be a blessing and a treasure in our social community, which we cannot part with and which, without injustice to any man we may affirm, if withdrawn from us, can never be replaced. If the removal to the proposed diocese would be conformable to his wishes, we would mourn over this in silence. . . . But if the removal can be referred to the principle of usefulness, we may safely assume that in no place, nor under any circumstances, can Bishop Cheverus be situated where his influence, whether spiritual, or social, can be so extensive as where he now is."[16]

So far as I know, there is no comparable case of such action anywhere in the world—at any time in the history of the Roman Catholic Church—or the general community! It is completely amazing that such a thing should have happened when one considers all the circumstances. I count the incident one of the highest and most proud points of New England history! It continually astonishes me that so exceptional and meaningful an incident should have been virtually forgotten in history which remembers so easily so much that is unpleasant.

Notwithstanding Bishop Cheverus' own feelings—and those of his good neighbors—the Prince de Croy made it clear that the King could not accept his refusal of the See of Montauban, and so in September 1823, after twenty-seven years in Boston, the much-loved Bishop Cheverus departed for France.

Before leaving Boston, however, he gave away most of his

personal possessions. He left Boston with nothing more than the old trunk with which he had arrived, as a refugee from the French Revolution.

To the Boston Athenaeum Library went the remainder of his books, accompanied by a letter to Theodore Lyman, Jr.:

Boston
September 25, 1823

Dear and honoured Sir:

Your kind letter written at the desire of the respectable Trustees of the Athenaeum has been duly and gratefully received. The Trustees, as well as my other fellow-citizens of Boston, are disposed to exaggerate the little I have been able to do, but they never can rate too high my love and devotedness to them, and nothing but what I believe to be an imperious duty could ever tear me from them.

I shall feel happy in being an agent and a correspondent of the Boston Athenaeum and to give some token to the proprietors of my affection and remembrance.

I send this with a Fac-Simile of the Testament of Louis XVI and his horribly calumniated consort. It will perhaps enhance the value of these interesting documents when my literary friends know that they have often been bedewed with my tears.

Assure the Trustees of my grateful sense of the honour they confer upon me by their letters, and accept my thanks for the handsome manner in which you have conveyed their sentiments.

I have the honour to be with sincere and affectionate respect,

Dear and honoured Sir,

Your obedient humble Servant

+ John Cheverus[17]

The parting scenes were touching, as Samuel Knapp recalled them: "At a very early hour in the morning, the vestry (of the cathedral) was filled with Protestants and Catholics, dissolved in tears to think they should never see him again. It required all his firmness to support himself in bidding them farewell. As he left the house for the carriage, lisping infancy and silver-haired age rushed forward to pluck his gown and share the good man's smile; and the last accents of his blessing were mingled with the moans of grief at his departure."[18] We are also told that Cheverus was accompanied along the Post Road toward New York by some three hundred carriages—and this in a day when his own people had few, if any, carriages.

After three years in the Diocese of Montauban, Bishop Cheverus was appointed Archbishop of Bordeaux. Charles X made him a Peer of France and conferred upon him the blue ribbon of a commander of the Order of the Saint-Esprit. Although these secular honors were swept away by the Revolution of 1830, King Louis Philippe requested the Pope to elevate Archbishop Cheverus to the College of Cardinals. On February 1, 1836 he was named a Cardinal of the Holy Roman Church. On July 19, 1836—six months later—Cheverus was dead!

A bronze statue of Cheverus, by David d'Angers, has stood for many decades in the square of his native Mayenne, but it was not until 1950—when a bronze plaque, contributed by a group of Protestant businessmen, was placed on the façade of the Chapel of Saint Thomas More, in Franklin Street, Boston—that any memorial to Cheverus could be seen in the streets of Boston.

Despite the tardiness of his commemoration in bronze, the memory of Bishop Cheverus was long cherished in Boston. During the thirteen years of his ministry in France, Cheverus corresponded with old friends and was ever kind to travelers from Boston. From Montauban, in 1826, he wrote to Major Quincy:

> If, as you have the goodness to assure me, I am not forgotten in Boston, I can say with truth, I do not forget Boston. So dear

and familiar is the name of the beloved city, that even in conversation I say Boston instead of Montauban, and this often; and I am then told, "You love Boston better than Montauban, but we defy the Bostonians to love you more than we do."[19]

When Samuel Knapp began the publication of the *Boston Monthly Magazine*, in June 1825, the first article, in volume I, number 1, was a "Memoir to Bishop Cheverus" and the frontispiece was an engraving of the Stuart portrait of the Bishop.

William Ellery Channing, reviewing in 1829 a life of Fénelon in the *Christian Examiner*, wrote:

Has not the metropolis of New England witnessed a sublime example of Christian fortitude in a Catholic Bishop? Who among our religious teachers would solicit a comparison between himself and the devoted Cheverus? This good man, whose virtues and talents have now raised him to high dignities in Church and State, and who now wears in his own country the joint honors of an Archbishop and a Peer, lived in the midst of us, devoting his days and nights, and his whole heart, to the service of a poor and uneducated congregation. We see him declining in a great degree the society of the cultivated and refined, that he might be the friend of the ignorant and friendless; leaving the circles of polished life, which he would have graced, for the meanest hovels; bearing with a father's sympathy the burdens and sorrows of his large spiritual family; charging himself alike with their temporal and spiritual concerns; and never discovering, by the faintest indication, that he felt his fine mind degraded by his seeming humble office. This good man, bent on his errands of mercy, was seen on our streets under the most burning sun of summer, and the fiercest storm of winter, as if armed against the elements by the power of charity.

He enjoys among us what to such a man must be dearer than fame. His name is cherished where the great of this world are unknown. It is pronounced with blessing, with grateful tears, with sighs for his return, in many an abode of sorrow and want. . . .[20]

I would hope that you might find the time to read all that Channing wrote of Cheverus. His essay is, again, one of those high points in community history which should completely counteract any less pleasant recollections for us all.

Well, so much for the story of Bishop Cheverus and the friendly spirit which prevailed between Channing, his flock, and the better of their New England contemporaries, and the French prelate. I submit that the story had and has a lesson for our times. I do not think the lesson need be labored.

Cheverus was, I assume, a Royalist in whatever political opinions he may have had. In Boston, he lived in a community committed passionately and permanently to the political ideas of the Republic, ideas which then were in some degree associated with those of the Revolution from which Cheverus was in flight. But the political *ideologies*, to use the awkward word which has become at once so common, so ominous, and so meaningless, which necessarily would have separated him from his neighbors and them from him, apparently in no way inhibited mutual respect, complete confidence, and genuine friendship.

Cheverus was an alien. In the parlance of our day he was what might be called a *displaced person*. For all his acquired love of America and most especially of Massachusetts, he was nonetheless deeply attached to his French fatherland, its ways and traditions. That fact and all its inevitable corollaries of a cultural and preferential kind appear to have been accepted by his neighbors as being no bar to cordial personal regard and warm mutual understanding.

Specifically, Channing on the one hand, and Cheverus on the other, necessarily disagreed profoundly on what both of them must have considered the most basic questions men must face. Channing's people held ideas which Cheverus could only consider heretical and sometimes even, I am sure, unintelligible. Cheverus preached a Faith which Channing assuredly did not believe in; in fact, Channing more than once said or wrote things about certain articles of the Faith that Cheverus held which strongly suggest that he had a restricted understanding of it.

Yet Cheverus and the people of whom Channing became the spokesman wished to be and were, as we have seen, the best of friends. Neither ever thought to plague the other with demands that he present any credentials, beyond the integrity of his own life, as to his honorable intentions, his neighborly spirit, and his ready acceptance, without unworthy qualification, of the social, political, and civic conventions under which they had all met one another and become friends in the free climate of the New World.

The Faith that Cheverus preached is still preached in the same essential terms and content in which he preached it. I, for example, preach it as the first Bishop of Worcester; I do so neither more nor less unqualifiedly than did he.[21] Cheverus belonged to the *open conspiracy* of Catholics everywhere to accomplish by prayer, persuasion, and every other constitutional means the "One Lord, one faith, and one baptism" which they believe to be God's Will for the followers of His Christ; so do all other bishops, priests, and devout people of Cheverus' Church.[22] His neighbors understood that . . . so do mine.

But neither he nor they supposed that these dogmatic and moral commitments, supremely important though they are and bound up with all that we are and all that we do, inhibited by so much as a degree the kindly spirit of neighborly cooperation in behalf of the common good we already share, or gave any ground for personal hostility or group suspicion in either direction.

There is another lesson which seems to me worth our reflection as we turn from these memories of old-time New England back to the preoccupations of our own day and place. It seems to me that if we emphasize and emulate the large-mindedness and greatness of heart of all these cultivated

236

spiritual ancestors whose names we have recalled this evening, we will better understand and more fervently repeat the prayer which their generation adopted as the motto of Boston back in those sometimes too-dead days: "As God Was with Our Fathers, So May He Be with Us."

Perhaps the frequent, devout, and sincere recollection of that prayer will be the best means of making it come true.

XVIII

The Common Good

One of the most basic questions in all social philosophy is this: Does society exist for each one of us, or does each one of us exist for society? Which, if either, of two goods provides the criterion of right or wrong, of morality and legality: the good which the *individual* needs and seeks for himself or the good which the *State* requires and seeks for itself?

Does the State, the organized society, exist for me; or do I, the individual citizen, exist for the State?

It is largely by their answers to these questions that many in our generation align themselves to the *Left* or to the *Right* on the social, economic, and political questions which agitate our thought. Moral and legal philosophies at the moment tend to polarize around one or the other of seemingly contrary and sometimes conflicting *goods*: the good of the *individual* and the good of the *collectivity*. Those who are preoccupied with the primacy of *individual* good tend to take their stand or find themselves accounted with the parties of the *Right* in our era of State Socialism. Those who opt for the *collective* good, and consequently give place of primacy to the rights of the State, turn up in our day in the ranks of the *Left*.

Unfortunately the social philosophies to the *Left* and those to the *Right* have polarized at their *extremes*, with a consequent antagonism, bitter in its sharpness, between those in both camps who might normally be reasonable moderates. This antagonism is reflected in the spirit of suspicion with which men approach one another who disagree, however slightly, on social legislation. It is reflected also in the intemperate

This address was delivered in Portland, Oregon, on October 5, 1954, before the Catholic Conference on Industrial Relations.

name-calling by which men of *conservative* instinct or judgment increasingly find themselves dismissed as *Fascists* or *Reactionaries*, while those of more liberal impulse or vision find themselves decried as if they were all *Revolutionaries* or *Anarchists*.

Even more disastrous is the manner in which, as a consequence, extremists on every side become the symbols and spokesmen of the camps with which they are identified, even when they are neither typical nor worthy representatives of these camps, being more often than not unwelcome nuisances to their own side of *center*.

Unfortunate, too, is the widespread sense of guilt, of *guilt by association*, among sincere political conservatives and honest social liberals who find themselves isolated from equally honorable and sincere citizens in opposite political or social camps, isolated from good men to whom they are inhibited from stretching out the hand of collaboration because of the sharply polarized divisions of contemporary opinion to which I refer. This paralyzing sense of guilt is intensified, to the great hurt of all concerned, by the embarrassment these same men find in the intellectual and moral company which they must keep on their *own* side as a result of this the polarized condition of which they are themselves the victims. And so, high-minded so-called *liberals* are too often associated in popular opinion, if not always in fact, with actual or potential traitors; while great-hearted *conservatives* are frequently distressed to find themselves tarred with the same stick as bigots, misanthropes, and the hard-of-heart generally.

Hence, it comes to pass, to the very great hurt, I repeat, of all concerned, that upright men find themselves unable to meet with one another on questions of either public or personal good, while they appear compelled to associate with evil companions almost fatally acquired in the pursuit of *good*: *individual* good in the case of the political *conservative*, the *collective* good in the case of the *social liberal*. Conscientious citizens find themselves discredited because they sought to

239

liberalize where a broader, more generous mood in social legislation was clearly necessary, or to *conserve* where a more cautious or critical spirit was the manifest need of the hour.

What to do? How find a formula which can reconcile good apparently in conflict, a formula under which we can rally to the service of America all the spiritual energies and intellectual resources which are now dissipated by polarized divisions disastrous alike to personal interest and to collective well-being?

What to do? The time-tested philosophy of Christendom, blending the *Hope* of Hebrew prophecy, the *Wisdom* of Greek speculation, the *Sanity* of Roman law and the *Charity* of Christian Revelation, had a phrase which provides the saving word. That philosophy spoke of a *third* good, a good wider than that of the individual and more warm than that of the collectivity; a good with richly personal elements, yet truly public in its nature. That third good, conciliating and unifying, is more humane than the mere good of the State; it is more generous than the good of the mere individual. It is, to repeat, both *personal* and *public*, though not merely *individual* on the one hand nor merely *political* on the other. It is what the scholastic philosophers of Christendom and the Founding Fathers of America called *the common good*. Perhaps it is time to ask for a reaffirmation of its nature and its claims.

We are not met this morning for a class in philosophy, and so we may only suggest points for meditation elsewhere on the notion of the *common good*. You will find it in Aristotle, who strove to set a happy balance between the general good and private good, between the obligation of the individual to yield to the honest good of the political State and the obligation of the political State in turn to serve the individual good of what he called the *contemplative*, i.e., the *spiritual*, *person*.

You will find it in Saint Thomas, who emphasizes the primacy of the *common good* in the practical or political order of the life of the community, but points out how the collective good and the State itself must ultimately subserve the nature and needs of the immortal person. Both the pagan Greek and the Christian philosopher understood that there is a sense in which the good of the whole is *more divine* than the good of the individual, but they also understood how the good of the social whole must be subordinated to the good of personality. They found the middle term for the equation between individual good and collective good, between the spiritual good of the person and the political good of the State, in the term *the common good*, a good which is not identified with any individual and yet which is not so identified with the collectivity, above all with the State, that it becomes detached from the good of the person.

What is this *common good*, devotion to which may yet rally in a single cooperative effort generous *conservatives* and thoughtful *liberals*? It is not, we have said, merely *individual*, though it is *personal*; it is not coldly political, though it is shared by all the body politic and includes many political elements. "That which constitutes the *common good* of political society," Maritain reminds us, "is not only the collection of public commodities and services—the roads, ports, schools, etc., which the organization of common life presupposes;" it is not merely "a sound fiscal condition of the state and its military power; the body of just laws, good customs and wise institutions which provide the nation with its structure; the heritage of its great historical remembrances, its symbols and its glories, its living traditions and cultural treasures. The common good includes all of these and something much more besides—something more profound, more concrete, and more human. For it includes also, and above all, the whole sum itself of these; a sum which is quite different from a simple collection of juxtaposed units. Even in the mathematical order, as Aristotle points out, 6 is not the same as 3 plus 3."[1] A victorious army is immeasurably more than the mere physical total of the strength or even the valor of the individuals who compose it. A symphony orchestra is made up of so many players plus the director, but the whole in this case is much more than the mere sum of its parts.

So the *common good* "includes the sum or sociological integration of all the civic conscience, political virtues, and sense of right and liberty; of all the activity, material prosperity, and spiritual riches; of unconsciously operative hereditary wisdom; of moral rectitude, justice, friendship, happiness, virtue, and heroism in the individual lives of its members. For these things all are, in a certain measure, *communicable* and so revert to each member, helping him to perfect his life and liberty as a person."[2]

The *common good* so conceived is not only a collection of advantages and utilities, it is strongly moral and ethical in its content. It includes elements of rectitude and honor, of morality and justice. Only on condition that it embrace these is the *common good* truly such, namely: the *good* of a *people* living in a *community*, the *good* of an *organized human city*, rather than the mere booty of a pack of thieves or common hoard of a mob of gangsters.[3]

"For this reason, perfidy, the scorn of treaties and of sworn oaths, political assassination and unjust war, even though they may be *useful*" or *advantageous* and in this sense practically good, actually contribute to the destruction of the true *common good*, the *bonum honestum* of which the ancients spoke.[4]

Let the French philosopher be here again our guide. The *common good*, Maritain reminds us, is always ethically good. "Included in it, as an essential element, is the maximum possible development, here and now, of the persons making up the united multitude to the end of forming a people organized not by force alone but by justice. Historical conditions and the still inferior development of human society make difficult the full achievement of the ends of social life. But the end to which it tends is to procure the common good of the multitude in such a way that the concrete person gains the greatest possible measure, compatible with the good of the whole, of real independence from the servitudes of nature. The economic guarantees of labor and capital, political rights, the moral virtues and the culture of the mind, all these contribute through the *common good* to the realization of this independence."[5]

The *common good* includes, we have seen, the cultural, historical, and spiritual heritage which is shared by the group, as opposed to the heritage particular to any individuals within the group. It is difficult to analyze the elements of this heritage, impossible to do so in a half-hour. But every now and again someone speaks out above the general din of dissident individual voices and utters ideals common to us all, words expressive of our heritage of common good. When such a one so speaks, his individual characteristics fade out completely; his words sum up a good that *all* deeply cherish; only the utterance is his alone, that and perhaps the beauty of the particular words by which he gives expression to the common thought.

For example, Abraham Lincoln was a Republican; he lived in a specific period of American history, he presents strongly individualistic traits; he was a partisan of the Northern cause in the War Between the States; it is difficult sometimes to appreciate that millions of sincere Americans profoundly disliked some of his ideas, deplored many of his policies, distrusted him personally. But when he spoke at Gettysburg, he spoke for us all; for all Americans, for our citizens in every epoch, every political party, every part of the country. There is no American who does not sense that the very stuff of our national *common good*—all its elements; its spiritual fiber and its political pattern—are woven into the things that Lincoln said at Gettysburg.

Woodrow Wilson was a Democrat. He, too, lived in a particular period of our national history and a specific phase of our emergence into the international community. He had marked individual traits, many of which his friends found amiable, others of which his critics found distasteful. Whole areas of his political philosophy were unacceptable to millions of his fellow citizens and some of his policies provoked the resentment of many. Yet in his public pronouncements he frequently transcended the inevitable limitations of himself, his times, and his political content. There is no one in this land who does not feel the tug of a common chord which runs through the hearts of us all when he reads the magnanimous phrasing of Wilson's declaration of war against the German government and not the German people; or the exalted address to the Military Academy at West Point in which Wilson summarized so many of the elements of our *common good* and linked them, as the common good must always be linked, to the benign purposes of God and to the secrets of God's Providence.[6]

So the *common good* is all the heritage from the past and all the hope for the future which good men share under God. Common to many, it is therefore public; perfective of the individual, it remains somehow *personal*. It calls the individual out of himself to share things with the general community, but it puts the resources of the general community at the service of the things closest to the personality of the individual. That is what Cicero meant when he defined the *common good*, the *res publica*, in terms of a nation's altars and hearths, of the *spiritual* and *domestic* values which center about these and which serve personality: *"in aris et focis est res publica."*[7]

It was out of this concept of the *common good* that our forefathers derived their notion of the great object of the State's existence. Hence their fine phrase the *common weal*, a phrase perpetuated in the name by which they designated this civil community, not by the cold collective name so dear to the totalitarian, *The State*, nor with any name of special interest or partisan emphasis as *The Duchy* or *The Realm*, but *The Commonwealth*, *The Commonwealth of Massachusetts*.

It is the concept behind warm words like *mutual* in the preambles of our national and state Constitutions, as that of

244

my own state which provides "that all shall be governed by certain laws for the common good."

It is the good which is preserved and promoted by the nurse who braves individual infection in order to serve the common good; by the scientist who forfeits individual convenience in order to increase that good; by the parent who forgoes individual advantage in order to rear future citizens to enhance that good; by the saint who renounces individual pleasure in order to sanctify the common good; by the soldier who disciplines individual preference in order to defend the good; by the party or regime or even the national State which abdicates particular claims or narrow prerogatives in order to conciliate those who share a common good.

It is the good which King Saint Louis of France loved when he subordinated both the instincts of self and the claims of his State to a higher *common good* shared with others. Perhaps you remember the incident; one thinks of it with wistful admiration as he reads the daily news. His counselors unanimously rebuked Saint Louis for excessive generosity in giving to the English king land which the French had regained from British conquest. King Saint Louis did not concede the English claims and he could easily have vindicated his own by force, but still he freely yielded the land. He said: "My Lords, the land that I give him I give not because I am under obligation either to him or to his heirs, but so that there may be mutual love between my children and his. And it seems to me that I am making good use of what I give him, since it makes us join hands in common love who were before at odds."

It is the good which another Catholic saint meant when he lamented those frozen words *mine* and *thine*—"frigida ista verba meum et tuum"—and rejoiced in the warm word *nostra*: "the things that are ours".

The *common good*: it is the mutual bond of all who love the good, the true, and the beautiful; who seek good things, not evil; who seek the private good of *persons* and the collective good of the *State*, but the good of *both* in and under and through the Supreme Good, which is God. It is the good which God gives us all in order to keep us together, as opposed to the good that He gives us each to keep to ourselves. It is the good before which, on due occasion, both individual and State are obliged to bow: the *common good*.

Out of a reaffirmation of the reality and claims of the *common good* there would come many results greatly to be desired. A quickened appreciation of the *common good* would turn the tide against the reckless setting of class against class, the irresponsible incitement of group against group. It would coordinate anew the interests and the efforts of labor *plus* management, tradesmen *plus* intellectuals, statesmen *plus* generals, as against the present so frequent pitting of good men against other good men in the conflicts of labor *versus* management, intellectuals *versus* tradesmen, statesmen *versus* generals within the same nation and presumably seeking the same good.

Such an appreciation of the *common good* which unites, as against—or, rather, as *above* all particular or factional or partisan goods which divide—would make possible the *Vital Center* for which certain political philosophers are pleading; a Vital Center which can exist only when honorable moderates of *Right* and *Left* prefer working with each other in behalf of the *common good* to working with extremists of their own respective camps, extremists who seek only the particular good after which their side aspires. Thus the present polarized condition of society would be eased and social *conservatives* anxious to preserve the heritage out of the past would have a common ground on which to meet and work with social *liberals* anxious to enlarge the hope of the future. The *common good* includes, in the phrase of Scripture, "nova et vetera": the old heritage and the new hopes.[8]

Thus the conscientious citizen who walks a little *Left* of center, freed from the embarrassment of constant association with senseless Revolutionaries, should be able to make common cause in the quest for the common good with the no less honorable citizen who steers his course a little *Right* of center and who is too often condemned as the friend of soulless Reaction.

A clearer concept of the reality and the rights of the *common good* may also suggest a formula for planning a better international order, an order which will conserve the values of the established nations, but be enriched by other, perhaps more basic and more humane supranational values, as little by little we come to appreciate how much, how *very much* of our heritage out of the past and our hopes for the future are shared within other nations by millions who seek the true *common good* of mankind.

Finally, a new emphasis on the nature of the *common good* will re-orient the minds of men toward other goods, higher goods which transcend mere private advantage or even temporal common weal. The longer men meditate the nature and the notion of the *common good*, the more surely will they come to understand that there is no true good so secular, so of the earth and earthly, but what it comes from God and has been hallowed by His Christ so that, by its consecrated use, it can be a means to Heaven. There is no *common good*, no truly human heritage or valid hope of any people, which lies outside God's Providence, which is not bound up with His purposes, which is not somehow predestined, however natural it be in itself, to find its place in the supernatural order which God has revealed and through which all things created are finally brought back to Him.

Reflecting on the nature of the *common good* and seeking always its more perfect accomplishment, minds and hearts will be lifted up afresh through the *bonum commune* to the *Summum Bonum*, the source of all good, God Himself, third and deciding partner in all enduring agreements, marital, industrial, or international.

XIX

Christ, the Divine Intellectual

The founding of educational institutions was from the beginning a primary preoccupation of the Church in America. In Baltimore, Emmitsburg, and Washington our first seminary, college, and university had their respective beginnings under the first bishop of the first diocese to be established in the United States. The first priest to be ordained in the United States, Father Stephen Badin, ordained in 1793, donated to the Bishop of Vincennes what is now the campus of Notre Dame University. One of the first dioceses to be cut off from the parent-diocese of the Church in the United States was Bardstown, and almost immediately there were established under its auspices a seminary of its own and then, in 1814, an institution for the education of young ladies, which became Nazareth College for Women.

It was appropriate, therefore, that in Missouri, the first of the states organized west of the Mississippi, there should have been founded the first University of the West, and that this University, growing out of a Jesuit school, as did Georgetown in the East, should have been under Catholic auspices.

Part of the motivation which prompted this early and so ambitious educational effort of the Catholic Church in America was, of course, protective. It sought to preserve the faith of young people who would otherwise have been obliged to seek their higher education in the aggressively Protestant seminaries of the East which were the colleges and budding universities of the day.

This sermon was preached at Saint Louis University, Saint Louis, Missouri, on November 16, 1955, on the occasion of Founders Day.

But a greater dynamic behind this heroic pioneer educational program was something more positive and permanent, something that is revealed in the quality of our early Catholic schools and colleges. It was an understanding of the kindred roles of the priest and the professor, of the mutual relationship among all the agencies which elevate the mind and perfect personality. This positive motivation behind the effort to build colleges and universities as soon as we had built our homes and our altars demonstrates the authentic Catholic attitude toward the things of the intellect and gives the lie to any idea that the Church herself—our Holy Mother the Church, as distinct from any or even most of her children at some given moment—is suspicious of the intellect, indifferent to learning, or unsympathetic with scholarship.

That this same positive dynamic behind the educational efforts of the American Church continued throughout the nineteenth century is reflected in the public pronouncements as well as personal labors of two typical prelates of the last century.

Father John Tracy Ellis recently took occasion to recall the convictions so admirably expressed by Bishop John Lancaster Spalding in the sermon he preached at the Third Plenary Council of Baltimore.[1] Spalding argued that all but the most unreasonable of our neighbors were even by his time persuaded of the depth and sincerity of Catholic loyalty, but on the intellectual level he found a less impressive situation and a much more urgent need. In 1884 John Spalding said: "when our zeal for intellectual excellence shall have raised up men who will take place among the first writers and thinkers of their day, their very presence will become the most persuasive of arguments to teach the world that no best gift is at war with the spirit of Catholic faith. . . ."[2]

So far John Spalding. It should be immediately evident that the converse proposition implied in his words is not less true, and that therefore the very absence of a generation of authentic intellectuals among us would constitute a serious embarrassment to arguments for the faith which are in themselves unanswerable but which, in the unfortunate circumstances of the absence of impressive intellectual vitality among those who advance them, might have little cogency to a generation rightly or wrongly enamored of the intellect.

Archbishop John Ireland understood this clearly. Speaking at the centenary of the American hierarchy, John Ireland linked his plea for the development of a vigorous intellectual life among our people to considerations of a pertinent and practical argument for the Faith. Archbishop Ireland said: "This is an intellectual age. It worships intellect. It tries all things by the touchstone of intellect. . . . The Church herself will be judged by the standard of the intellect. Catholics must excel in religious knowledge. . . . They must be in the foreground of intellectual movements of all kinds. The age will not take kindly to religious knowledge separated from secular knowledge."[3]

So far John Ireland. Lest anyone be tempted to minimize his contentions as perhaps reflecting the special American circumstances of time and place in which Archbishop Ireland spoke, let us note the example given us in our own day by the Holy See and notably by the reigning Chief Shepherd who so luminously blends the intellectual with the pastoral apostolate in the incomparable conferences which he gives the world week in, week out, on philosophy, on the physical sciences, on literature, law, and the widest range of secular subjects, all to the end that he may demonstrate how congenial are sound religious and secular sciences, how interrelated are the truths of both, and how he who holds the place of primacy among those who pray, or rule, or sanctify, holds also the place of primacy among those who teach and therefore is at home with the intellectuals—the poets and prophets—as well as with the priests and princes.[4]

And yet, there have been grave reasons in recent years to fear that in our newspapers and our forums, not to say even on our campuses, we have frequently revealed a nervous spirit of impatient and sullen anti-intellectualism. Such a spirit is surely inconsistent with the enlightened understanding and eloquent insistence of our forefathers concerning what must be the attitudes and accomplishments of Catholics in the realm of intellectual life if our Holy Mother, the Church, is to achieve her divinely intended growth in this land of privileged opportunity for her influence and action.

It makes little difference and there is room for much debate as to why so many Catholics have conformed to the prevailing mood of anti-intellectualism in our land. Perhaps Father John Tracy Ellis is accurate in his suggestion that such conformity may be part of the pattern by which our people have in all things sought to demonstrate how thoroughly *American* they are. In any case, it is unfortunate both for us and for America that we Catholics should so often qualify under the *witty extravagance*, quoted by Father Ellis, by which a certain dean differentiated the attitudes of Europeans and Americans toward intellectuals. The dean remarked that "in the Old World an ordinary mortal, on seeing a professor, tipped his hat, while in America he tapped his head."

Such a suspicious contempt for the intellectual life is far from being an exclusively Catholic phenomenon in the United States. It is, as Father Ellis notes, a kink in the American character fairly generally. It is the more unbecoming in Catholics, however, because it is so utterly out of harmony with any authentic Catholic tradition, and it is therefore the more painful that it should so often reveal itself on public questions and in community life as so entrenched among us.

There are, of course, refreshing signs of a requickened appreciation of the intellectual apostolate and of a re-valuation of intellectual interests among Catholics. In recent months one may observe several indications that the question of the role

251

and the responsibilities of the intellectual, both in the apostolic life of the Church and in the affairs of the general community, is, to risk a pathetic pun, at last coming to a head. One notes with joy a fresh solicitude among Catholics for a proper evaluation of the intellectual and his potential contribution to both the Kingdom of God and the City of Man.

I have already mentioned the valiant conference on Catholic Intellectualism in America by which Father Ellis braved the wrath of the unthinking. A young lay columnist, writing in the Davenport, Iowa *Catholic Messenger*, has been groping with admirable earnestness, if sometimes uneven results, to find a few definitions in this problem of the apostolic responsibilities of the Catholic intellectual. A monthly magazine, published by priests for priests, editorialized in a recent issue on the *intellectual*. It remarked that the word *intellectual* has become almost an expletive among us. It is so synonymous with *egghead* and *bubble-head* that many of us would rather have reflections cast on the honesty of our ancestry than be designated *intellectuals* at the moment.

It is healthy that Catholics are saying such things with increasing urgency and apostolic emphasis. It would be not only disastrous but also a bitter irony if any school of voluntarists, preoccupied exclusively with the virtues of the will, even sublime virtues so saving as obedience and so noble as loyalty, were to gain such ascendancy among the sons and daughters of the Church as to set at naught or almost annihilate the intellectual tradition in the household of the Faith.

So many of the heresies which have wounded Our Holy Mother, the Church, and robbed her of so many of her children have been voluntarist heresies, anti-intellectual in their roots and pretensions, that it would be pathetic indeed if anti-intellectualism now became a characteristic of those who have remained faithful to her obedience.

From the *stat pro ratione voluntas* of Luther and the *fides fiduciatis* of Lutheranism, through the blind fatalism of Calvin and the perverse austerities of Jansenism, to the sentimentality and exaltation of instinct or feeling which, for all its superficial show of scholarship, characterized religious Modernism, the heresies which have divided the Christian flock in these last four centuries have been chiefly voluntarist and anti-intellectual. By the same token, the inspired witness of our Holy Mother, the Church, from the Counter-Reformation, the Council of Trent and the *Ratio Studiorum*, to the Council of the Vatican and the Syllabus against Modernism, has been a witness at once to the reality of Revelation and to the validity of Reason, to the essential part of rational elements even in the supernatural act of faith and to the divine origin of the primacy and rights of the intellect in the natural order.

What a doubly tragic irony it would be, then, if, after centuries of battling for the natural law and the rights and function of reason, as well as for the primacy of the intellect over passion, emotion, instinct, or even will, the Church should find herself represented in the world of the college, the press, or the forum by sons and daughters contemptuous of that wild, living intellect of man of which Newman spoke, and cynical about the slow, sometimes faltering, but patient, persevering processes by which intellectuals seek to wrest some measure of order from the chaos about us.

How to prevent the spread of such a spirit of anti-intellectualism? How to uproot and annul it where it may have gained ground? How to foster anew a truly Catholic reverence for the gifts of the intellect and a wholesome vigilance for their proper use and growth? These are timely questions for our universities to face.

Our theme this morning suggests the spiritual and theological context within which the question of the dignity and the vocation of the intellectual should be evaluated by persons of truly Catholic mentality: "Christ Jesus, in Whom are hid all the treasures of wisdom and knowledge. . . ."[5] Does not this description of the Eternal Son of God incarnate among us

253

impel meditation on Christ as the inspiration and the exemplar of all intellectuals worthy of the name? Because He was reared in the home of Joseph and Mary subjecting Himself to them in all things, we have proposed Him in our schools as the model of obedient adolescence. Because He was reputed to be the carpenter's son and plied the trade of His foster-father, we have asked ourselves what He would do as a worker and we have hallowed the cause of Labor by the memory of His human toil. Because He shed tears of predilection over the capital city of His nation and paid the coin of tribute to Caesar, we have seen in Him the example of the good citizen. Because He preached a gospel destined to reach and unite all men, because He placed at the equal disposition of mankind without exception the treasures He came to share, we have sought in Him the qualities of the Christian internationalist. Christ the King, Christ the Priest, Christ the Judge, Christ the Friend—all these we have studied in our classes and meditated in our chapels. As a result, these human offices and callings have been cleansed of their dross in our eyes and placed in their proper supernatural and eternal perspectives.

At a moment when the word *intellectual* has become a reproach and when the vocation of the intellectual has become obscured or even discredited, is it not time to reflect prayerfully on Christ the Divine Intellectual, the Eternal Logos of the Father, all Divinity summed up in one Divine Idea and then made Man, that Person of the Adorable Trinity Who is best described in terms of the Thought of the Divine Intellect, as the Third Person is best described in terms of the Love of the Divine Will—the Word of God, "Christ Jesus, in Whom are hid all the treasures of wisdom and knowledge"![6]

Meditation on Christ so understood may help sanctify and inspire the work of intellectuals even as our preaching on Christ the Worker or Christ the Loyal Son of His Nation has done so much to elevate and hallow Christian labor or patriotism. It will throw new light on the Christ-like function of the genuine intellectual, called to imitate Christ by making incarnate in each generation and each culture something at least of the treasures of eternal wisdom and knowledge, the divine ideas summed up totally and perfectly in the Person of the Son, the Logos, the *Verbum caro factum est et habitavit in nobis*, that we might see His glory and be guided by it.[7]

Obviously such an understanding of the sublime vocation and preeminent dignity of the intellectual involves no plea for intellectual license or academic irresponsibility. But it does imply that the living intellect has a certain divinely appointed autonomy and that every valid word of truth has rights analogous to that freedom which Saint Paul proclaimed for the word of God: *verbum Dei non est alligatum*.[8] We make no plea for disloyalty and we hold the will in no contempt when we warn against the voluntarism which is at the core of all Fascism, Red or Black, and when we lament an anti-intellectualism which mocks that spiritual faculty by which the sons of men most nearly reflect the image of the Eternal Son of God.

To this needed spiritual and theological emphasis our schools and colleges can add other means of rehabilitating the name and nature of the intellectual vocation. Perhaps it is necessary at the moment for us teachers and priests to develop a special patience with the bright and the sometimes irritatingly brilliant, a patience comparable to that which we have always virtuously tried to have toward the dull. Perhaps it is needed that we be slow to label revolutionaries or liberals in any unfavorable sense those who have many ideas, including occasional disturbing ideas, instead of a mere comfortable few—or none! Perhaps it were well if for a season or two we preached as often on intellectual sloth as we tend to preach on intellectual pride.

The dangers of intellectual pride are many and grave, and we do well to discipline ourselves and our students in the moral and ascetical controls of this as of all other vices. But the dangers of intellectual stagnation are not less grievous both for individual personality, for the common good and for the Church. The wrath of the stupid has laid waste the world quite as often as has any craft of the bright.

Pride is not more the necessary concomitant of the intellect than humility is necessarily the adornment of those lacking in intellectual gifts. Teachers and spiritual directors among us may be well advised to remember that while it is doubtless better to feel compunction than to know its definition,[9] still the grace to repent and to repent humbly is not necessarily impeded by an informed understanding of what compunction is, or even by a knowledge of the bibliography on the subject, or of the history of those who have felt compunction to their own profit and ours—or of those who have failed to do so, with resultant grave loss to themselves and injury to mankind.

A typical Catholic university can do a great service toward correcting the prevailing prejudice against intellectualism by demonstrating that there is no *intellectual class* in the divisive and exclusive senses in which we speak of a *proletarian* or *peasant* or so-called *noble* class. Our students tend to come from many *classes* and especially from working and middle class families. When our universities develop the intellectuality which is latent in the common sense, good taste, and alert minds found more or less equally among all classes, they produce authentic intellectuals in the fullest and fairest sense of the term, whatever the subsequent special vocations or interests of the genuine intellectual.

Possibly it would break the spell and ease the tension which surround the word *intellectuals* if we stopped using the word for a while, and used instead the more rugged word *scholars*, a more solid word, perhaps, and so easily associated with the word *saints*. In another day, men aspired to be known as good scholars, and perhaps we would have more sturdy and more respected intellectuals if we intensified our efforts to make our students *good scholars* again. If the word *intellectual* has a recent history of effeteness and ineptness, the word *scholar* still keeps its ancient and honorable repute.

In any case, we cannot work too urgently for the highest effectiveness of our universities in graduating lovers of ideas, intellectual scholars, or scholarly intellectuals, as you choose. Pope Pius XI is quoted as calling the loss of the European worker the great tragedy of the nineteenth century, and the recent history of the part of the workers in the great struggles of the twentieth century confirms his melancholy judgment. The loss of any class or any notable part of any class is a source of embarrassment and grief to our Holy Mother, the Church. But given the nature of the new struggles which lie ahead, the struggles we describe by the awkward but significant word *ideological*, no tragedy could be greater than the loss to the Church of intellectuals, those who deal in ideologies and who love ideas.

Speaking at the mid-century convocation at Massachusetts Tech five years ago, Winston Churchill spoke of the great battles of the future. He said they would no longer be fought on the level of colonial empires, or political empires, or for the dominance of empires of oil, precious metal, or vast populations. The struggles of the future, he said, will be on the level of the empires of the mind.

The phrase is striking and it has the ring of prophecy. The battle for the minds of men, for the furtherance of ideas rather than political boundaries or military spheres of influence, is a battle in which the Holy Catholic Church not only belongs but must be victorious if God's Will is to prevail. In such a battle our schools, colleges, and universities are the indispensable arsenals and training grounds, our intellectuals are the soldiers and lieutenants. Of these may Christ be the Commander, Christ Jesus the Divine Intellectual, "in Whom are hid all the treasures of wisdom and knowledge".[10]

257

XX

Youth, the Hope of Christ and the Church

In the year that King Uzziah died I saw the Lord. . . . Then said I, 'Woe is me! for I am a man of unclean lips . . . and I have seen with my eyes the King, the Lord of hosts.' Then flew one of the seraphim unto me, having a live coal in his hand, which he had taken with the tongs from off the altar: and he touched my mouth, and said, 'Behold! this hath touched thy lips; and thine iniquity shall be taken away, and thy sin shall be cleansed.' And then I heard the voice of the Lord, saying, 'Whom shall I send, and who will go for us?' Then said I, 'Here am I! Send me!'[1]

The theme of your great congress echoes a point repeated so often that it must seem almost trite to you. It is the idea that youth is the hope at once of the Church, the spiritual family of us all and of the nations, our temporal fatherlands and political communities.

Even more bold, yet not less true, is the assertion I make to you tonight. It is implicit in this same proposition that you, as devout and dedicated young men and women, are the hope of the Church. It is the assertion that you are *also* and *even* the hope of *Christ*.

How dare we utter a sentence like that? *You are the hope of Christ?* The reverse contention we readily understand and immediately *accept*: that is, that Christ is the hope of the world and therefore of us, young and old alike; that Christ is the source of our hope of salvation and Christ is the object of our hope in all else that matters. In His grace only lies our protection and by His name alone are we saved, saved from ourselves and from the evil about us, saved for Heaven and for the best that is in us —Christ is indeed *our* hope!

This sermon was preached at Saint Louis, Missouri, on December 1, 1955, before a Youth Congress.

But we are also the hope of Christ. Saint Paul used a phrase about the apostles which may give the clue as to why we say this. He said: *apostoli ecclesiarum gloria Christi*—the apostles are the glory of Christ.[2] Like ourselves, the apostles were sinners, at the worst unworthy of Christ, His friendship and His grace; at best only His agents, chosen without reference to their merits to do *His* work in the world. Christ was their Savior, their Lord, the Source alike to their strength, their work, and such dignity as they possessed. Yet Paul calls them the glory of Christ, clearly implying that somehow they *add* to Christ something which otherwise even the Son of God would lack, that they do for Him something He somehow cannot do for Himself, *Apostoli ecclesiarum gloria Christi*.

And Saint Paul is right! For by the apostles, the work they do and the gospel they preach, the otherwise invisible good-ness and glory of Christ are made visibly manifest among the nations. However imperfect the apostles may be, still by *their rude voices* the saving truth of Christ is made audible to the scattered tribes of men. However weak the apostles may be, still by *their faltering steps* the strong help of Christ is carried to the ends of the earth. However unattractive or even unworthy the apostles may personally be, *their mission* is that of Christ, *their efforts* are of and by and for Himself and what they do, not of themselves but through Him, makes them *the visible agents* of Christ's invisible power: *apostoli ecclesiarum gloria Christi*.

All this is not less true of the devoted Christian who labors mindful of the effects of his Baptism and conscious of the relationship to Christ which becomes his at Confirmation. Baptism made the brethren of Christ co-heirs of His Kingdom. Confirmation commissioned the most imperfect of us agents of Christ, co-workers with Him in bringing to pass on earth that Holy Will of God which is the essence of Heaven. Saint Teresa had all this in mind when she spoke of how we Christians, however weak or unworthy we may be *singly*, owe it to Christ to put to work within the visible, tangible, audible world about us the hidden spiritual, *secret riches of Christ* ascended to the Father and relying on *us* to bring to pass the triumph of His Kingdom here below. Christ has *no eyes but mine* to see what needs to be done *today* and in this *place* with the grace He sends *me* from eternity. Christ has *no hands but mine* to transform the dying world with the energies He shares with me from Heaven. Christ has *no feet but mine* to run His errands here below; *no heart but mine* to bring human understanding and the sympathetic aid of a blood–brother to those who need Him here below; *no body now but mine* to spend its strength and perhaps be broken in accomplishing purposes, at once human and divine, for which He, in the hour appointed by the Father, became Incarnate, taking on the flesh of human nature Himself that we might see His glory, be guided by it and, by long, arduous, and even heroic effort, one day reproduce some part of it in ourselves.

The apostles are the glory of Christ. We, too, are mirrors of His beauty, stained and imperfect though we be. We are the agents of His power, however frail and fumbling our personal endeavors.

All this throws light on what we mean when we say that youth are the hope of Christ. You are in the springtime of life, that period of youth in which Isaiah of old found himself "in the year that King Uzziah died. . . ." Isaiah was young and all too conscious, as high-minded youth can often be, of his own unworthiness. He said: "Woe is me! . . . for I am a man with unclean lips!" And yet, in that same year there was opened before him the vision of what he should be and what he should do. "In the year that King Uzziah died, I saw the Lord."[3]

Isaiah was touched with the grace of God, in a manner perhaps different from you or me, but no less really. Sparks from that same celestial fire which has inflamed each Christian heart since Pentecost were on the coal by which the seraphim purged his lips, as God's grace cleanses us when we repent and give ourselves to Christ. "Behold this hath touched thy lips, and thine iniquity shall be taken away."

And in that hour of dawning maturity, as in the hour when

we consecrate ourselves and our strength to God, vocation came to the fiery young prophet. "And then I heard the voice of the Lord, saying, Whom shall I send, and who will go for us? Then I said: Here am I! Send me!"

The work of God is still so incomplete. And so, too, there is a tremendous need in our day for the restoration of the sense of individual vocation, the realization that not blind fate, nor mere fortuitous circumstances, but the *particular will* and *individual call* of God for every one of us sets *the work that each should do*, the use that each is called to make of his life.

And so *today* no less than in the day of Isaiah, the King sends forth His call: "Whom shall I send, and who will go for us?" *Here is the essence of vocation*: a cry from Christ to do some work, different for each of us, a work which Jesus needs; some work essential to the building up of His Kingdom here below, to the perfection of His glory in the world to come. And the sense of personal vocation is the most important quality we can beg God to develop in each of you, you who mean so much to Him, to His Christ, and to His Church.

"Whom shall I send, and who will go for us?" Whom shall God send to sanctify the homes and families which should be other Bethlehems and memories of Nazareth? Who will go for Christ as righteous fathers, faithful spouses, loyal kinsmen on the front of Christian family life? To this divine vocation the Catholic youth who seek human love consistent with the love of God answers with disciplined passion: "Here am I! Send me!"

"Whom shall I send, and who will go for us?" Whom shall God send to exert His refining, ennobling influence among the diplomats, the merchants, the chieftains of a divided world? Who will go for Christ bringing independent minds but loyal hearts into teaching, journalism, the professions, the trade unions, the armed services, political life, commerce, and business—and wherever else His doctrines and ideals are needed to elevate what is already good and to redeem what may be evil? To these potentially holy vocations, each according to his

261

choice and talent, the Catholic youth who seeks a career in the world, aspiring so to use the benefits of this world as not to lose the blessings of the next, answers with generous energy: "Here am I! send me!"

"Whom shall I send, and who will go for us?" Whom shall God send to tell our race of Heaven when earth grows too drab to be endured? Who will go for Christ to bring His mercy to the wounded, His pardon to the repentant, His supernatural wisdom to the fool and the wise alike? To this sublime vocation the Catholic youth who dares ask priestly ordination or pronounces religious vows, answers with confident humility: "Here am I! Send me!"

In the year that King Uzziah died, the young Isaiah saw the Lord. He heard the King of Heaven cry for help that he, Isaiah, alone could give. He knew his own frailty and confessed his own sin. But he lifted his lips to the purging, healing, energizing touch of the fire of God's grace, and he gave himself over entirely to God's will.

Every year, everywhere, our young people, restless to be rid of childhood and to discover *God's will* for their adult lives, somehow see the Lord. They, too, hear Christ cry out for help that each of them, personally and alone, must give or some part of God's great work will go undone. They know their weaknesses, their limitations, and their sins; they, too, confess them as humbly as ever did Isaiah. But their lips also, and ever more their minds and hearts lie open to the redeeming, regenerating, inflaming grace of God, and one by one they make the choices of vocation by which they in their turn are *sent by God* and are thus *the hope of Christ*.

Here am I—the boy or girl with a keen mind, a lively intellect, a good head that God has given me. *Send me*—that I may put to work for God my fund of ideas, may think the thoughts of Christ and speak His truth in terms intelligible to the bright of our day.

Here am I—the young man or woman of ardent will, eager

to spend self and to serve others, with a generous heart that God has given. *Send me*—that imitating Christ's own self-giving, I may not be wasted, but may use my enthusiasms, my good will, and my passions to my own salvation and the inspiration of all who love me in a manner attractive to all who need God—and me.

Here am I—the skilled craftsman, the talented artist, the man who can speak, the woman who can sing, the strong who can lead where victory waits, the repentant sinner, even, who at least can warn of where lies danger. *Send me*—that I may play my part, however humble, however blindly, however poor, in manifesting the glory of Christ, performing His work, fulfilling His hopes.

O Lord Jesus Christ, *here are we*, your youth. Whatever our faults, whatever the work you need to have done, *send us*. Be thou our vision. Make us thy hope, thine agents, the earthly authors of Thy glory—so that we, like Isaiah, may hear Thy voice and do thy will, and serve thy Kingdom and save our souls.

XXI

The Isaiah Thomas Award

The only part that I can properly play in this evening's program is that of a sincerely grateful beneficiary of the great generosity of the Advertising Club of Worcester and so my few words can only be of humble thanks.

Before thanking the thoughtful Worcester people who have made this evening possible, I cannot resist a word of affectionate salute to the large number of Boston friends who have made the long journey from the seacoast to the Heart of the Commonwealth to be with us tonight. I have not seen so many Bostonians in Worcester since the adjournment of the Republican and Democratic State Conventions last summer and I rejoice that a greater unanimity dominates this evening's meeting than did either of the other historic Worcester gatherings.

The sad circumstances of the death of his mother deprives us of the honor and happiness of Mayor O'Brien's genial presence this evening. I speak for all, I know, in pledging affectionate prayers for the Mayor's dearly loved mother and our sincere sympathy with her devoted son and his family.

No representative of the municipal authority could be more welcome in the Mayor's stead than Mr. Holmstrom, whose neighborly and amiable part in this evening's program brings back cherished memories of how these same qualities in the then-Mayor made the first days of my service here in Worcester so memorable for me and so proud for all our people. I am grateful to Vice-Mayor Holmstrom for his courtesy to me again this evening.

The Isaiah Thomas Award has become so coveted in our

These remarks were delivered at Worcester, Massachusetts, on April 22, 1957, on the occasion of accepting the Isaiah Thomas Award.

city because of the high level of character and accomplishment represented in the previous recipients of the award. You will appreciate, therefore, with what becoming embarrassment I thank so many previous recipients of the Isaiah Thomas Award for their presence at the head table this evening. It must be apparent that, in contrast with recipients like Mrs. Johnson, Mr. Stoddard, Mr. Jeppson, and Mr. Fuller, to name only those who are with us this evening, I am in the position of the eleventh hour laborer in Our Lord's parable who received, through the sheer bounty of the master of the vineyard, the same honor as those who had borne the heavier burdens and greater heat of the longer day of so much more arduous service.[1]

To the thanks I owe them for their gracious presence here this evening, I owe them a special word of appreciation that they have not grumbled against me, as the full-time workers complained against the late-comers in the Gospel, saying: "These last fellows have only put in one hour's work and you've treated them exactly the same as us who have gone through all the hard work and heat of the day."[2] By their presence they do me great honor and at the same time confirm the community's impression of their own magnanimous, truly Christian spirit. They win our renewed tribute, and escape any danger that the captious might paraphrase the word of Scripture against them by saying: "Must you be jealous because the Advertising Club is generous?"[3]

The other previous recipients will pardon me if I recall with special gratitude and personal appreciation two Isaiah Thomas Award winners who are no longer with us, George Francis Booth and Everett Francis Merrill. It would be difficult to measure, and even out of order to attempt to detail here, how indebted to them I am both personally, as one whom they befriended from the first moment of my coming to Worcester, and officially, as one who found in them unasked and un-qualified allies in whatever pertained to those aspects of my office which touch on the common good of this community. Suffice it to say that not the least ground for my natural pleasure in accepting this distinction is the further bond it gives me with two now historic Worcester personalities, neither of whom I ever asked for a favor, who contributed mightily to the good will in Worcester of which this evening's program is the most recent typical expression. These two Protestant gentlemen gave the first Bishop of Worcester understanding, encouragement, and cordial cooperation which were beyond price to a Catholic bishop who tries to take himself lightly, but his work seriously.

In that same spirit, I express my gratitude to the Reverend Wallace W. Robbins, who has opened and will close this evening's program with his prayers for us all. A couple of years ago I had the privilege of addressing the men's club at the Court House Church of which Dr. Robbins is the new pastor. That evening I spoke of the friendship between his people and mine in the days of William Ellery Channing, the eloquent Unitarian divine, and John Cheverus, the first Catholic bishop in New England. We recalled the great mutual respect between Cheverus and Channing, and the common solicitude for so many good things, happily shared in the midst of inevitable and necessary differences, which made their chapter in New England religious history so gratifying and luminous.

Dr. Robbins' presence this evening is a pledge that our own days, whatever the occasional stresses and strains of a mixed and complex society, are still blessed with such friendships and far-sighted vision as those which brought so close together in their personal relations and affections the Unitarian preacher and the Catholic prelate.

The choice of Mr. Robert Stoddard to serve as toastmaster to our festivities is one for which I am also deeply grateful. Mr. Stoddard bears a name that must always stir nostalgic and appreciative memories in my heart when I recall the evening in

266

the Municipal Auditorium seven years ago when his father, speaking with a deserved paternal primacy, welcomed me to the Worcester community and bade me Godspeed in a work he has since encouraged so often and so cordially.

I shall best demonstrate to you the grounds for my admiration of and gratitude to our speaker this evening, Dr. Paul Dudley White, by deferring to him in maximum degree by yielding as much time as possible for the wise and mellow message that he will bring you. I was worried when I read that he was in Puerto Rico only a matter of hours ago, but I reflected with relief and rejoicing that these last few years have found him in just about every corner of the world without on that account depriving New England of the prestige and the rich benefit of his presence. I was happy when the Advertising Club chose him to speak to us, and I am grateful to Dr. White for coming, for two principal reasons. First of all, the pace at which he travels at his age is a rebuke to those who chide me for frequent journeyings at my lesser years. Second, Dr. White and certain of his works, of which I hope he will tell us, symbolize the wonderful harmony that is constantly growing between the realms of the spirit and of science. A half-century ago people used to speak of the conflict between science and religion—indeed a man named White wrote a history of precisely such an alleged conflict—but men like Paul Dudley White, in the camps of the theologians and the scientists alike, are daily demonstrating in our more favored times that, whatever the remaining skirmishes, both are battling for the same objectives: the greater knowledge of God's will for men and the more perfect service of God's children.

In expressing gratitude to Dr. White for what he is and what he has done, I speak for an increasingly wider circle of people in every land who directly and indirectly are the beneficiaries of such untiring zeal for service as brings him here tonight.

Mr. Philip Warren and his associates in the Advertising

Club deserve the grateful salute of us all for making Isaiah Thomas a symbol of the values they hope to see perpetuated in the Worcester community. I am indebted to them for their kindness to me personally in choosing me as this year's recipient of their coveted award. I am not sure precisely what I have in common with Isaiah Thomas. He and I were both born in Boston, but of somewhat different descendancy, background, and interests. He was a craftsman; I am not. He was the first Master of the first Masonic Lodge in Worcester; I am the least likely candidate for that office. He became quite rich and so was able to retire; I look forward to neither happy fate.

Perhaps, however, we have in common something which should characterize every American and of which a community like ours needs constantly to be reminded. Every American will always be a bit of a revolutionary, as every Christian should also be. We speak of benevolent despots and sometimes we see a certain justification for them in the historical circumstances which produce them. We should speak not less of the need for benevolent irritants or mild revolutionaries who are useful as spurs or stimulants to the changes which are so essential to temporal as well as spiritual progress.

Isaiah Thomas was such an irritant. He was not a very radical revolutionary, especially in the light of the description of his personality, intellect, style, and manners as these were described by Governor Levi Lincoln of Worcester. But he was one of those men who always thought things could have been better and always sought to have them done perfectly and therefore differently. He had that divine discontent which, not less than stability of principle and purpose, is indispensable to temporal civilization or eternal salvation.

The memory of Isaiah Thomas is particularly important to a community like ours. We have so many and such excellent established traditions. We have so much that is good to cherish and to hold that we are in perpetual danger of complacency. We are so blessed in the things which make a community worthwhile and enduring that we might easily become strong in our own conceit. This, of course, would be fatal—and it is the function of those who share the spirit of Isaiah Thomas, whether they be businessmen or bishops, every now and again to upset us a bit, lest we settle for less than God and our best natures would have us accomplish.

XXII

Christian Charity
And Intellectual Clarity

The word *crossroads* in the theme of this Newman Club gathering, *The Catholic Student at the Crossroads*, implies a journey and a journey, in turn, implies motivation and direction.

It has been suggested that we might keynote our convention by turning to your saintly patron, Cardinal Newman, for something of the motivation and the direction needed to choose and to journey wisely the way of your vocations as devout intellectuals.

Cardinal Newman has been praised, beyond what would be his endurance, for many and wonderful qualities. Two of these I select as pertinent to our times and to your vocation. These two are particularly concerned with the motivaton and direction in the life of the Catholic intellectual.

Cardinal Newman had a passionate love for the spiritual beauty of Christian charity; he had no less a passion for the intellectual clarity of Christian conviction. The first of these qualities, love for the shining charity of the Church, he acquired, I think, from his studies of the apostolic Church, that age when the flame of charity burned so luminously among Catholic Christians that our love for one another, rather than any legal or philosophical hallmark, was the outstanding mark of the Church, the infallible clue to Christ's people. The second of these qualities, his luminous intellectual clarity, I like to think he inherited from his own Catholic tradition, from the days of medieval Catholicism in England.

Suppose we consider these two qualities, reflect on their

This address was delivered at the Waldorf-Astoria Hotel, New York City, on August 29, 1957, on the occasion of the annual convention of the National Newman Club Federation.

pertinence to our generation, to the work that we must do, and to the problems which confront us as we stand, in the phrase of the time of the convention, at the *crossroads* of our careers as Christians and as scholars.

How greatly would the cause of Christ and the growth of His Church be served in modern times if we could recapture in full measure the enthusiastic charity of Catholic wills in apostolic times and the luminous clarity of Catholic minds in medieval times! Charity pertains to the motivation and the action of the will. Generously espoused, it would purge our relations with our own times of such self-seeking, such preoccupation with vested interests or attachment to our own ends, personal or partisan, rather than those of Christ, as now so often discolor and even discredit our Catholic appeal to the heart of our generation.

Clarity pertains to the intellect. If we had manifest clarity in our convictions and clarity in our expression of them, our appeal to the mind of our generation would be enormously more cogent.

Of apostolic charity and its power to move hearts, your patron spoke in moving terms when he was discussing the faith that justifies. He spoke of the manner in which the Apostles, in the springtime of the Church's history, won people over to the cause of Christ and of how the Apostles presented their doctrines. They argued, defined, even debated so as to win men to their convictions. But argument, debate, and definition, controversy and polemic, formed a relatively subordinate part of the approach of the Apostles to the generation they won to the cause of Christ. Certainly as opposed to the place that polemic, argument, and mere verbal debate hold in our relations with the generation we would convert, the place of these in apostolic times was, as contrasted with charity, very subordinate, indeed. We argue so much; they followed a more persuasive pattern.

Let me quote to you your patron. He said:

271

The Apostles then proceeded thus: They did not rest their cause on argument; they did not rely on eloquence, wisdom, or reputation; nay, nor did they make miracles necessary to the enforcement of their claims. They did not resolve faith into sight or reason; they contrasted it with both, and bade their hearers believe, sometimes in spite, sometimes in default, sometimes in aid, of sight and reason. They exhorted them to make trial of the Gospel, since they would find their account in so doing. And of their hearers, "some believed the things which were spoken, some believed not." Those believed whose hearts were "opened", who were "ordained to eternal life"; those did not whose hearts were hardened. . . . The Apostles appealed to men's hearts, and, according to their hearts, so they answered them. They appealed to their secret belief in a superintending providence, to their hopes and fears thence resulting; and they professed to reveal to them the nature, personality, attributes, will, and works of Him Whom their hearers ignorantly worshipped. They came as commissioned from Him, and declared that mankind was a guilty and outcast race, that sin was a misery, that God was everlasting, that His law was holy and true and its sanctions certain and terrible; that He also was all-merciful, that He had appointed a Mediator between Him and them, who had removed all obstacles, and was desirous to restore them, and that He had sent themselves to explain how. They said that Mediator had come and gone; but had left behind Him what was to be His representative till the end of all things, His mystical Body, the Church, in joining which lay the salvation of the world. So they preached, and so they prevailed; using indeed persuasives of every kind as they were given them, but resting at bottom on a principle higher than the sense or the reason. They used many arguments, but as outward forms of something beyond argument. Thus they appealed to the miracles they wrought, as sufficient signs of their power, and assuredly divine, in spite of those which other systems could show or pretended. They expostulated with the better sort on the ground of their instinctive longings and dim visions of something greater than the world. They awed and overcame the passionate by means of what remained of Heaven in them, and of the involuntary homage which such men pay to the more realized tokens of heaven in others. They asked the more generous-minded whether it was not worthwhile to risk something on the chance of augmenting and perfecting those precious elements of good which their hearts still held; and they could not hide what they cared not to "glory in", their own disinterested sufferings, their high deeds, and their sanctity of life. They won over the affectionate and gentle by the beauty of holiness, and the embodied mercies of Christ as seen in the ministrations and ordinances of His Church. Thus they spread their nets for disciples, and caught thousands at a cast; thus they roused and inflamed their hearers into enthusiasm, until the Kingdom of Heaven suffered violence, and the violent took it by force.[1]

These first spokesmen for Catholicism were not merely intellectuals, if indeed they were intellectuals in any technical sense at all, but their sound went forth to the ends of the earth. It did so not because of any debating in which they were proficient, nor of any skill they had at nice or knotty definition, but because they spoke with a commanding and beautiful charity. They won the hearts of those who heard them, and won these, in Newman's phrase, "by the beauty of holiness and the embodied mercies of Christ", not mercies that one explains only, but mercies that one manifests. The living eloquence of their lives opened hearts thus made glad to listen to the logic of their preaching, a logic which reached few minds, so long as hearts were untouched.

In our own day, the great Cardinal Suhard has said something similar about what must be the primary and preeminent impact you have on your generation if you are to have men listen to your truth, let alone believe and accept it. The Cardinal uses the same word that the Apostles would have used, indeed the word that the New Testament does use. The New Testament has no word which corresponds to our word polemicist. It has no word which corresponds to our word debater. It has no word which corresponds to our word propagandist, at least in

273

its present so largely verbal and argumentative sense. The New Testament word for what you must be, the word that Suhard uses, is the word *witness*. To be a witness, says Cardinal Suhard, does not consist in engaging in propaganda, nor even in stirring people up, but in being a living mystery. It means to live in such a way that one's life would not make sense if God did not exist![2]

So far Suhard. In Newman's phrasing, it means to win for Christ the affections and loyalty of men by the beauty of holiness and the mercies of Christ embodied in you.

Our first great need, then, is for the apostolic charity by which the Apostles and their generation of Christians not merely made their sound go forth to the ends of the earth (we can do better than they, thanks to the techniques of contemporary communication!) but made their sound beautiful, made it resound in the welcoming hearts of all who heard it, because of its charm and the charity with which it was presented, the apostolic charity that we must recapture.

The need for intellectual charity, luminous and cogent, could not possibly be greater than it is at the moment. Surely to young scholars, to intellectuals by declared intent and vocation (for such you are, whatever the report cards may say), we have the right to address the urgent appeal for a clarity of judgment and thought, a Newmanian firmness in conviction, which will resist and offset that too-long established cult of uncertainty which paralyzes intellectual life in our day.

For several generations of university and collegiate life, there has been a veritable cult of uncertainty, a studied abstinence from convictions. As a result, there has grown up in those areas of the mind where clarity should be the supreme virtue, a cultivated cloudiness, an almost systematic fogginess. As against this state of mind, your great patron stood for medieval clarity and the lucidity of the great ages of Faith.

If it be said that medieval clarity of thought sometimes produced an unfeeling objectivity which could be cruel on occasion and even require martyrdom, as it did, in the name of its convictions, one can only answer that our generation still requires its *martyrs*, *martyrs* by the million on a dozen battlefields from Korea across the five continents back to China.

There is one great difference between those who died as martyrs in a sometimes excessive medieval clarity and those who die as martyrs in the modern fogginess concerning objectives and concepts. The modern martyr, the conscripted soldier, the victim in the concentration camps, the exile or displaced person, must usually die deprived of the consolation of any conviction as to why he is dying, there ordinarily being scant clear conviction either on the part of the one who dies or on the part of those who put him to death. It is some consolation, it is even a great glory, to die prematurely for something about which one is clear and certain, convinced and proud, to die for something which one could state or which, at least, has been stated to one, if only by the executioner. But it is a brutal stupidity that people should die as soldiers, as they often do in our day, for something which they do not themselves understand and which those who send them forth to die cannot even state in clear, convincing, or even grammatical terms.

It is human, even somehow divine, to die for a faith or a conviction; but who wants to die for a foggy, ill-conceived theory or a cloudy, inconclusive half-truth, stupidly expressed by a man who can't even spell the words, let alone define them, which invoke values he may not even accept, certainly does not properly grasp, yet in the name of which he bids men die?

In moral philosophy, including political philosophy, just as in faith, the trumpet that sounds an uncertain note commands neither the devotion of friends and allies nor the fear or respect of the enemy. Indeed, a false philosophy, even an evil and unfounded philosophy, may easily prevail if only it be boldly and clearly proclaimed, while a true and decent political system,

275

foggily understood and ineptly expressed by its adherents and chieftains, will meet with indifference and be summarily repudiated by a generation which demands clarity and cogency of those who would lead it. Any political or other philosophy may be as humane and as accurate as you choose, but if it is set forth in fumbling, foggy terms, it cannot possibly gain the day, save by a miracle. And when the fogginess of our concepts and the fumbling of our presentations are culpable, then we forfeit the right to expect a miracle.

Foggy concepts and stumbling expression of them are culpable when these are the result of undisciplined thought, undisciplined study, slothful, slovenly preparation, whether for examinations or for the business of life—or for a press conference.

Perhaps the greatest single danger which threatens our civilization at the moment derives precisely from the foggy thinking and inept speech of those upon whom, God help us, we must rely to set our directions, to state our philosophy, to plot our course, to sound our battle cry, and to lead us in the defense of our heritage.

Let me illustrate what I mean by certain contrasts which I know you will find diverting, and I hope you will find disturbing—so disturbing that, as scholars, and please God as future leaders, you will be determined to cleanse your own thinking and purge your own manner of speaking of all the mental gunk and verbal gobbledygook which obfuscate the thought and talk of those who too often are the spokesmen for our part of the world before the human community.

A wag has put in parallel columns the paragraphs written in the days when those who spoke for our country—they may have been wrong or they may have been right, but in every instance they were clear—with paragraphs caricaturing the manner in which like things would be said in our day.

Take for example, the Declaration of Independence. You

remember the clear, cogent, luminous phrases in which its philosophy and claims were set forth:

"We hold these truths to be self-evident, that all men are created equal, that they are endowed by their Creator with certain unalienable Rights, that among these are Life, Liberty, and the pursuit of Happiness. . ."

Now, I'm not concerned with whether those propositions are true. All I state for the moment is that they are clear. They were clear to the people who declared them and they were capable of making them clear to us; as a result, politically we have lived on and by them for all these decades. How would they be worded now by the people who hold corresponding posts? Is this caricature too far from what would be said straightface:

"When after continuous study and joint consultation the peoples of one country liquidate their obligations to another and are determined to play a role among the Great Powers of the globe to which they are authorized by the concepts of natural and divine law, it is expedient to spell out the unifying principles on which their action is based.

"We accept these facts as data, namely that all peoples are equal as regards national sovereignty, that they are empowered to exercise certain prerogatives, numbered among which are life, freedoms, and the struggle for happiness."

Now, tell me: where does that kind of confused and confusing verbiage, the bewildering expression of thought already thrice bewildered, chiefly flourish? Is it in the factories among workers? Is it on docks? Is it in kitchens of ordinary homes? You, more than any one else, know better. It flourishes on campuses, in classrooms, wherever *experts* and *brain trusts* are recruited. It is the sort of jargon indulged in by committees of professors, including us theologians all too often, and it spreads its smog into the body politic through students echoing the rambling thought and talk not of their hardworking

277

fathers, but of their Ph.D. professors. It is the characteristic talk, only slightly caricatured, of a generation of leaders who, if they themselves know what they're talking about, have lost all semblance of ability to let others in on the secret by clear, convincing expression of their thought.

Let me offer you another sample. Do you remember the words of Tom Paine in *The Crisis*? Now, I do not agree with what Tom Paine said on many subjects, but I do know what he said, and I know what he said because he knew what he meant—and knew how to express it. Typical of his clear, compelling style was the following:

"These are the times that try men's souls. The summer soldier and the sunshine patriot will, in this crisis, shrink from the service of their country; but he that stands it *now* deserves the love and thanks of man and woman."[3]

How would that be written now, say by a *philosopher* such as might grace by his presence a telecast symposium on the tensions of the hour?

"This is the epoch of the neurotic personality. Those persons whose psychodynamic structure can be equilibrated only in the context of an absence of external anxiety will in this era of socio-economic convulsion manifest an inability to discharge their social responsibilities; while those who can assimilate the impact of exogenous pressures will legitimately command the respect of the community."

What does that mean? It means absolutely nothing.

One final example. Someone in Washington, perhaps a reporter who had attended too many press conferences and who is worried about how our case is being put across to a world in peril, recently composed a satire that is a bit cruel, a bit amusing, but more than a bit depressing because of the frightening insights it affords to the bewildered thought and bewildering talk against which we beg you to develop a moral defense and an intellectual offensive. Any one who thinks he recognizes the original behind this satire will be expelled from the hall, not for lèse-majesté as you might suspect, but for the injustice of imputing to one man alone a confusion that is shared by all too many of us. This piece might be entitled *The Gettysburg Address as a Modern Lincoln Would Have Written It*, and it goes:

I haven't checked these figures but eighty-seven years ago, I think it was, a number of individuals organized a governmental set-up here in this country, I believe it covered certain Eastern areas, with this idea they were following up based on a sort of national independence arrangement and the program that every individual is just as good as every other individual. Well, now, of course, we are dealing with this big difference of opinion, you might almost call it a civil disturbance, although I don't like to appear to take sides or name any individuals, and the point is naturally to check up, by actual experience in the field, to see whether any governmental set-up with a basis like the one I was mentioning has any validity and find out whether that dedication by those early individuals will pay off in lasting values and things of that kind.

Well, here we are, at the scene where one of these disturbances between different sides got going. We want to pay our tribute to those loved ones, those departed individuals who made the supreme sacrifice here on the basis of their opinions about how this thing ought to be handled. And I would say this. It is absolutely in order to do this.

But if you look at the over-all picture of this, we can't pay any tribute—we can't sanctify this area, you might say—we can't hallow according to whatever individual creeds or faiths or sort of religious outlooks are involved about this very particular area. It was those individuals themselves, including the enlisted men, very brave individuals, who have given this religious character to the area. The way I see it, the rest of the world will not remember any statements issued here but it will never forget how these men put their shoulders to the wheel and carried out this idea.

Now, frankly, our job, the living individuals' job here, is to pick up the burden they made these big efforts here for. It is our job to get on with the assignment—and from these deceased fine individuals to take extra inspiration for the same theories for which they made such a big contribution. We have to make up our minds right here and now, as I see it, that they didn't put out all the blood, perspiration, and—well—that they didn't just make a dry run here, and that all of us here under God, that is, the God of our choice, shall beef up this idea about freedom and liberty and those kind of arrangements, and that government of all individuals, by all individuals, and for all individuals, shall not pass out of the world-picture at this particular time.

Funny, isn't it? Funny, but very, very sad. Very sad. Sad, because nothing of the basic goodness and rightness of the men who talk like that shines through their chaotic confusion. Obscurity, ineptness, lack of precision, and finality like that have nothing to do with whether the man who speaks is good or bad, right or wrong. But it has much, very much to do with whether the values of which he is the spokesman will gain effective hearing and even survive in our day. A generation of which the thought and expression can be so satirized—and, I repeat, we are talking now of a whole generation of leaders, not of one man—is a generation without the slightest idea of what it is trying to say. It is a generation incapable of disciplining its own action and accomplishment by ideas clearly grasped and firmly held. It is, of course, incapable of influencing the action and accomplishment of others, friend or foe, through the persuasive and lucid expression of its own ideas and ideals. It is a generation that can ill afford to laugh at the pretended *obscurantism* of ages past or to lament the *intellectual martyrdom* allegedly imposed by the oversimple clarities of other times.

Was it worse to suffer contradiction, perhaps even *intellectual martyrdom*, because of the excessive clarity, on occasion, of the Middle Ages than it is to go marching off to the atomic murder of wars fought for obscurely understood half-values fumblingly expressed in the circumlocutions of men whose personal bewilderment makes one lose heart for the causes they publicly bespeak?

We are told that it was bad for men to think and speak so patly and so definitely about Heaven and Hell that their controversies over these led, on sad occasion, to mutual executions among people who, it is said, tried to think too precisely and to act in too exact literalness about these remote places and the other-world personalities who dwell in them. But what shall we say about the battles of modern warfare which might have been prevented if certain of our diplomats were not obliged to confess, in rare bursts of humility, that they cannot even spell the names of the cities here below in which they represent us, or pronounce the names of the men with whom they must here and now do intellectual battle if millions are not to die military victims of the tragic spiritual chaos and intellectual confusion of which such spokesmen are the distressing symbols?

Is it not your clear duty, as intellectuals who are the heirs to American freedom and Catholic faith, to prepare yourselves to provide a better, more convinced and more convincing presentation of the case for faith and freedom than is provided in samples like those which have been satirized this morning?

You will so prepare yourselves by developing the charity of will and clarity of intellect of which Cardinal Newman was the herald and the example in his period of modern times. You will develop these by inflaming your hearts and wills by the enthusiastic following of Jesus Christ, Who made manifest for all the ages the mercies of God which you must embody and reveal to your own generation.

You will develop the intellectual gifts of clarity and cogency by taking the trouble so to study, so to speak, so to spell, even, that your performances on these modest levels of achievement will be evidence of your competence to the more lofty levels of Church and State where enlightened, dedicated, and effective leadership are always needed.

The contemporary urgency of that need demands of you the charity of will and clarity of intellect which Cardinal Newman expected people pursuing your vocations to possess. God grant that you who share his name may share also his virtues—and may have something of his inspiring influence in our bewildering times.

XXIII

Interview with John Deedy, Jr.

Deedy: Does the Church have a view on science?
Wright: Of course it does. The Church has a *view* on all
           things created, not merely because of the place
           they hold in the spiritual universe, by reason of
           the moral use men must make of them in order
           to find and to serve God, but also because of the
           place they have in the cultural order of which the
           Church is at all times a patroness and often a
           teacher.
Deedy: How can we learn what this view is?
Wright: The view of the Church on science finds ex-
           pression on many levels and through many
           channels. It is set forth authoritatively in the
           magisterial pronouncements of the duly con-
           stituted teachers in the Church, above all, the Holy
           Father. It is significant how large a proportion of
           the public discourses of the present Pope have
           been concerned with science and, directly or
           indirectly, scientific issues. It is also significant,
           by the way, how progressive, not to say ad-
           vanced guard, so many of the Holy Father's
           public positions on these questions prove to be.
               The view of the Church is reflected also on the
           broader, grass-roots level of popular Catholic
           interest and pride in the contribution to science
           of the sons and daughters of the Church. These
           evidences of pride range from the relatively
           scholarly books which Catholic authors write
           about great Catholic scientists, the Popes and

This interview was published in the April 1958 issue of *Ave Maria*.

science, and the like, to the familiar popular stories, so dear to Catholic newspapers, of which scientists are Catholics and how edifying or otherwise attractive to believers are the lives of men like Pasteur.

This same popular Catholic pride in scientific accomplishments reveals itself, somewhat more seriously, in the identification of great Catholic religious orders with specific areas of scientific research. Traditionally, the Jesuits have been noted for an interest in seismography, anthropology, and certain other branches of science. The Franciscans have a heritage of interest in botany and the scientific areas pioneered by their Roger Bacon. The Trappists have traditionally taken a keen interest in various branches of husbandry and the agricultural sciences generally. One of the most remarkable chapters in the stories of the modern missionary orders, particularly those of women, is that which tells of their competence in medical, public health, and biological sciences.

Finally, the view of the Church on science is mirrored in the liturgy. The created things which form the objects of scientific interest are constantly recalled in the liturgy, all through the year, as when the liturgy speaks of those *temporal goods*, *visible things of creation* or *things of this world*, in the study, love, and use of which the devout come to the attainment of *eternal goods*, *the invisible things of God*, and *the things of the world to come*.

From these three sources, and many others, the thoughtful will glean a view of the Church on science which is, in its essence and its permanent characteristics, broadly humanistic, devoutly sympathetic and, so to say, Franciscan in its spirit. The pertinence of each of these words would take a whole essay to develop but I think you will understand what I mean.

Deedy: How then should the Catholic react to the recent scientific breakthroughs?

Wright: If his reaction is in the spirit of the Church, then it will be essentially enthusiastic. The enthusiasm of the Catholic in the presence of new discoveries of science will have roots of delight in the new stimulation and satisfaction of intellectual curiosity about the world in which we live. It will also have roots of piety and spiritual joy in the increased insight which scientific discoveries give into the omnipotence, majesty, and wonder of God. The devout Catholic, like the prudent man generally, will frequently have a healthy suspicion of the claims of individual scientists, as he will have of the claims of occasional individual statesmen or artists—but he will always be enthusiastically receptive to new contacts with truth, goodness, or beauty. Scientists may be woefully mistaken, as may other mortals in any field. But science is concerned with truth, as art with beauty, and Catholics cannot possibly encounter new statements of truth or expressions of beauty without enthusiasm, gratitude, and reverence.

Deedy: Is there any danger that emphasis on science might detract from the humanities in our educational system? How can we meet this threat?

Wright: Surely there is such a danger. It is inherent in the very nature of things. All the wisdom of mankind warns against such a danger. The frequent spiritual admonitions of the Church against forgetting God in the midst of our fascination with the works of His hands are confirmed and paralleled by countless proverbs in which mankind warns itself not to let the bewitchery of (relative) trifles obscure good things, and not to let the trees cause us to lose sight of the forest.

In other words, there is the obvious danger that a period of intense preoccupation with particular positive sciences may be a period of forgetfulness or even lack of sensitivity to transcendental realities and spiritual values. A generation fascinated by things we can measure, stockpile, and build or destroy is in danger of indifference to things which are immeasurable, intangible, and beyond our power to change. That is a grave danger, of course. But the danger does not make invalid or negligible the truths and realities of science, even though these are only parts of a greater whole which it is the business of the poets, philosophers, and theologians to reveal to us, and our duty, as mystical and rational animals, to discover and acknowledge.

Deedy: How can we meet this threat of preoccupation with science?

Wright: The great need is that our scientists be themselves spiritual and scholarly men, not merely human robots. Also there is need that those responsible for the planning of educational systems and curricula, whether they be trustees of particular schools, politicians, or administrators, be endowed with a sense of proportion and an ability to keep a balanced emphasis among the humanities and the scientific branches, the arts and the sciences, the ancient classics and the modern researches in our educational systems. Finally, there is the urgent obligation incumbent upon those called to be our prophets and spiritual directors—the poets, artists, philosophers, and, above all, priests—to do their job in an age of science with all the heroism, diligence, and all-out dedication—and even more, too, which characterize so many scientists in their labors and accomplishments.

In other words, it will be the fault of the teachers and preachers of super-scientific values if they default the enthusiasm of our generation to the scientists. Who can blame the scientists for hawking their own wares? If we do not consume ourselves in doing as good a job as they, to whom the blame?

Deedy: Are the theologians, to narrow the problem to them, doing their part in making an impact on an age preoccupied with science?

Wright: I think that many are and I think the prospects are excellent that many more will. The ranking *theologian* in the Church is always our Holy Father, the Pope. We may well rejoice that our generation has been blessed with chief shepherds of Christendom who have not been content with the primacy in teaching authority which is theirs officially, but have achieved a primacy in teaching zeal as a result of their personal energy and brilliance in the exposition and defense of the Faith, together with the application of its teachings to the problems of the day.

Jacques Maritain once observed that the teaching pronouncements of the contemporary Popes are among the most eloquent evidences of the operation of the Holy Spirit in history. The reigning Holy Father, with his indefatigable, luminous, and so truly universal contribution to the spiritual direction and intellectual understanding of the great issues of our day—historical, political, scientific, theological, even artistic—is a providential example of what Maritain meant. His efforts to make the Gospel and the wisdom of Catholicism pertinent to the interests and activities of so many groups of scholars, scientists, and statesmen are an inspiration and an example to all others who teach, study, or preach in the Church.

A like apostolic spirit—intrepid, intelligent, and fruitful—has revealed itself among the theologians of France, Germany, Italy, frequently England and, on occasion, Spain. There are encouraging signs that in our own country, despite its relative youth and the practical problems of building the Church in a largely non-Catholic atmosphere, the Spirit is breathing with that freedom and fire which belong to it.

Deedy: Do you have any predictions on how all the emphasis on science will affect the religious life of people in the future?

Wright: Predictions involve both the unknown and the future. Accordingly, anyone's guess is as good as anyone else's prophecy. Who can know the answer to this question?

However, one may venture an opinion which may be a prophecy and may be wishful thinking. Certain aspects of the new scientific developments, particularly their orientation and the social, and therefore moral, questions involved in them, incline one to the belief that the new age of science may be the prelude to a future age of faith requickened.

Deedy: What do you base this hope on?

Wright: The principal areas of scientific interest in the era that seems to be opening are quite literally in the heavens. The orientation of scientific discovery at the moment is into interstellar space. Such an era of fascination with the skies, the planets, and the universe almost instinctively lifts the minds and hearts of men out of the self-centered confines of the psychological and biological sciences which have so largely taken up men's attention for over a century.

We may not realize the extent to which studies in psychiatry, experimental psychology, anthropology, and even sociology—the sciences which, together with biology and other microscope sciences, dominated recent decades—have riveted man's attention on himself. They have turned his gaze inward, downward and, in the case of psychiatry, even backward, and all to a point which has long since become a little morbid, a lot self-centered, and altogether too materialistic.

Suddenly the orientation has shifted and the shift may prove not only healthy, but even holy. From ancient times the contemplation of the stars has led men to speculation about God. Contemplation of ourselves, particularly on a studious, scientific basis such as that which characterizes so much modern psychology and sociology, is necessarily depressing stuff and, without the grace of God, could lead to despair. That sometimes seems to be precisely what has happened.

The new age of science, using telescopes instead of microscopes and gazing out into God's clear space instead of back into our own murky psychological depths, may let fresh air into modern thought. In such air it may be easier for the Spirit, moving where It will, to evoke more ready response. Astronomy, the prospect of interplanetary studies and even journeys—these are far removed from the introspective broodings and negative agnosticism which were the frequent by-products of the recent sciences gone to seed. These new directions in science may easily recapture the mood of mingled joy and reverence in which the psalmist wrote: "I look up at those heavens of Thine, the work of Thy hands, at the moon and the stars, which Thou has set in their places; what is man that Thou shouldst remember him? What is Adam's breed, that it should claim Thy care? Thou has placed him only a little below the angels, crowning him with glory and honor, and bidding him rule over the works of Thy hand!"

Deedy: Do you think this will take long?

Wright: I think this mood of mingled awe, yet joy in the face of a universe opening before us has already set in. Perhaps it will prove a natural predisposition to supernatural faith. It is a much more healthy atmosphere for religion than that which has dominated some corners, at least, of the world of science since Darwin and Freud. This mood is more likely to prove theocentric, rather than narrowly humanistic in any man-centered, materialistic sense. It is the mood in which a new Saint Bonaventure or John Duns Scotus could talk to us of the Christocentric universe. It is the mood of a generation with its eyes on the stars, not inverted toward the depths, shallow or profound, of its own self.

Deedy: Do you envision a new Golden Age for the Church in all this and a greater interest in her teaching?

Wright: Again, who knows the secrets of God? And yet, if only for the mood these new scientific developments help create—a mood of awe, humility, and praise—one sees grounds for hope of a wonderful revival of faith in and love for God. The opening up of the Americas and the Orient to discovery and exploration saw the raising up within the Church of missionary heroes whose vision and prophetic spirit profoundly revitalized the faith of whole nations at a time when faith might otherwise have been eclipsed.

What like marvels of zeal and inflamed vision may be stimulated by the opening up of almost cosmic frontiers made possible by the new scientific developments? What Raymond Lull may turn his Franciscan dreams of conquest for Christ toward the new worlds dawning in the universe of that Brother Sun and Sister Moon who have not seemed so close to us since the days of Saint Francis? Who will be the Marquettes, Joliets, and Riccis of the age of interplanetary exploration? What devout pioneers may carry the cross to the new ends of creation? Who will aspire to offer the Holy Sacrifice of the Mass in what corners of space?

These questions stagger the imagination,

perhaps, but they also recall the challenges which of old raised up saints who gave new direction to the energies and imagination of the Church when once before an old order was dying and new sciences were making inevitable a new concept of the world in which we live.

Deedy: Could you develop this further?

Wright: There is another reason why one thinks the new scientific directions give grounds for optimism about a growth in religious fervor among the nations. These reasons are broadly moral. The older sciences of the present and the immediately preceding century—anthropology, biology, experimental psychology—had certain unfortunate social by-products, quite apart from and independent of their valid conclusions and great content of truth. They unintentionally fed vocabulary to the social theories of racism, blood emphasis, Nordic-supremacy nonsense and like absurdities, which so bitterly divided mankind under the myth of the twentieth century, as the Nazi pseudoscientist called his particular theory of racial supremacy. The truths of authentic science are bonds among the nations and the valid conclusions of the recent sciences are, of course, part of the common patrimony which unites mankind. But the mood of experimental psychology, anthropology, and materialistic sociology was a mood that fostered division among men, the bitter divisions which plague us still.

Once the silly spirit of partisanship which temporarily worries about who *first* launched what space satellite or projectile has passed, the dynamic of the new scientific developments should be unitive. The mere presence of these objects in space, plus the prospect of exploring the depths beyond the margins of the skies, should tend to shrink the earth and subordinate its divisions. Mankind should henceforth function in a new perspective, one much more consistent with dreams of social unity among men and therefore more consistent with that moral law by which God desires and His Church seeks the unity under law of all the tribes of men.

Deedy: What effects will this new perspective you speak of have on the Church?

Wright: Such a social and moral climate would give the Church a chance to preach our unity as sons of Adam and as brethren of Christ with a prospect for attentive listening which she has not had since the rise of nationalism and the spirit of religious division in the fifteenth, sixteenth, and seventeenth centuries. We should pray God that His grace will be poured out abundantly on those who preach, as well as on those who listen, in such an age of opportunity for His Kingdom on earth.

Some such reflections as these may have been in the mind of the Holy Father when he apparently speculated—concepts so thrilling to both imagination and intellect—on the possibility that the opening up of the realms of space might even bring, one way or another, solutions to problems of an eventually overcrowded earth, problems which, in the mood of the nineteenth-century sciences, have so often been invoked by the dismal prophets of race suicide, the survival of the fittest, and contraception as the justification of their gloomy ethics. The new sciences, with

293

more radiant, broad, and thrilling vision, may talk with more optimism and morality than did the bleak, inhibiting sciences of Darwin, Malthus, and their disciples.

True enough, no matter how vast the distances which may open to our vision and venturing, the man who travels them could carry with him all his preoccupations, problems and limitations. Riding among the stars a man might be as morbid with self-centered brooding as he would be in a psychiatrist's ten-by-twelve foot waiting room, but it seems less likely. Even soaring beyond the Pleiades, a man might still be less aware of the majesty of God than of his own weary partisan commitments and petty personal pride. Some might, but most wouldn't. At least, so we may hope—and pray!

XXIV

The Roman Spirit

The practice governing the appointment and consecration of bishops in the Holy Catholic Church presupposes the Roman loyalty of our prelates. Nowhere does the phrase *communion with Rome* have more relevance or force. Church discipline assumes that those consecrated and those who consecrate them be *in communion with Rome*.

The theology of Catholic Christianity requires no less. Peter, having once turned forever back to Christ, confirms his brethren among the Apostles, even as Christ planned and prayed that he would do.[1] Peter's successor remains the Prince of the Apostles, the Chief Shepherd of the shepherds of Christendom, and the visible, living pledge of the unity of the Catholic episcopate. It is from Rome that Peter still governs the world-wide Church, holding that presidency of charity and primacy of jurisdiction to which the bishops, as successors of the apostolic college, have deferred in word and deed from the beginning.[2]

Our bishops, then, are Catholic in their faith and Roman in their loyalty. The Catholic faith that they preach throughout the world gives the Church its universality; the loyalty to Rome of which they give example gives the Church its indestructible unity. It could not be otherwise and be as Christ intended.

These canonical and theological realities take on greater warmth and more lively meaning when they are matched by the strong Roman sympathies, keen Roman insights and, so to say, natural Roman temperament of an individual bishop. All

This sermon was preached at Davenport, Iowa, on September 24, 1958, on the occasion of the Silver Jubilee Mass of the Most Reverend Ralph L. Hayes.

priests and prelates, indeed all the faithful worthy of the name of Catholic, are Roman in their obedience; some are Romans by every disposition of mind and heart. It is of such a bishop that we are privileged to speak this morning as, after a quarter century of work as a bishop and almost a half century of priestly labors, a gracious custom permits him to pause for a day of jubilee so that friends may speak his praise out of their grateful hearts.

This Bishop of Davenport is a Roman by obedience; the decrees which appointed him to this See fourteen years ago, as those which called him to consecration eleven years before then, bore the sign and the seal of the Roman Pontiff. Bishop Hayes is a Roman by priestly formation; his character as a priest bears the imprint of a Roman seminary, a Roman university, and the influences of his years of study in a disciplined Roman atmosphere and of sojourn under the serene Roman sky. To the office of a bishop, as originally to his ordination as a priest, he brought a personality adorned with qualities which, in classical and Christian times, have merited the name of Roman.[3]

Sixteen centuries ago a man who blended in himself the influences of pre-Christian Rome and those of the Roman Christianity to which he became a convert, Paulinus of Nola, summed up those proud, virile qualities in what he called a *Roman heart*. He bade a brother-bishop, setting forth for a diocese distant from Rome, to teach his flock to follow Christ with a Roman heart . . . *resonare Christum corde Romano*.[4]

These same qualities an American cardinal, recollecting his years as a student and later a prelate in Rome, described in an eloquent autobiographical chapter entitled "Student Days in Rome".[5]

The spiritual qualities of the Roman heart and the intellectual characteristics of the Roman mind were introduced to many of our generation of Roman seminarians by Bishop Hayes, who spoke to us of what Paulinus loved and Cardinal

O'Connell meant in terms of something the Bishop called *the Roman spirit, lo spirito Romano*. As priest and as bishop, Bishop Hayes has diligently fostered and nobly exemplified that spirit, and so we do well to mark his jubilee by reflecting on the Roman spirit that is so essential to Catholicism and so needed in our times.

The authentic Roman spirit is cosmopolitan, *catholic* in every sense. It is not Italian, nor German, nor Irish, nor Spanish, nor American. Neither is it exclusively identified with any period or time; the perennial spirit of Eternal Rome is neither ancient, nor medieval, nor modern. It ranges in its interests and its influence far beyond the confines of the Mediterranean world, Latin culture, and Western civilization in the almost regional sense that this phrase necessarily suggests. Even the pagan Roman had something of the world-mindedness proper to the Roman spirit; he felt, as did the Roman soldier in Chesterton's poem, that "all the earth is Roman earth", and, so feeling, possessed a natural counterpart to the supernatural cosmopolitanism of the Christian Roman who knows that his High Priest has all the world for his parish.[6]

The Roman spirit is never partisan or petty. In its Christian development it derives an intensified universality from the spirit of the Church, as the Church, in turn, partakes of the all-embracing spirit of Christ. Wherefore, the Roman spirit instinctively repudiates whatever would place the part above the whole, the transient above the eternal. Hence the inevitable opposition and tension between the Roman spirit and the spirit of division, whether revealed in sectarianism, Gallicanism, racism, or parochialism. It is the Rome of this universalism, papal Rome, the Rome of Peter alive and at work in his successors, not the Rome of the dead Caesars nor Rome the mere capital of contemporary Italy, that Dante could describe without exaggeration or irreverence as . . . *di quelle Roma onde Cristo è Romano*, that Rome of which Christ is first citizen.[7]

The Roman spirit is patient. Rome can always wait; its spirit does not impel to impetuous conclusions, nor does it rail at the inevitable limitations of human nature as these manifest themselves in individuals and institutions. The patience of the Roman spirit at its best comes from the mingling of Christian charity with the sophisticated experience of the centuries and accounts for the characteristic tolerance of Rome. Roman tolerance is patient with persons, not opinions. It does not derive from obscurity about ideas, carelessness about values, or apathy about principles; it is born of patience.

Hence in its dealings with individuals the Roman spirit, like that of Christ, acts with a patience that frequently scandalizes the self-righteous; Rome often irritates the Pharisee by taking the part of the Publican. Hence, too, Rome is more disposed than many of her children abroad to await with tolerant patience the perfection of human institutions, social, economic, or cultural, and to view with patient tolerance the failures, disappointments, and frustrations of merely human efforts, regional or international. The spirit of Rome is that of Gamaliel, wisest of the teachers in Israel who knew that if the revolutions of his day were of men they would quickly pass, and if they were of God no intemperate action or violent denunciation would suffice to destroy them.[8]

And so, the spirit of Rome is realistic. It listens to the visionary and even inspires the dreamer. But it is ultimately down-to-earth, inclined to be skeptical and to prefer the decently practical to the unlikely perfect solution. No wonder that one of the patron saints of Rome is shrewd Saint Philip Neri, the saint of common sense, allergic to illusions disguised as reality and to abnormality posing as a miracle. The honest, clear-headed piety of the veritable spirit of Rome partakes of this Roman realism; it desires no part of the novel, the fanciful, and the ephemeral.

Finally, the Roman spirit, so catholic and cosmopolitan in its premises and its aspirations, has a genius for becoming identified with, indeed incarnate within, the regional in order to accomplish universal objectives in particular places. In this respect, too, Christian Rome built in part on a pre-Christian Roman pattern. Imperial Rome knew how to adopt to its universal purposes whatever was native and necessary to particular places or preferences, while adapting its universal resources to the special needs of each region. Catholicism, diocesan and provincial in its programs and administration, world-wide in its vision and its spiritual resources, has brought to perfection the Roman spirit of universal accomplishment through appropriate local action.

In all these Roman qualities Bishop Hayes aspired to school us when, as Rector of the American College in Rome, he spoke of *lo spirito Romano*. These same qualities of the Roman spirit he has brought to the works of his priesthood and episcopate.

His diocesans here in Davenport have witnessed and been grateful for his Roman spirit in conforming himself to the pattern of his people and applying the universal resources of Catholic teaching to the particular needs of this region. One of his discerning laymen paid tribute to this quality of the Bishop by observing that, although born in an *Eastern* industrial city, Bishop Hayes has completely identified himself with the interests of his Middle Western diocese and given alert, energetic leadership to the rural life programs, rural liturgical observances, and studies of rural problems which mean so much to so many of his flock. His thoroughly American and modern understanding of the place of good schools in the attainment of the Catholic Christian ideal of perfection reflects the Roman spirit; so does his militant encouragement of native vocations to provide his people priests and teachers in years to come.

His priests in Helena and here, as his students in Rome, will recognize the Roman spirit of practical piety and forthright realism with which the Bishop cuts through cant and dismisses nonsense. One of his students will long remember the day he asked Bishop Hayes for vacation time to visit a Bavarian mystic whose rumored revelations were attracting attention at the time. Said the student: "I would like to go to Germany to see this saint", whereon the Bishop commented: "I belong to a Church which calls no one a saint until she is safely dead!" It was a gentle rebuke in the Roman spirit of Philip Neri.

Bishop Hayes brings the equanimity of the Roman spirit to the consideration of certain problems which so often unduly agitate others. At least one American bishop is indebted to him for a typical lesson he gave in tolerant patience with the inevitable imperfections of the trade union movement, then still struggling through the period of its growing pains. To the exasperation expressed by a young priest, annoyed by some excessive demand on the part of organized labor during an inconvenient strike, the Bishop replied with a defense of the labor movement; he put the excessive demand in proper perspective, all with a Roman tolerance, the patient wisdom of which he documented out of memories of his youth in Pittsburgh.

But it is in his personification and fostering of the broad, universal outlook of *lo spirito Romano* that Bishop Hayes has preeminently demonstrated his own Roman spirit. His diocesan newspaper is widely admired for the documentation by which it brings an intellectual emphasis on papal teaching into American diocesan journalism and for the cosmopolitan viewpoint by which, avoiding narrow factionalism and the spirit of nervous reaction, it reflects a Roman universalism and optimism. The educational system under his patronage, with a flourishing diocesan college at its apex, reveals the same Roman breadth of spirit and Roman disposition to give new, vital expression to the old, invincible truths. Above all, the Bishop's pastoral preaching and public addresses invariably echo the mind of the Holy See; his priests and people have heard from him no purely personal teaching, no partisan opinion, but always the lofty, permanently valid Roman doctrine on the wide range of subjects to which the pronouncements of the Popes have directed the thought and action of the Church in our day.

We began by recalling that it is the divinely appointed privilege of the Bishop of Rome, as heir to the dignity and duties of Peter, to confirm the faith of his brethren, the other bishops who perpetuate the mission of the Apostles.[9] We recalled that, in so doing, the Bishops of Rome accomplish and guarantee that visible unity that Christ coveted for His Church.

We end by rejoicing that it is the proud vocation of the bishops in the various nations of the world to proclaim to their peoples the Catholic faith confirmed by Peter and thus, by fidelity to their own apostolic calling, to achieve and make manifest for the Church that universality that Christ commanded. We rejoice today in the example given us by a bishop who, for twenty-five years of his episcopate, nearly fifty of his priesthood, has taught us how best a bishop serves Roman unity while spreading Catholic faith, remains at once close to the Chief Shepherd and yet close also to the scattered flock, by being, as Bishop Hayes has been, a man of Roman spirit, an American fellow-servant of the Roman servant of the servants of God.

XXV

Interview with Donald McDonald

McDonald: Bishop Wright, a couple of years ago, at the St. Louis University Founders Day celebration, you said that the term 'intellectual' seems to have become a term of reproach and that this need not be and should not be, especially in Catholic circles.[1] Would you say that that anti-intellectualism, which seemed to be so much in the air then, is now abating?

Wright: I think the air has cleared around that argument, rather more rapidly than many people thought it would. I'd like to insist, by the way, that I never shared the contention that our Catholic colleges and universities, or our schools on any level, had proved notably deficient in turning out people appreciative of the intellectual life. I never went along with the thesis of some who seemed to feel that our schools had let us down by a failure to produce competent intellectuals.

   Nonetheless, I thought that whole argument very important because it speeded the end of an anti–intellectualism that was indubitably abroad in the land; it still is, but it has largely gone underground precisely because of the attention focused on it by the debate stirred up two and three years ago by Msgr. Ellis and others.[2]

   I think there was an unfortunate equivocation in the discussion with respect to what, exactly, we mean by an *intellectual*? Our schools and colleges and universities, by and large, probably

This interview was published in the July 9, 1959, issue of *The Catholic Messenger*.

do not turn out as many professional intellectuals as other institutions of a more specialized kind do. But I am not at all sure that this is lamentable. I believe that our colleges, and in perhaps proportionate degree our universities, are turning out people who, whatever their work may be, have authentic intellectual interests; they love music and like to read; they enjoy the conversations and ideas which I take to be the joy of the intellectual, as opposed to the formulae and skills which I suppose are the delight of the craftsman.

I derive satisfaction, not regret, from the thought that my own college back in Boston has turned out a large number of men who are quite content to work as insurance men, furniture salesmen, or at other useful occupations to earn their living, but who never made the mistake of supposing that's why they came into the world. They go home at night to good books, good conversation, good intellectual company, but they are not professional intellectuals, nor would they wish to be.

McDonald: Your distinction, then, is between specialists and intellectuals in general?

Wright: I am distinguishing between people who live by their intellectual pursuits and those who are nourished by them and live by something else. And I think our schools have turned out and do turn out a very notable number of the latter group, and that these are the best intellectual leaven of the good society.

McDonald: Do you think we should be turning out more of the others, the professional intellectuals?

Wright: I'm not at all certain, and one reason I'm not certain is because I'm not sure but what society may have too many of the others, the mere professional intellectuals. I'm not sure but what they have given intellectuality a bad name. For example, when Frenchmen were talking about the treason of the intellectuals, they were talking precisely about professional intellectuals who became divorced from the everyday business of having babies, buying homes, planning communities, living in parishes, and meeting people.

McDonald: Meeting their political responsibilities . . .

Wright: . . . and taking part in the general life of the community. The debate over the *trahison des clercs* in France was along that line exactly. Whereas, I think the Catholic community is producing people who properly subordinate their intellectual life to their total personal life, as they subordinate their economic life, sometimes in a manner which seems heroic, to their total personal life, and as they subordinate, or try to, everything to the total business of personal perfection and of serving God in this world that they may be happy with Him in the next. In other words, I think the emphasis on the need for specialists who have the kudos attached to professional intellectualism may be a passing thing. When one meets some such specialists he hopes it is [a passing thing], because it is hard to imagine a good society made up of these Magi. I can't imagine it being humane, that's my point.

McDonald: Do you think we are spreading ourselves out too thin on the graduate school level? I think it was George Shuster, among others, who recently said that what Catholic higher education should have in this country is one or two very fine graduate schools, on the level, say, of

304

	Harvard, rather than everybody trying to have a little piece of the graduate work.
Wright:	That makes a good deal of sense, but I would like to underscore that you don't produce intellectuals, in my opinion, on the graduate level. If people don't arrive on the graduate level as intellectuals already they're never going to be such. They may become specialists of some species, but they're not going to be intellectuals. I often reflect on a memory from my seminary days—I mention this not to give the thing a folksy turn, but because there is validity in the point of the example I have in mind, as I think most of the men who were at Saint John's Seminary in my time would agree. I think the most authentic intellectual who lived on our campus at that time was the porter. This is not to say that we did not have many and excellent intellectuals on the faculty and many potential intellectuals among the students. But it is to say that Jim Moriarty was an authentic intellectual, and many of us were less so. We were specialists.

Jim had come over from Ireland as a young fellow. I think he had no formal education beyond perhaps the equivalent of a secondary school. He became porter at the seminary because it gave him access to a library which he thought infinitely more important than anything else one could be near. He lived to be almost ninety and it used to be a source of embarrassment to those of us who were college graduates and now post-graduate students to find Jim quoting out of the poets, historians, and philosophers when he probably wasn't getting more than twenty-five or thirty dollars a week. It never crossed his mind that his salary was significant; Jim lived richly on the level of ideas.

I am not asserting that it would be economically desirable that the Catholic people of the United States be getting the same average income that Jim Moriarty got. But I would think we had a superb intellectual, educational, and cultural system, if any large part of them had distilled as much of the experiences of our race as Jim Moriarty did by his hours and hours of reading. I am not offering him as the ideal of the intellectual life, but I do say that it's somewhere in this direction that the norm lies as to what constitutes an intellectual in the European sense and in the Christian sense, as opposed to what I think is a somewhat narrow and technical sense of the word.

McDonald: Father Hesburgh of Notre Dame said last year—and it's one of many similar statements we've been hearing lately—that what we need is more Catholic scientists. He had just left the Conference on the Peaceful Uses of Atomic Energy in Geneva and he was commenting on the small number of Catholic scientists among the three thousand at the Conference. Is it true that we need more Catholic scientists? We know, of course, that more knowledge will not necessarily make a man wise. But you're not saying, of course, we should not be active on the graduate level.

Wright: Not by any means. But I am saying that I am not sure I know what is meant by the term *Catholic scientist*, as I'm not sure what is meant by a *Catholic mathematician*. I know what's meant by a *Catholic intellectual*. It means a man whose

306

thoughts and values are colored by his Catholicism as mathematics could never be. In other words, I would be more worried by a lack of Catholic material scientists, because poetry and philosophy are concerned with values rather than with formulae, with thoughts rather than things, and there is where the battle for human and divine civilization is ultimately won.

McDonald: I suppose what Father Hesburgh is thinking about is the apologetic value of having Catholic scientists mixing with non-Catholic scientists.

Wright: Perhaps, in which case he's thinking about a prestige point, too, and a perfectly legitimate one. But it happens to be one that leaves me a little cold. I remember as a youngster that every church porch was filled with pamphlets about all the great scientists who were Catholics, about how Louis Pasteur would rather have the faith of a Breton peasant than pasteurized milk or whatever his scientific preoccupation was, but I must say that it didn't bring me any closer to the altar or to the Communion of Saints, although it perhaps made me grateful for Pasteur. I am afraid that the point, in terms of its apologetic value, is sometimes overdone.

I am not at all sure that the criterion of Faith has much to do with the number of scientists or technicians who have wisdom enough to know and love God. I take such a criterion to be a false measuring stick of the worthwhileness of a culture or an education.

I hope we play our proper and proud part in producing scientists but I would be much more interested in Catholic historians, and other useful citizens—Catholic poets, Catholic short story writers, Catholic journalists, and Catholic philosophers—than I would be in a mere flood of Catholic mathematicians.

One hesitates to say this in print, but there are good reasons to wonder if in the ideal civilization the people who run turbines and handle test tubes would be recruited from the serf levels of the population rather than . . .

McDonald: You mean the Greeks' distinction between the servile and the liberal arts?

Wright: Perhaps that's what I had in mind. I think the Greeks had a civilization and I'm not at all sure that what Father Hesburgh is talking about would be as truly such. I think it would be fine if all our scientists and all our generals were devout men, but their piety and insight would have little necessary connection with anything they had learned precisely as scientists or as generals. One fears we have over-labored the connection between the two.

McDonald: Well, I suppose if there is a lack of Catholic scientists, that may reflect a lack of interest in science.

Wright: Perhaps that's true.

McDonald: And then all of a sudden we have the bomb and we don't know what to do with it. . . .

Wright: That's right. But I'm still not sure that a lack of dominant interest in science is a lack that I personally would passionately regret. I might as well admit that I would much prefer that Catholics wrote the poetry and philosophy that will orient men's minds after the bomb has done its damage than that a Catholic had played any great part in producing the thing.

McDonald: Bishop Wright, we've had a number of stories

recently, some from our own News Service, in which certain people, including seminary people, are talking about what they call the culture gap between priests and laity today. Now obviously a priest is ordained not to be a great philosopher or poet, but to bless and consecrate and offer sacrifice and administer the sacraments. Nevertheless, a number of seminary people are becoming concerned about this so-called culture gap. They say they discern a two-fold trend: the priests' training is becoming more specialized in the area of theology, the sacred sciences; whereas the lay people, more and more of them, are getting a college education that is more and more technological and secular. They think the priest could possibly be more effective, even in his priestly ministry, if he could talk more fluently, I suppose, more realistically, about the things that concern his people.

Would you say our seminaries have become overspecialized in theology, that we have to strike a balance between theology and liberal arts, a balance that hasn't yet been struck?

Wright: Sometimes my worry runs in the other direction. I'm gravely afraid that in our effort to get inside the minds of our neighbors, or inside the minds of our flocks and find out what it is that makes our businessmen tick, we have included, both in the collegiate and seminary education of our young men, all manner of courses designed to equip them to understand their parishioners, some of which courses take time and use talent that might better be given to their theological and liberal arts preparation to increase their people's understanding.

Viewed in terms of society, the clergy should be one of the so-called learned professions, together with law and teaching. I'm not sure that our people expect them to have any more than any cultured man's superficial acquaintance with the fields of specialization of their parishioners. I think our people want them to be good theologians, particularly in the fields of dogmatic and ascetical theology. Far from thinking there's too great specialization in the seminaries in these fields, I think we have a tremendous job to do in perfecting these ancient disciplines.

McDonald: You mean to go deeper into theology, into ascetical theology.

Wright: Far deeper and more intensively. We do not need priests who are able to help out with the parishioners' bookkeeping problems or help out the parishioners with their specialized professional problems.

McDonald: I don't think this is quite what these people are talking about when they use the term culture gap between priests and laity. They say that the priests don't have this general liberal arts background. I should think, however, that they would get that in their college work, in their pre-theology training.

Wright: I agree. That's the problem, you see. It isn't in the seminary that the liberal arts job should be done. The difficulty goes all the way back to high school. And it's bound up with this tragic disappearance of Latin and Greek from secondary schools and colleges.

I talked the other day with a man who is head of a language department in the New York public school system. He told me that in that tremendous school system, embracing as it does a population of many millions, there are somewhere around a score of students studying classical Greek this year. He told me that there is only one high school where there is a serious Latin department this year.

McDonald: Do you think the schools should assert themselves more against parental or student wishes and say, 'All right, we are going to have Latin'?

Wright: I assuredly do. And I think, above all, that it's the obligation of priests and the Church to see to it that Latin studies, Greek studies, and the liberal arts curriculum are made inescapable in the lives of gifted children in our schools.

McDonald: You wouldn't make Latin and Greek optional?

Wright: Not at all, certainly not for future priests or members of the learned professions, because it's not at all optional in terms of whether a person is educated or not. Moreover, if there is a cultural lag between clergy and laity it is not because lay people are stronger in the liberal arts and the clergy weaker, but rather because lay people, being also ignorant in the liberal arts, are strong only in their fields of specialization, while the clergy, alas too often ignorant in the liberal arts nowadays, are strong only in their field of specialization, and thus there is no common intellectual ground, such as the liberal arts used to provide, among the members of the learned professions. Once upon a time a well-educated businessman, a well-educated editor and a well-educated diplomat could meet and spend whole evenings in a rich exchange of ideas without once bringing up their respective fields of specialization. That's no longer likely.

As it is now, there is no cultural lag of one group behind the other—clergy behind the laity or the laity behind the clergy. It's simply that they're building parallel towers reaching up to God knows where from completely different grounds. It seems to me that it's not a lag as much as it is a chasm which separates people on the level of ideas.

I can't think of a doctor of my acquaintance who would nowadays write the kind of humanistic book about his profession that was written in the days of Harvey Cushing. One exception would be a man like Dr. Paul Dudley White who loves to read up about the Dead Sea Scrolls and who takes long journeys to read Renaissance Latin treatises in the Biblioteca Corsiniana in Rome, but who, as a consequence, is sometimes looked upon as off-beat in the medical profession.

McDonald: Bishop Wright, there is a good deal of discussion nowadays about the future shape of the parish. Now I realize there is a trend to suburbia and that there is, in fact, a good deal of vitality in the new suburban parishes, such as Father Longley's parish in Minneapolis and Msgr. Chatham's parish down in Jackson, Mississippi.

On the other hand, we have testimony from some of the religious sociologists who emphasize the new mobility of the people, the breakdown of former ethnological bonds that used to be cohesive in so many of our parishes and the question is raised: Is the present parish structure outmoded? Can the parish serve as more than just the place where people go to Mass and receive the Sacraments—the service station idea?

312

What can the parish do with people so spread out and so very mobile?

Take something as mundane as parking facilities on Sunday: the Masses, it is said, must be scheduled an hour apart, one right after the other, because the parking lot must be emptied for the next Mass. If we are getting gigantism in the parishes, is that good or bad?

Wright: I don't think it's possible yet to answer the question: What's becoming of the parish? The *revolution* in the concept of the parish has, in point of fact, hardly started among us. In one or two places it has, as in Paris, where the groupings of the devout according to their vocational interest rather than their geographical area are causing changes in parish patterns. To a certain extent there is a process under way in some of our large cities. As a boy in Boston I used to be fascinated by the night-workers' Mass. All the men who worked on the newspapers late Saturday nights went to Mass together at Saint James' Church; they constituted a kind of *parish* without reference to the parish in which their families lived.

All this introduces immediately a problem, namely, whether the parish is something with which one is individually affiliated because of his individual interests, vocation, profession, or perhaps social class, or whether the parish is a *family of families*, whether it's a family thing. Along with the trend toward the former idea, the emphasis on family Communion and family activity seems to constitute a contrary trend. I know many small parishes where it is popular for whole families to go to Mass together all the time on the principle that the family that prays together should pray together, above all, in church, where prayer is or should be at its best.

So I think that the revolution in parish structure has a long way to go before the general lines of it will be clear. I think, too, that it will be very different in different parts of our own country, as well as in different parts of the world. I would be extremely suspicious of any generalization about the breakdown of the parish and its reorganization, because even within a single diocese the patterns of parish life are so very, very different.

McDonald: Is size a factor? I know some scholars say that the smaller the parish obviously the closer . . .

Wright: More cohesive . . .

McDonald: . . . yes, and the closer the priest to the people.

Wright: Yes, we try to break down our parishes to achieve just that, our territorial parishes. But before it will be possible to generalize about any revolution in the concept of the parish, and before any sociological or other processes will act as catalytic agents in any transformation of the parish, we must face a further question: Are we going to think of the parish, as we have come traditionally to do, chiefly as an administrative unit or are we going to think of it as an educative unit?

Now every parish is, of course, an administrative unit of the praying community and an educative unit of that same praying community. But whereas in the immigrant days of the Church in America, the parish perforce had to be primarily an administrative unit and to take its structure and emphasis from that fact, now the

314

parish is more and more an educative unit. The administrative unit in most parts of the country is becoming more emphatically the diocese. People are much closer to the bishop than they used to be, sometimes as close as to the parish priest.

Bishops now work directly all over the diocese and are available to people more than ever before. The telephone numbers of the bishop are listed now. They have office hours. They no longer receive in throne rooms; they see people across desks. The administrative aspect of the diocese is stronger. Diocesan programs of the NCWC, Diocesan Council of Catholic Men, Youth Council impinge their administrative apparatus on areas that used to be confined to the parish, the parish lyceum and the special administrative programs of the city or rural parish.

What, therefore, does the function of the parish tend to become? Perhaps the parish will be less and less the administrative unit and more and more the educative and, please God, above all, more and more the liturgical center of Catholic lives.

McDonald: Do you think the Catholic laity in general then should draw their vitality and their educational material—some of it at any rate—from the parish and under parish auspices?

Wright: The parish altar remains the most effective center of worship, it seems to me. For the indefinite future the ideal pattern in worship will make the parish altar the center of our liturgical lives; the parish tabernacle, the parish baptismal font, the parish confessional, the center of our sacramental lives. I say this even though well aware of the tremendous part played in the spiritual lives of our people by the various non-parochial groups to which they belong, retreat leagues or specialized professional guilds.

McDonald: Pastors, then, should probably not be doing a great many things which their laymen could do.

Wright: Pastors would be the first to agree. Note the number of parishes which now bring in professional fund-raisers to do what a lot of pastors put themselves prematurely in the grave trying to do: raise money. Many bring in professionals now to do that; the pastor offers grace at the kick-off dinner, as indeed he should do, and says a word of pastoral encouragement.

It's impressive the number of parish priests who now have secretaries to do things that once a man did by himself and in longhand. It's noteworthy, too, how certain aspects of the mere administration of the parish are taken care of by devout laymen in the Legion of Mary, the [St.] Vincent de Paul and other groups wherein some of the laity can do some of what the pastor couldn't hope to do in an administrative way and at the same time accomplish a part of the vocation of the laity in the life of the Church.

All of this will contribute, it seems to me, to the shaping of the parish of the future. But the strength of the parish will be that it is the liturgical unit of the life of the Church, at least as far ahead as one can see.

McDonald: To come back to size again for a moment. Some scholars note that sermons, for example, can't be over six or seven minutes long because you've got to get the people out. And, since the sermon is frequently the only educative contact between

	priest and people, it should be of a reasonable length, allowing time for the priest to develop a point.

Wright: I think certain requirements of our civilization are going to take care of that. If we're going to have a different economic, social, and industrial set-up from what our forefathers had, we're going to have a different understanding of where instruction has to be done and of where it's best done. Back in the days when people worked six days a week and on the seventh day rested, on that day they heard an hour's sermon and heard it gladly.

They heard it gladly for a hundred reasons. First of all, it was almost the only instruction they ever had, in the absence of television, radio, and widely diffused periodical and other literature. Secondly, it was so much better than the bang of the machine and the other things they heard all week that it was welcome. Third, they had no place else to go. Moreover, Sunday was the day they left aside for just that—the Mass, the sermon, and Sunday school.

When I was a boy the afternoon Sunday school from two to three o'clock was jammed with hundreds of kids who came back in the afternoon after having been to Mass in the morning. You could never get attendance like that now for any purpose whatsoever, no matter what it might be, all the year round.

In other words, the whole civilization has changed and since this question of when you give instruction is a peripheral matter and the instruction is the substance of the thing, the influence of civilization need not be feared. I

317

anticipate, then, that we may reach the blessed day where at Sunday Mass there'll be no sermon, perhaps a brief homily, but, please God, no announcements. There'll be the reading of the Gospel and then a homily on that Gospel, not a developed instruction. It wasn't expected that the few minutes between the reading of the Gospel and the Creed would be the time when we would teach theology, inspire to the good life, reprove the sinner, encourage the saint, and do all the things that have to be done by instruction.

I think the time will come when the Sunday Mass, in line with what we've been saying about the parish as the liturgical unit, will include a homily of a pastoral kind, and then, with the present forty-hour week, and now the four-day week under consideration in some circles, it may become possible to figure out a pattern whereby study clubs, parish instruction hours, schools of religion, something like the old lyceum program will come back into parish life. The CCD could bring this to pass. I hope it does.

People are going to get so sick of television and of all the present uses of leisure time that an alert clergy will have a golden opportunity to instruct them in CCD, adult, and specialized groups—if only we have the vision and vitality.

McDonald: Then people don't expect a college-type lecture from the pulpit?

Wright: They're not interested in their priests being dons, they're interested in them being divines in the root sense of the word.

McDonald: You say a homily is what they want.

318

Wright: Homily is the word. You see, the rebirth of the homily will bring with it a whetting of the appetite to study the Faith. We don't love things until we know them, but we're not likely to take the trouble to know them until we've fallen a bit in love with the beginnings of them. And it's the function of the homily to fire love of the Faith.

McDonald: That brings up, it seems to me, the whole general problem of lay spirituality. Take a professional man, for example—a doctor, a professor, editor, lawyer—and if he is married, he has certain obligations—to his wife, to his children, to his work, and, of course, to his own spiritual life. He has a problem, it seems to me, of keeping things in balance and not just in balance but so that these things nourish each other and so that his work is also spiritual and so that his family isn't slighted. And it comes down, sometimes, to something seemingly as simple as budgeting one's time, of which there never seems to be a sufficiency.

Now is there any one pattern—whether it be Third Orders, secular institutes, specialized Catholic Action—which will help a layman who wants to ascend to God and also to meet all of his temporal obligations and do all the things he must do in the temporal order?

Wright: Well, you've left out the thing that I would most wish to talk about. It's the lay retreat movement. I don't know anything more likely, properly utilized, to accomplish what I think you mean than is the lay retreat movement. Nor do I know, by the way, any more encouraging sign of the vitality and the spirituality of our laity than, again, the lay retreat movement.

319

Sometime ago I went to the biennial convention of the men's retreat movement. I went to it, and to the laywomen's retreat movement convention, because I am episcopal moderator for both. One is perpetually astonished by the kind of men one meets there and the kind of women met in their retreat movement. They are people who are identified with all manner of widely diverse apostolic interests. They have almost nothing in common except existence and the Faith; they cut across all manner of professional and social lines. They make their annual retreat, some of them in retreat houses which are very inadequate, which fall far short of the ideal and far wide of the mark; others in circumstances which are ideal. But all have recognized the great necessity, precisely in order to meet one's essential obligations, of withdrawing periodically for that thinking in the heart without which the world grows desolate.

McDonald: Well, that is once a year, or at most twice a year. Can they develop a pattern from that?

Wright: Well, it's once a year like the income tax return is once a year but it dominates one's budgeting for all the rest of the year.

McDonald: Will that carry them through a year?

Wright: I think it would if a man were able to pick the place and the company of his annual retreat. I think it would accomplish wonders for him in providing him a solid, three-day spiritual checkup on what he did during the year gone by and on what he intends to do during the coming year. It gives him an opportunity to meditate on the duties of one's state in life, which should be the first question we ask ourselves when we prepare for our weekly confession. If a retreat were properly made each year, it would gravitate around the man's vocation; it would highlight the duties of his state in life for the year to come.

McDonald: You'd have to get a homogeneous group in a retreat, people with somewhat similar problems?

Wright: Ideally, perhaps, people would make their retreats by professional groups, or at any rate by broad groupings of an intellectual, trade union, or social kind. Any grouping may be advisable or helpful.

I am always happy when I see a group of Alcoholics Anonymous make a retreat together; the grouping reflects a common preoccupation. I enjoy giving retreats to groups of students. Each year I try to give a retreat to groups like the students at the Harvard Law School. That's a homogeneous group; it's proper that it should be.

It is not proper that parish life should be thus segregated, but it is good that their retreat should be, because a retreat, it seems to me, should be concerned precisely with the weighing of the duties of one's state in life, and we do differ in our states in life.

McDonald: I suppose it takes a great deal of training in the art of giving a retreat. Is the supply of retreat-masters adequate?

Wright: No, it's not; there's another great need. But that doesn't make the program less essential. We must begin with the recognition of how essential it is. It's encouraging that more and more dioceses are now providing diocesan retreat houses.

321

The diocese of Covington, where the late Bishop Mulloy was so forward-looking in so many areas, has just finished a diocesan retreat house. It isn't a Jesuit retreat house, a Redemptorist house, or a Passionist one, but all schools of spirituality will, from time to time, have the opportunity to make their contribution of spirituality there. It's a diocesan retreat house; it recognizes that the men of the diocese, precisely as good diocesans, have the same need for an annual retreat as do the priests.

McDonald: Not everyone can give a retreat, I suppose; it takes experience.

Wright: That's true, very true. A retreat, again, is not a series of lectures; it's not an instruction course. Nor should it be the same as a parish mission. It isn't to de-alkalyze drunks or to bring sinners to repentance. It is to take men who are leading completely normal, integrated Catholic lives, and provide them with the annual opportunity to consider their greater perfection in their own state in life. That aspect of the retreat movement is growing and I mention it first as one of the signs of the vitality of modern lay spirituality.

McDonald: When you speak of retreat, you mean the closed retreat.

Wright: Closed retreat, yes, I don't mean Days of Recollection or the new Evenings of Recollection. I mean the formal closed retreat for which Pope Pius XI pleaded in his encyclical on the Spiritual Exercises.[3]

McDonald: Certainly it's difficult to know in a particular instance whether spending more time on something connected with one's work is proper if it

322

means a lessening of one's time with one's family or spiritual life. It is difficult to know, with any great degree of confidence, that a particular allocation of time is proper.

I know it is true that if one is doing a good and competent job as a doctor or a lawyer or a teacher or a journalist, that that in itself has spiritual validity, but it has always seemed to me that simply to state that is a bit facile because obligations do conflict and compete. Perhaps there should be no conflicts, perhaps good intention covers everything. . . .

Wright: I am inclined to doubt it. I don't know of any old saw that's more true than the one about the place which is paved with good intentions.

McDonald: If you wanted to make a hierarchy, what would you do—put God, family, and work in that order?

Wright: Hierarchy of values?

McDonald: Yes.

Wright: Yes, except that, you see, the moment you begin to say God, family, and work, you imply that there are sharply distinct and isolated responsibilities involved, or levels cut off from one another like the cells of a honeycomb or like the floors of a steel-girded building. There's something the matter with that concept of the spiritual life.

It seems to me that the member of a learned profession, in some degree every Christian, but certainly a member of a learned profession has to have a rule of life, a spiritual philosophy and ascetical code which is humanistic and which, therefore, doesn't make that dichotomy of *God*

323

and family or *God and my work* but rather makes him the servant of God in the law, a lover of God in his wife and family, and so on.

I mean that an incarnational spirituality eliminates the necessity of thinking of God and family and work in such distinct and almost conflicting, even antagonistic, terms.

McDonald: It eliminates the tension between the obligations?

Wright: The duty that the Catholic spouse owes his wife is also his duty to God in a real sense, and if he understands that sense he keeps both duties. One isn't likely to be forgotten in the other. The "thank-you" he says to his wife is a "thank-you" to God and his *"Deo gratias"* is a "thank-you" for his wife. Our failure to realize the humanistic aspects of the Incarnation and its effect on spirituality accounts for this tension of which you speak. You see, we've been haunted by the absence of a humanistic spirit, born of appreciation of the Incarnation, in Christian spirituality.

McDonald: Are you suggesting there is an anti-naturalistic strain running through this thing?

Wright: Well, it is anti-humanistic, certainly. It's the *two loves have I* idea that, pressed far enough, is Manichean. Claudel has a good handling of it; he protests that there are not two loves, there is only one. With the same love by which my heart of flesh embraces the created order, he asserts, my heart of spirit loves its God. The human personality involves a psycho-physical unity, and the God we love is immanent in creation as well as transcendent to it.

Sometimes some of our disjunctions bedevil this question at every turn. For example, the constant disjunction that we imply in some of our spiritual direction—*seeing things in the light of reason and seeing them in the light of time*—almost suggests that these lights were lights bearing against one another, as if they admitted of no synchronizing.

McDonald: I suppose Saint Thomas would be the best example of one who brought in both Faith and Reason and produced something new and unified.

Wright: Yes, and that is why he gives such aid and comfort to Christian humanism. He talked of *The Apostle* and *The Philosopher*, and capitalized both words. The Philosopher was Aristotle and the Apostle was Paul. He continually starts off with "the Philosopher says" and appeals to what "the Apostle says", bringing their testimony together without this hideous dichotomy that has haunted even Catholics since Descartes pitted Faith and Reason against one another and made the spiritual life somehow schizoid. "Lest, having Him, I must have naught besides"—and all this business.[4]

We build up with spurious and disastrous romanticism the spiritual choices involved in the vocations of our children, for example. If they elect to be nuns, we say *they have rejected the world* or *died to the world*, which can be vicious talk, since you can't die to anything that God so loves that He identified His only begotten Son with it, so that whosoever believeth in Him might not die, but have life everlasting.

This humanistic aspect of the Incarnation— the fact that Pilate did not need to send God

325

to death (since he couldn't anyway) in order to be guilty of deicide, but only had to send unjustly to death the man before him, deserves immeasurably greater place in our preaching and meditation. It would unify and purify our concepts concerning spirituality.

McDonald: Spirituality won't take care of itself, though, will it? You have to work at it. There is that categorization that is inevitable and that brings you back to the retreat, of course.

Wright: It brings you back to the retreat as the annual opportunity to balance your books in the light of your rule of life, and of your understanding of yourself, and your answer to "what does it profit a man", etc. That's the business of the retreat.

McDonald: As you were speaking of the anti-humanistic element, I was thinking of perhaps a taint of it in some of the thinking of the program at Catholic University of America, their *Guiding Growth in Christian Social Living* textbooks in which we find what are called *Catholic essays* and *Catholic short stories* and *Catholic poems*, bringing in immediately, it seems to me, this disjunction between religion and life, bringing in denominationalism where it doesn't seem to me to be pertinent.

Wright: You see, one of the results of the Incarnation should be that those who conform themselves to Christ and therefore develop the full image of Christ could say something far better than what the pagan humanists said. They could say, not merely as the best of the pagans could, "I am a man and therefore nothing human is alien to me", but they could also say, "I am like to God, the God of the Incarnation, and therefore nothing human is beyond the range of my interest, my influence, my desires, or my love. . . ."

McDonald: A few years ago the Pope spoke to a group of Catholic book publishers and he said the term *Catholic* per se excludes not only sin and error, but that it embraces everything else. But it seems to me that we may be teaching our children to think—when they bring some of these Catholic text-books home from school—that everything that hasn't got a Catholic label on it is somehow bad, or at least not worth their attention.

Wright: What does one mean by a *Catholic hexameter*? A *Catholic couplet*? Did Alexander Pope write Catholic couplets, and Swinburne write Protestant couplets? That isn't where the Catholicism enters.

McDonald: I wonder if we could go to the subject of Catholics and international life and international relations. A few years ago one of the authors in the book, *The Catholic Mind Through Fifty Years*, commented that there is frequently a gap between what we Catholics believe and what we do, and he said that nowhere is that gap so large and formidable as in the area of international relations. And he pointed out that Catholicism of its very nature is international, or supra-national.[5]

Now, I know that you are interested and active in the Catholic Association for International Peace. Do you think this gap between Catholic belief and Catholic action is as wide today as apparently it was thirty to thirty-five years ago when that statement was made following the first World War? Or are we closing it?

And, relating to that, you spoke a few years ago at the National Liturgical Week about "The

327

	Mass and the International Order" and I believe you said then that Catholic universality is primarily moral and religious in its postulates and that the Catholic sees that, discerns it, in the liturgy and in the Mass.[6] Now do you think we can give political expression to this moral and religious solidarity and universality?
Wright:	First of all, on this suggestion that there is a seeming apathy among Catholics with respect to international interests and international movements, I am afraid there is no more irrefutable proof of that than the half-starved condition of our little Catholic Association for International Peace, by all odds the smallest organization in the whole set-up of the NCWC. That is perhaps a symbol of the situation that exists among us, I'm afraid.

If one goes to meetings where people get together to talk about the possible organization of the human community, he invariably discovers that if he's not the only Catholic present, the only other Catholic is probably someone who is believed to be on the eccentric side. On the other hand, he finds there, to his scandal from a Catholic point of view, all manner of Episcopalians, Quakers above all, a few Congregationalists, many Unitarians, and, appropriately enough, practically all the Universalists there are. But any semantic reason which explains the presence of the Universalists should apply even more to us on account of the meaning of the word *Catholic*. We know why the Universalists are there. We don't know why the Catholics aren't.

The more you think of it, and sometimes during the long keynote addresses at peace conferences you think quite a bit on it, one possible explanation occurs to you. One almost dislikes accepting the explanation because it doesn't seem fair to our dissident neighbors and, in a way, it doesn't seem fair to our own people either. But I think it's part of the explanation.

I've often reflected that while Catholics are, in theological and religious matters, the most cosmopolitan and world-minded people on earth, somehow in political, social, and economic matters they turn out to be ultra-nationalists.

On the contrary, those who are so ultra-nationalist theologically that their very church names reflect the names of their nations—the Church of Scotland, the Church of England, the Boston Unitarians—are, as a matter of fact, usually among the most international-minded in what pertains to politics, problems of peace and war, and like temporal problems of a cultural or social kind.

Isn't it a strange paradox that finds those who are world-wide in their religious loyalty so fiercely nationalist in their political sentiments? No one is more pro-Papal nor more completely British than a British Catholic, impatient, as my friend Douglas Woodruff tends to be, with the gross manifestations of American Catholicism; ultra-Papal, ultramontane in the extreme, sometimes to the bewilderment of the Italians and even of the Spaniards, in religious matters, yet ultra-insular in economic, political, and social matters. Whereas the Anglican, whose very

329

name means that he has broken with world Catholicism, is in temporal matters more likely to have a world view.

McDonald: Are these compensations, on both sides?

Wright: Perhaps. But I think there is another explanation. Possibly it is unjust to the Protestants, but I think that the Messianic vision and the world impulse that belong in religion and which some Protestants no longer find in religion, finds its expression in a secularized form, in interest in belonging to peace movements and seeking a better world order on the political and social level.

Meanwhile, the Catholic has been put on the defensive in terms of his national loyalties precisely because of his ecumenicism and his worldwide religious unity. He has spent three hundred years saying that one mustn't think he isn't a good American, a good Englishman, or a good German simply because he doesn't go along with religious *Americanism* or *Anglicanism* or the *los von Rom Kulturkampf* as a result of his having a world loyalty in his relationship to the Pope and to the "one Lord, one Faith, one Baptism" essence of Catholicism, while at the same time, to make himself acceptable in the Protestant-dominated political and intellectual community, he has hammered away on what was Catholic in Thomas Jefferson's library and on how Catholic it is to be a good American.

As a result, the discerning Protestant politician was quite prepared to exploit that Catholic nationalism and he garnered, by the basketful, Irish Catholic votes on the grounds that he was opposed to the League of Nations! The sectarian

330

	Protestant, I regret to say, has until recently cared little about what became of world Christianity, but has taken keen interest in world social organization.
McDonald:	Will Herberg made the remark in that Fund for the Republic seminar on religion in 1958 that he shocked a group of students at a Catholic university when he criticized Jack Kennedy for, as he said, "bending over backwards" to prove he is four hundred per cent American.
Wright:	He was quite right; it's a characteristic Catholic pattern.
McDonald:	And it seemed to Herberg that Kennedy seemed to epitomize Catholics in general who are so anxious to show they are American that they are going to an unnecessary extreme.
Wright:	But you see the historical explanation of it. I shouldn't be at all surprised but we may some day see little colored children saying they had white ancestors, and yet being proud of their pretty color, perhaps saying, "You know, we get our particular blend of black from the fact that remotely we were white." Just as Catholics go around trying to show that Bellarmine was actually the author of whatever at the moment is considered truly American.

We're perpetually scandalized to discover that the Protestants apparently do not take these things as seriously as we do, and that they sometimes seem less interested in what is one hundred per cent American than in a wider world community of which America is but a part. Catholic Americans are sometimes shocked by this wider interest, despite the fact that it is really part of our moral heritage more than theirs!

McDonald: My own feeling would be to blame some of my fellow-editors for some of this ultranationalism, aside from the historical reasons here.

Wright: But you must remember that your fellow-editors are also readers and subject to all the pressures of the rest of the crowd. I think the responsibility of Catholic editors in this department is greater than in any other, as is that of a priest, or that of a bishop, as it is the Pope's.

The Popes seem to be meeting theirs admirably. They almost never say things that are specifically Italian. Each knows that he is an Italian and he may look like one or have the gestures of one. I am sure that he has something of a preferential charity for Italy. He should have. Nevertheless, one marvels at the manner with which they rise above their *Italianness* in their churchmanship and in their pastoral office. I think they should be our norm.

McDonald: What do you mean when you say, "editors are also readers"?

Wright: We sometimes think of the priest or the editor as being up on the mountain apart from the mob in the plain. The fact is that the editor is putting out a paper down in the plain. The further fact is that he goes home every night to the plain, back to his nationalistic relatives and friends. He goes out to lunch with business men or the fellow in the shop next door, and he is perpetually being influenced by them even as once a week he influences them. He doesn't, as a matter of fact, do his thinking up on the mountain, even if he withdraws to an ivory tower to do his writing. He is conditioned by all the things that con-

332

dition the rest of us lowly folk—even though he should strive for greater detachment.

So the priest goes into the pulpit. It would be wonderful if he came down every Sunday from Sinai and spoke to us of what God had just said to him, but the fact is that he often goes into the pulpit and talks of what we said to him at clubs or in conversations, of what we were saying all week in the office and of what was said when he went home for a day off to his mother, his brothers, and his sisters. These colonies of thought are very real.

Hence the function of the retreat movement and of like means to pull us up to Sinai for a few days every now and again, and of the liturgy to give us the mind of the Church and of eternity, thus offsetting the partisan and temporal influences all around us.

McDonald: Do you think the priest should give more explicit expression to this moral and religious solidarity that seems to be a corollary of Catholic belief?

Wright: I think he should, and I think he will if he really goes up to Sinai and listens there for a while. The theological and spiritual realities behind those corollaries are the things that we pick up on Sinai.

But, remember, while Moses was up on the mountain, the people were down on the plain doing business and worshipping the golden calf. And so, when he came down, he seemed so strange that he looked as if he had horns. Alas, often Moses speedily talks their language, as the expression is, so that he won't seem too strange and be repudiated or ignored. That's the fear of the good priest. So he talks their language, and there the compromise and dilution set in.

But the more often the theological and spiritual realities picked up on the mountain are brought down into the market place or the more frequently the crowd is brought up into the mountain, as by the Mass liturgically celebrated, as in the retreat movement, as in the worthwhile study club, the more the jargon and the coin of the market place are subordinated and the influence of the mountaintop is felt.

McDonald: It isn't so much, I suppose, that a direct harangue is needed. It's rather that the implications of this moral and religious solidarity start to become evident.

Wright: It's a process of osmosis more than it is of elocution or instruction. The love of divine things makes us divine and the love of vile things makes us vile. The more our love for these transcendent things is nurtured by the transcendental aspects of the Church—the Mass, the Sacraments, the "one Lord, one Faith, one Baptism" emphasis, the better the spirit of Sinai flourishes and the sordid mood of the market place is controlled.

McDonald: I hope there's still a place for the journalist here.

Wright: There is, of course—to record and encourage our progress and to point out the occasions when we fall away from our own ideal.

McDonald: And I suppose to keep the Papal messages clear, to keep the lines of communication open.

Wright: Surely. All this the journalist is called to do.

McDonald: Saint Thomas discussed at one point in his writings the common origin and common destiny of

	man and I suppose that is relevant in any discussion of the international community, but there again you find yourself on the mountaintop.
Wright:	But it is to the mountaintop that we have to make periodic excursions lest we talk exclusively the jargon of the crowd which is always the jargon of division. Thence, of course, comes the terrible temptation to the preacher or to the journalist. He thinks: "I must talk their language without saying the things they say." Now there's a problem!
McDonald:	Here's another problem. Father Gustave Weigel recently wrote that it seemed to him the best way for religious leaders to approach statesmen faced with moral problems is not through religious tenets but through the natural law. On the other hand, Dr. Michaelsen, the Protestant director of the School of Religion at Iowa City, says that, outside of Catholics, there seems to be no basic agreement as to what is the natural law, or whether it is acceptable. Isn't this a problem, then, that goes deeper, that goes into theories of knowledge and criteria of truth and so on?
Wright:	I think we have a couple of problems in connection with this business of the natural law. First of all, I don't think that outside of the Catholic Church many people any longer *believe* in the natural law.

I use the word *believe* because I think that's the word they would use, which shows right away that they don't even know what it is. The natural law is something that one recognizes; it is not an article of faith.

By what curious, collective astigmatism it has come to pass that men do not recognize the

335

natural law that was so clear to Cicero, to Aristotle, and to Aquinas, and to the founding fathers of America, I don't know. But the fact is, men don't. I think the probable explanation is that the founding fathers, Aristotle, Thomas Aquinas, and Cicero, whatever else they may have been, were not subjectivists, as our generation is.

There's been a rise of subjectivism not only in religion—for Protestantism historically has appealed to strongly subjective elements as opposed to what they would probably declare improperly objective or *extrinsic* elements, but you also have, of course, the rise of subjective schools of epistemology, ethics, psychology, ontology, and comparative religion. Whatever is by its every emphasis non-subjective has hard acceptance in so subjectively-conditioned a generation as ours.

McDonald: Descartes' influence is felt here.

Wright: Yes. And when we no longer talk in medicine about objective germs causing objective diseases, but more and more about psychosomatic conditions causing symptoms of disease and so on, natural law concepts do not have the cogency they had in a generation of *the laws of nature and of nature's God*. They could and should have, of course, but the subjective emphasis in every area stands in the way of clear thinking. I would think it likely that there isn't a single member of the Supreme Court as of this moment who is a natural law legal philosopher.

McDonald: There is one Catholic on the Court.

Wright: I would be quite prepared to learn that he didn't have a natural law approach to cases. Surely Mr.

336

	Murphy didn't have. Probably the most brilliant mind on the Court is Frankfurter, and he would be quite candid in saying that he has no notion of the natural law.
McDonald:	Learned Hand said much the same thing when he bowed out from the New York judiciary several years ago, that "I don't know what you mean by natural law."
Wright:	Chief Justice Holmes found the concept laughable. One of the few men in the Harvard Law School faculty in the last generation who was a natural law legal philosopher was Dean Pound.

Time was when the Massachusetts Supreme Court was graced with men who were of different political parties or creeds, but who were natural law judges. For example, Chief Justice Rugg, who was a Unitarian, was a natural law philosopher. In his decisions, he was constantly invoking the precepts or dictates of the natural law.

But at the moment the defense of the natural law has been left largely to the Church. Pope Pius XI once said to the editor of a French periodical: "I look upon the Papacy as the last defense and militant champion both of supernatural Revelation and of natural law." The Holy Father described ours as a generation which repudiates both.

They don't repudiate one, as some Catholic polemicists assert, because they have repudiated the other. But the same thing that made them repudiate one, helped them repudiate the other. They haven't given up the natural law because they lost the Faith. The subjectivism that weakened the Faith also undermined the natural law

337

concept. Objective considerations—supernatural and natural—went out the window together once subjectivism gained the day.

What, therefore, to do in order to get a bridge-head with a generation that has repudiated the natural law as well as the ancient Faith, though continuing to call themselves Christians? How to reach them? What's the ground on which to stand? It's not the acceptance of the natural law that we have in common with these separated brethren. Nor is it the natural law that Catholics can now think of as our bond with them. Ed Marciniak probably said the correct thing when he remarked that the bond we have with them is not the natural law, it's charity.

McDonald: Maritain has said that repeatedly.

Wright: Of course, we can always have as an optimistic objective the hope that we can perhaps reach common natural law agreements again. Bliss Perry used to say something like this: "If in my fellow-feeling and in your charity we can stick with one another long enough, can keep the dialogue going long enough to arrive at agreements which don't involve me in supernatural beliefs or involve you in heresy, then we may have achieved a foundation on which to build some order."

But even that is a long way from agreement on the natural law. Outside the Catholic community any widespread grasp of natural law has gone totally down the drain.

Any great intellectual agreement is at the moment, in my opinion, illusory. We're using the same words to mean totally different things.

338

	We use the word *freedom* to say totally different things.
McDonald:	Or *authority*.
Wright:	We certainly don't mean the same thing by *authority*. We certainly don't mean the same thing by *Faith*. We don't mean the same thing by *brotherhood of man*. We don't mean the same thing by *fatherhood of God*.

We assuredly don't mean the same thing by *children of God*. We are not all God's *children*. We are all God's *creatures* in a natural-law concept, but that is quite another matter. Some of those creatures have received the spirit of adoption by which they are enabled to say, "Abba, Pater", and therefore become His *children*. Some of His creatures through no fault of their own, and some through fault of their own, are not children of God, but only creatures of God.

When we meet and we say we are all *children of the same God*, we are in danger of defrauding one another, and we delay a showdown which, if it be in all charity, need not result in bitterness or non-cooperation, but might easily result in fruitful dialogue on the level of mutual sympathy and forebearance.

McDonald:	Father Weigel raised this question at a recent Catholic Press Association convention. He said: "Why meet with one another at all, since the Catholic cannot hope to convert the Protestant, and the Protestant certainly cannot expect the Catholic to join with him in some higher form of unified Protestantism. . . ." Father Weigel then gave the answer in his talk: it's because we have to live together.

339

Wright: We have to use the same public buses, the same public library. Therefore, we have to reach a practical formula under which we can use those things which are in common while having few ideas in common.

I think it's dangerous to focus on such things as the birth control argument, or on any aspect of sex, because there are overtones there of highly charged tension, passion, even guilt, and therefore both sides get worked up more rapidly and the dialogue breaks down, whether it's on birth control or companionate marriage . . . or filthy pictures.

It seems to me that the general problem has to be faced in a more calm and quite literally cold area so that we can there discern the principles which can then transfer to the more heated moral arguments.

It's in another area that we shall best face our differences and where they may be more fruitfully approached. Suppose we could agree for a generation, or a century, to direct our attention away from these differences except where they involve police action. We might say, in effect, to our neighbors: "If you find us actually hard at work nullifying the actions of the Congress, or rulings of the courts, as your relatives do in the South, arrest us by all means in the name of precisely what you find us doing. And if we find you handing corrupting stuff to our people, we shall arrest you, certainly. But in the meantime, for purposes of this Catholic-Protestant dialogue which is needed in order to restore something like Christian order to the world, suppose we leave off mutual suspicion and recrimination long enough to face the basic questions in the dialogue—What is God? What think ye of Christ?—before we come to grips with questions of a peripheral kind."

If we could only agree, as the Christians we profess to be, that our rights are entirely subordinate to the discovery of the will of God. If we met occasionally to ask ourselves what the words in that sentence mean—*God*, *God's will*, and *discover*—and these bring us face to face with the ultimate problems of ethics and epistemology as well as theology, isn't that a worthwhile dialogue? It is certainly the inevitable one.

Saint Paul said God made us out of one that we may dwell on the whole face of the earth to seek Him. That's the essential thing.

McDonald: Do you think American theologians are ready to converse on this level as they do in Germany, Catholics there with Lutherans? We seem rather cautious about doing so here.

Wright: We're cautious for good reasons, but justified caution does not require total non-cooperation. We're cautious because in these matters there are such titanic values involved, values with eternal implications. Then, too, as I have tried to say, we are really so far apart, so very far apart—and this fact imposes caution.

Caution is entirely called for, but some effort at dialogue is not less called for. The dialogue, however, must be on the ultimates, rather than on the proximates, because it is the ultimates which have become obscured.

We tend to assume that on the ultimates we all

341

agree, and that it is only on these little practical applications—birth control, a Catholic President, etc.—that we disagree. Nothing could be further from the truth. We're more likely to agree on some of these than we are on the ultimates.

XXVI

Our Patriotic Debt to Our Dead

Modern patriotism makes the nation the object of its most passionate and proud devotion. But other forms of civic piety than national patriotism alone still happily survive. Among these more ancient forms of patriotism is that by which people are individually moved and collectively united by an intense local love of that city from which they come or which for them is home.

The Apostle Paul was proud to be a Jew, a Hebrew of the Hebrews, but we catch echoes of his special patriotic pride in his home town when he speaks of his native city. "I am Saul of Tarsus, no mean city!" boasted the man who came to loom so large in great Jerusalem itself and one day would dominate even mighty Rome.[1]

Paul's patriotic attachment to Tarsus has its counterpart in the pride of millions in their home cities, a pride which is more conscious in some than are their ties with the larger societies which have politically engulfed our towns, as the modern national state has tended to absorb the cities. Certain cities have kept a powerful hold on the patriotism of their sons and daughters. Once I heard a girl answer "Naples" when someone asked what was her country. Some people are Parisians more than Frenchmen; they are loyal to France, but love Paris. Not long ago a shrewd writer commented that it wasn't so much his religious loyalty to Rome as his sentimental attachment to New York that made Al Smith somehow *alien* and unintelligible to many Americans. We all know people who

This address was delivered at the Worcester Memorial Auditorium, Worcester, Massachusetts, on September 25, 1958, at the rededication ceremonies of the auditorium.

would rather be Dubliners or Corkonians than Irish; whose warmest memories go back to London more than to England, to Quebec rather than Canada; or who will join in any criticism of the United States, but cut you dead if you pass remarks about Texas, or Brooklyn, or South Boston.

Perhaps the strongest patriotism ever to center around a single city was that of the Athenians in the age of Pericles two thousand and five hundred years ago. The patriotic love for their city of those Greeks who were also Athenians included all the emotions, interests, and obligations, spiritual and cultural, by which a civilized man is bound to the whole society of which he is a part; Athenian patriotism was focused exclusively on the City of Athens. The patriotism of ancient Athens was no mere sentimental or nostalgic attachment; it was the all-time model of perfect patriotic love for one's city.

Athenian patriotism found its most sublime expression in a speech given by Pericles in ancient Athens under circumstances somewhat like to those which bring us together tonight in Worcester.[2] The neo-classical style of our magnificent Memorial Auditorium recalls the very architecture of which Athens was so proud and is in the tradition of the superb public buildings which Pericles built, sometimes amid the moaning and groanings of taxpayers, to make so beautiful the Athens of twenty-five centuries ago.

But it is the fact that our municipal auditorium commemorates the men whom Worcester has given to the Armed Services and to the defense of our land which chiefly calls to mind the oration of Pericles that summed up the elements of patriotic love for one's city. At the rededication of an auditorium built in a style reminiscent of ancient Athens, and serving as a symbol of our patriotic debt to those who brought honor in war to the name of Worcester, I cannot do better than recall the words by which Pericles taught the Athenians how to prove their patriotic piety toward the dead and their patriotic pride in their city.

True, Pericles spoke as a pagan. The element of revenge

which was part of the spirit in which his heroes fought and died is one which we, taught by the Hebrew prophets and the Christian Gospel, must always purge from our hearts and motives, even when we go to war. But much of the idealism that Pericles praised in the brave men who defended ancient Athens was born of a spirit which we rejoice to find present in our heroes, too, and which every Hebrew hope and Christian faith can only applaud, praying that such a spirit of valor will always be strong among us.

Pericles paid tribute in his memorial oration to the valor of the men and boys who loved Athens so much that they could not bear to think of her in enemy hands, and so died in her defense. He said: "they thought fit to act boldly . . . thus choosing to die resisting, rather than to live submitting. So died these men as became Athenians."[3]

Then turning to the living relatives, friends, and neighbors gathered to mourn the dead of Athens as you are met tonight to commemorate Worcester's heroes, Pericles said, "You, their survivors, must determine to have as unfaltering a resolution in the field" as did these heroes. "Not content with ideas derived only from words about why it is good to defend your city . . . you must yourselves realize the worth of Athens and feed your eyes on her from day to day, till love of her fills your hearts; and then, when all her greatness shall break upon you, you must reflect that it was by courage, by sense of duty, and by a keen feeling of honor in action that men became capable of accomplishing all this." "These [men and their virtues] take as your models, and remember that happiness is the fruit of freedom, and freedom is the fruit of valor; then you will never decline the dangers of war."[4]

Pericles' praise of military courage and his passionate reminder that happiness is born of freedom and that freedom is bought with bravery carry timely lessons for us in days so rightly appalled by the horrors of war, but often wrongly tempted by the fallacies of pacifism.

All of us wish we could live by a wisdom less martial than

that of Pericles. Surely a priest is the first to wish it were not necessary to maintain the armed vigilance that remains the patriotic price of our freedom as citizens and our happiness as humans. We all pray—or should, as a priest assuredly does— that saner, more moral times may come in which it will be possible to let down our guard without ungrateful treason to our war-dead.

But that time is not yet, nor should the devout—though our religious piety be more refined than that of the pagan Greek— be tempted to put aside yet the prudent, patriotic spirit of military preparedness that Pericles warned ancient Athens always to keep alive. Religion does not require us to be political fools—and it would be supreme folly, at this stage in the emergence of the reign of law over recourse to arms, if we were to de-emphasize unduly those militant aspects of patriotism which pacifism pretends to find unholy.

It was not because he loved war, but because he loved Athens, that Pericles held up to living patriots the example of those who had died resisting, rather than live submitting, and bade their survivors to have as unfaltering a resolution in the field as those soldiers had manifested who, loving Athens more than self, and virtue more than life, had died, if not gladly at least courageously, in order that Athens might be free, and beautiful, and honorable, and happy.

We live in times that are avid in their desire for peace. That desire has been inspired by a religious vision more clear than that of pagan antiquity; it is impossible to have lived in Christian times and not be more impatient with the evil of war than Pericles could ever have been. Our desire for peace has been further intensified by sheer weariness with the demands of war and sheer disgust with its brutalities.

Such times and such desires properly make us prefer to work for peace rather than prepare for war, but we would be great fools if, while striving with all our hearts to make possible the ways of peace, we were to forget the sad, but sane, lessons of the patriotism of those who died in war.

It is good that we can use this splendid building for music, laughter, and song, the words and the works of peace; but it would be criminal madness to forget not only that this building is their memorial, but that it would be impossible either to build or to use it were it not for the citizens who were willing to risk the dangers of war, understanding that, even in days of war so dreadful, it is not always true that peace at any price is good.

Pacifism is always attractive to the sensitive of spirit, but there has been much nonsense talked about the idealism of pacifists and the alleged moral blindness of those who recognize that wars are sometimes still imposed upon us by moral obligation as well as by military necessity. We are all bound by religion and humanity to be workers for peace; devout and decent people have always preferred peace to war. Pagan philosophers, Hebrew prophets, and Christian saints have been unanimous in their prayerful hope for a society in which there will be no war, and have placed upon the consciences of us all the obligation to work, unrelentingly and uncompromisingly, for the day when men "shall change their swords into plowshares and their spears into pruning-hooks, and they shall not learn war any more."[5]

These prayers of the best of men and efforts of most of men have, in fact, borne fruit. As we have grown more fraternal under the influence of our philosophers and the spiritual direction of our saints, peace has become much more the normal condition of mankind than people sometimes realize. The teenage gang fights we have been reading about strike us as outrageous, hardly believable, because we are no longer accustomed, as men were for centuries, to fighting as the daily occupation of mankind. A small police force spends a lot of time in the relatively routine, peaceful business of directing traffic and maintaining order among friendly citizens, instead of there being whole regiments of police all over the place protecting people from one another, as in many lands was necessary for many centuries. We are able to own personal property without maintaining private armies to protect us, as used to be necessary even in relatively civilized communities. Skirmishes go on more or less constantly between the great powers, but now our diplomats are able to carry on the cold war of debate and of bargaining for years, where once our generals would have been exchanging gunfire in a matter of days or even hours. Peace becomes steadily less a Utopian dream and more a blessed reality.

But it is not so much to pacifists that we are indebted for this happy progress as it is to workers for peace who were willing, if need be, to risk the dangers of war rather than see destroyed the very institutions and ideals which make peace possible. Can you imagine how much worse would be the condition of the world today, bad as it sometimes seems, if pacifists, rather than workers for peace prepared to fight for their ideals, had been able to have their way when the heartbreaking but world-building decisions had to be made concerning the declaration of the wars to which Worcester men have gone, from the days of the Revolution that made America possible, through the days of the Civil War that made America united and strong, to the days of the dreadful World Wars which kept America free? If the pacifists had had their way, it is appalling to imagine what would be the condition of mankind made slaves by unrebuked despots, divided by rival tyrants, and made stupid by the brutal dominion, so hostile to intellect and to freedom alike, of the Nazi, the Fascist, or the Red dictator. That is why, as had been noted, there has always been a historic distinction between the worker for peace and the pacifist.

Never forget that the same Good Book which tells us to work for peace, reminding us of the Prince of Peace Who said, "Blessed are the peacemakers, for they shall be called the children of God", is the same book that quotes from Christ this lesson for our times: "When the strong man, fully armed, guards his courtyard, his property is undisturbed. But if a stronger than he attacks and overcomes him, he will take away his whole armor on which he was depending, and will divide his spoils."[6]

It is holy to use this hall, dedicated to strong men who guarded our courtyards, in order to work for peace; it would be hypocrisy, as well as madness, to use a hall made possible by peace defended with arms in order to preach a pacifism that mocks the faith of the dead and imperils the freedom of the living.

On the other hand, it is precisely because our warriors, while willing to fight, would have preferred to be workers for peace, that we best honor their memories with joyful works of peace rather than melancholy tokens of war. To remind us of our daily debt to our heroes, memorial buildings like this are built. But these are not the only or even the best dwelling places of their memories. Pericles, praising the heroes of Athens, said: "The whole earth is the monument of brave men; and their story is not one graven on stone of their native earth, but lives on everywhere, without visible symbol, woven into the stuff of other men's lives."[7]

So we, with even better understanding than that of Pericles, should express our gratitude to the dead by increasing everywhere the spiritual and civic good of the community that was the object of their patriotic pride. So, wherever good things are done in the faith and freedom they made possible, there the blessed dead should be daily remembered. Wherever true things are taught or said in the faith and freedom they made possible, there the blessed dead should be daily thanked. Wherever beautiful things are admired with the faith and freedom they made possible, there the blessed dead should be daily beloved.

The loving generosity that impels us to memorialize the heroes who have defended our patriotic patrimony should prompt us to increase the opportunities of the living to have better access to the good, the true, and the beautiful as the best memorials to the dead.

349

So in the spirit that built this auditorium a quarter century ago, we should contribute to the works of healing and of research in our Worcester hospitals, to the support of our Worcester charitable agencies, to the perfection of our Worcester schools and libraries, to the adornment of our Worcester churches, to the enrichment of our Worcester museums and the improvement unto greater beauty of our Worcester parks and Worcester streets, all as the most perfect way to perpetuate the memory of our Worcester heroes.

One wishes that the good money of good people had always been used to provide such increased blessings for the living as the best tribute to the dead, rather than so often wasted on the ill-considered and ill-kept war memorials that, in their neglect, so speedily cease to grace the memory of the dead and soon stand as a disgrace to the neighborhood out of which the dead came. It is shocking to see in many corners of the city today war memorials covered with evidences of neglect on the part of the old and vandalism on the part of the young, shameful reproaches to our patriotism, symbols of our unworthiness and ingratitude, rather than our fidelity to the ideals of the dead and our respect for their memories.

But if, instead of wasting pennies on cheap memorials that so easily turn to trash, we were always to act in the spirit of those who built this auditorium, then grateful dollars, gladly given, would make possible new wonders in our hospitals, greater good deeds in our charitable agencies, better stores of books and improved facilities in our libraries and schools, organs to give music more noble in our churches and shrines to nourish the pieties that inspire heroism and patriotism, treasures more lovely in our museums, and flowers, fountains, and quiet places in our parks. All these would daily tell the dead that we remember and teach the living why they must be grateful to the dead. All this would be done, and unworthy blemishes would be removed from the face of our city, if the instinct to memorialize the blessed dead were always obeyed in the spirit of those who built this auditorium.

In this memorial auditorium, the type and symbol of the monuments an intelligent people erect to those whom they remember with grateful affection, all things should be kept clean, fresh, and perfectly functioning, effective and beautiful, that those who come after us may see in the way we kept this building the proof of our worthiness of those in whose memory it was built. This building should be in the daily life of our city a reminder to our resolution to be as unfaltering in the field of battle as were our soldiers, should occasion again require. It should be a gathering place for growth among our citizens of the goodness, truth, and beauty, which are the values served by the heroic dead, values bound up with those works of peace which promote the common good of living. This building should be a proof that in modern Worcester the piety and patriotism that were the glory of ancient Athens remain the strength of a proud city and the joy of a peaceful people.

XXVII

Peace, the Work of Justice

The theme of our deliberations, *Peace, the Work of Justice*, the motto of our late, so lamented Pope Pius XII, *Opus Iustitiae Pax*, illustrates the manner in which this great Pope, though dead, will continue to teach us for long years to come.[1] *Etsi mortuus, adhuc loquitur!*

The Holy Father, who spoke so often and so eloquently of peace, is now dead. Deprived of his living example of the personal charity which he brought to the problem of promoting peace, we are given a sad but salutary opportunity to consider more soberly the objective content of the late Holy Father's reflections, suggestions, and positive teachings on questions of peace and war.

One result of such sober consideration of the pronouncements of the Pope of Peace, (in all their objectivity and, now that he is dead, of study of these apart from the great warmth and color that his personal charity and profoundly spiritual optimism gave to them while he was alive) is that one becomes perhaps more acutely aware of the radical distinction in papal teaching and in the very nature of things between the respective parts and functions in the effort to promote a peaceful world order of two essential, indispensable, but distinct virtues: the virtue of *charity* and the virtue of *justice*.

The personal example and the eloquent pronouncements of the late Holy Father made us all, I think, aware as never before of the tremendous need and mighty role of charity in the promotion of peace. His own charity and his passionate exposition

---

This address was delivered at the Sheraton Park Hotel, Washington, D.C., on October 24, 1958, on the occasion of the thirty-first annual conference of the Catholic Association for International Peace.

of the social and spiritual potential of charity opened millions of hearts and minds to the possibility of peace, the progress toward peace, the universal desire for peace, and even the hope that a peaceful world order may be close at hand. To this dramatization of the part of charity, the Holy Father brought a prophetic touch so contagious in its optimism, so enthusiastic in its vision, that even the most reactionary, discouraged, or even misanthropic must occasionally have felt that, with God in His Heaven and His Church in the hands of leadership so buoyant and so confident, all must soon be right with the world if only divine charity, so incarnate and contagious in this human Vicar of God, could catch fire on ever wider human fronts and spread in beneficent, life-giving epidemic.

Other than reactionaries and misanthropes, people of instinctively generous heart and magnanimous, venturesome mind found the Holy Father's emphasis on the creative, reconciling, constructive power of charity a most welcome inspiration to their own idealism and a spur to their own confidence that a new age of peace must be in the making, perhaps even a matter of just so many prayers, just so many penances, just so many more dynamic acts of charity away. Surely this was the heart-warming effect that certain of the Holy Father's allocutions had on some of us, and that the constant tenor of the flaming charity in his discourses and documents on peace and war, as well as in his very personality, tended to have at all times, even during the most dark days of these fratricidal, frightening nineteen years.

No one could have been insensible to the Pope's supernatural confidence in the social power of charity to pacify, to unite, and to inspire even the most bitterly divided peoples after reading such allocutions as his Easter Message of this very year, with its Paschal themes of Light, Life, Hope, and Peace; or the almost incredibly youthful and optimistic address on our age as "the springtime of history", in which only last March the aging Holy Father spoke to the youth of Italian

353

Catholic Action about the tranquility and peace which should be in their hearts, the joy of living in their souls, the untroubled enthusiasm and full confidence with which they should live in a world torn apart by horrible wars, confident that the *winter* of history is now passed, that *summer* is near, and that men, not only aware of their increasing interdependence, but also of their marvelous unity, will now find in the charity of the Mystical Body of Christ the obvious solution to the problems which have so long held the world in anguish! This same incandescent spirit of charity, making one almost ashamed of so much as a misgiving about the immediacy of the reign of divine peace and human good will, shone through countless such documents as the Holy Father's letter to the International Military Pilgrimage to Lourdes and his 1944 Christmas radio message to the world, as brilliantly as it did from his very eyes and his instinctively friendly gestures.

Those who love peace can well be pardoned if they found in the spirit of charity of this most passionate lover of peace a sometimes *heady* inspiration to their own most ardent hopes and a confirmation of their own sanguine proposals.

But in this sobering period during which we now recall, in all their objectivity, the words of the Pope now dead, sterner realities, never absent from either the doctrine or the personal preoccupations of the Pope alive, force themselves more urgently on our attention. They make us mindful that the spirit of charity, so incandescent and so contagious in the Chief Shepherd of Christendom, was matched at all times, as matched it must be in integral Christian doctrine and the very nature of things, by a rigorous sense of justice.

Peace is the fruit and the flower of *charity*, but, alas, peace involves, by strict necessity, the painful, persevering, sometimes discouraging *work of justice*. From the beginning of his pontificate to the end, Pope Pius XII prayed and pleaded in that spirit of charity without which peace can have no organic, life-giving soul; but all his pontificate was dominated and his

354

unrelenting efforts were motivated by the basic recognition, set forth in his motto, that without the complex, sometimes uninspiring work of justice, peace has no possibility of an organized, life-bearing, vigorous body. *Opus iustitiae pax*!

These sober reflections, one might almost call them second thoughts on an inspiring, even exhilarating, pontificate, suggest the need that lovers of peace, like the members of the Catholic Association for International Peace, reassess the respective parts of charity and justice in the attainment of world order and in the pursuit of that peace which is the happy by-product, not the cause, of such an order. That is the first point I would urge as our deliberations begin.

Against the background of this always real and sometimes sharp distinction between the respective demands and functions of charity and justice, one suggests that we must clarify our thinking with respect to certain related but distinct contributions of the Christian citizen to the promotion of peace. If we are deeply and effectively aware of the role of charity in the creation of the moral climate in which alone a peaceful political order can flourish, then our prayers will be at once more fervent and more effective. We will follow the example of Pope Pius XII in making peace a constant and dominant intention in our prayers, our spiritual reflections, and our charitable works. Far from despising the need and the powerful part of prayer, we will multiply our intercessions increasingly and will storm Heaven, each of us alone and all of us together, in petition for that peace which the world cannot give because it does not possess it. We shall regret, as deeply as some of our brethren deplore and condemn, the unfortunate absence, not to say scandalous exclusion, of prayer from the programs of assemblies, organizations, or agencies which are appointed or which profess to promote the political, economic, or cultural conditions of a peaceful world society; indeed, we shall regret such indifference to prayer for reasons more profound than those of our brethren whose condemnation of the absence of prayer from peacemaking bodies sometimes seems based on prejudices more closely related to partisan commitments of a human kind than to prayerful considerations of a spiritual order. We shall be no less mindful than any of our most *realistic* brethren of that wisdom which from apostolic times has impelled Christians to put not their trust in princes or statesmen, if only because our ultimate reliance must at all times and in all things be on God and that grace of God to which prayer gives us such claim as we may have.[2]

But, still in accordance with the example of the prayerful and luminously charitable Pope Pius XII, we shall not be misunderstood when we insist that prayers for peace are not enough.

No peace will ever drop from Heaven ready made. God does not normally intervene miraculously in the social and political movements by which peace is made possible and the conditions for peace are created and sustained. God works through secondary causes, and we must be His instruments, conscious and untiring, if the world is to be bent to that Will in which is our peace.[3] Too many of us take it for granted that we have done all we need or can do when we sue Heaven for peace in our more or less fervent prayers. This is not merely hopeless politics, it is bad theology. Prayer has its best chance of being efficacious when it is implemented and supplemented by consecrated action on the part of those who pray. That is what the spiritual writers mean when they bid us to pray as if everything depended on God, and work as if everything depended on us.

Let not the devout be deceived; no peace will ever drop from Heaven ready made. No less than war, indeed far more, peace calls for heroic strategy, untiring vigils, generous sacrifice, and an all-out effort. Peace is the work of justice; so proclaimed the Holy Father's motto and the word to be emphasized was the word *work*.

Something of the magnitude of the work to be done in

obedience to justice, as well as the prayers to be said, before we shall have so organized the human political community that divine charity will adequately function as its abiding organic soul, may be guessed from a preview of the titanic problems to be considered even in this brief annual conference. The inevitable human rivalries, the real jurisdictional conflicts and the almost infinitely varied prudential judgments involved in the questions of space exploration and control, far from immediately wiping out our accumulation of inherited and new international, interracial, and interclass tensions, may not merely momentarily add to these further problems of another kind, but even further complications of another degree within the existing problems. Your discussion of the problem of *theology and modern warfare* will bring you face to face with practical issues, for the patient facing of which all the charity in Heaven and on earth will be needed, but which no amount of charity, in the absence of the other virtues and of the gifts of the Holy Ghost, will resolve. Even the most superficial analysis of that international economic common good and international political common good, the study of which you contemplate, will remind you at every turn of problems in justice and equity which we can sustain, but cannot solve by charity alone, even though charity must inspire, motivate, and inform all the many virtues and works, above all the work of justice, by which, through tortuous, persevering generations, perhaps centuries, we shall press forward toward the peace which is the fruit and flower of charity, but the rigorous work of justice.

There is one final and delicate suggestion which, I fear, is further required by a re-focused study of the respective roles of charity and justice in the promotion of a peaceful world order as a result of the sober reassessment of the dual emphasis of papal teaching on charity and justice. This further suggestion is one for which I, at least, am indebted in part to a point made by Angier Biddle Duke in an address to the Council of

357

Catholic Men in the Diocese of Raleigh last spring, but which also follows from a realistic reading of papal pronouncements on peace. It is a point which one has felt bound, painfully but inescapably, to make in recent discussions on problems of peace and war, even though in doing so one has been obliged to brave the paradoxical, yet unmistakable, wrath of the pacifists.

Speaking precisely on papal principles of peace and work for peace, Biddle Duke points out that there is an historic distinction between the worker for peace and the pacifist. It goes without saying that there is also an historic distinction between the Christian soldier, defending his native land or a wider human good, and the militarist. Such distinctions are basic to papal policy and clearly present in the premises of papal pronouncements. This is true whether we consider the paternal, sympathetic insight into the destiny of the loyal soldier which continues to reveal itself even in documents or allocutions condemning without qualification the intentions, spirit, and actions of warlords, warmongers, and militarists generally, or whether we note the reserve with which the Holy See necessarily touches on the contentions of pacifists or even acknowledges in word or deed the justice of specific historic cases of recourse to arms, even while pleading and working, with passion second to none, for the elimination of war and the promotion of peace.

Here, too, we are face to face with one of the requirements of the clear and necessary distinction between the respective natures and functions of the virtues of *charity* and of *justice*. The virtue of patriotism is one of the subordinate but clear parts of the virtue of justice; the tragic military necessities which patriotism continues, at least on occasion, to impose are as pathetic, as heartbreaking, and as regrettable as any pacifist cares to call them. Unfortunately, it is not yet possible for theologians, mindful not only of the realities that some pacifists profess to find unencompassed by moral idealism, but also of the Christian ideals which sometimes make such stern and heroic demands, to deny the possibility that justice may require of us duties from which charity would prefer to shrink. It goes without saying that the requirements of justice and charity, perfectly reconciled in God, are even among imperfect men capable of ultimate synthesis; I am merely recalling how, on occasion, the sense of justice still must make demands, not merely in the name of military necessity but even in the name of Christian morality, which momentarily may appall the sensitive spirit of charity. It is neither good morality nor good politics to pretend differently.

Hence the urgent need for workers for peace who will avoid the theoretically dubious and practically perilous extremes of pacifism, as well as for valiant men (in the pattern of that *strong man* of whom Jesus spoke who, "fully armed, guards his courtyard, his property undisturbed"), as opposed to the militarists and like *strong-arm men* who cannot possibly merit the blessing Jesus gave the peacemakers.[4]

Hence, too, the need that we bear with greater patience, greater than that of some pacifists, and with great understanding, greater than that of any militarists, the necessity that time, events, and the grace of God help clarify some of the issues which have cast into new and unfamiliar forms the old problems of the morality of a just war and the means to the defense of the common good, including the tremendous progress toward peaceful world order which has, in simple fact, already been made and which may easily be forfeited if, seduced by illusory hopes of peaceful charity, we fail to meet the stern but saving duties of justice—and the more heroic charity which prompts us to risk life itself to save honor, to vindicate faith, or to preserve freedom.

A case in point may well be the sometimes bewildering contrast between the positions taken by good men on certain of the peace-or-war issues of the hour. For example, *America* magazine carried an editorial that deserves attention at a conference such as this and that suggests the necessity for a sharp distinction between pacifists and workers for peace.[5]

Many sensitive souls were no doubt greatly moved by Dr. Albert Schweitzer's well-publicized appeal to the nuclear powers. From his remote home in French Equatorial Africa, this respected humanitarian with the voice of a prophet called upon both East and West to cease testing nuclear weapons and to renounce their use. He urged them to this course in the name of their responsibility to their own peoples and to all mankind. Such an appeal was bound to awake a sympathetic echo in the hearts of troubled men in the free nations now embarked on a program of nuclear armaments.

This much can be said for Dr. Schweitzer's message: it dramatizes a conscience problem which must be met. It would be an injustice to the moral sentiment of Western civilization to suggest that the ghastly potentialities of nuclear warfare do not stir grave doubts about the rectitude of our course. World opinion is entitled to guidance from its moral leaders if these doubts are not to gnaw away at the inner fabric of our society and undermine our capacity to resist Soviet aggression.

In this respect the Easter sermon of Archbishop Godfrey of Westminster provides more valid moral norms than the appeal to the heart which marks the call of Doctor Schweitzer. In Great Britain, during the past months, as that country has been carrying on H-bomb experiments in the Pacific, public opinion has manifested more than ordinary disquiet as to the moral issues involved. To meet this rising demand for peace of mind, the ranking English Catholic prelate laid down a few essential points. These points are valid for American as well as for English Catholics.

Three key principles emerged from Archbishop Godfrey's sermon: 1) In a war of self-defense the use of even the most powerful nuclear weapons against a legitimate target can be justified; 2) testing of such weapons is therefore permissible; 3) but the use of indiscriminate nuclear weapons on areas preponderantly civilian is unlawful. One portion of the Archbishop's sermon deserves explicit quotation. "We do not believe," he said, "that it has yet been conclusively shown that there can be no conceivable circumstance in which there might be a legitimate target for even the most powerful nuclear weapon." Obviously, if the use of such weapons is permissible, it is also lawful to test them, particularly if the testing diminishes the amount of dangerous fallout.

This is no blanket endorsement of nuclear warfare but a carefully weighed guide to consciences facing a specific situation in a given period of time. In the context of the debate now going forward in English Catholic circles and in Britain generally, the Archbishop's meaning is unmistakable. The present nuclear armaments program of the Western Allies is not inherently repugnant to the principles of Christian morality or of natural ethics. Provided that earnest and not merely perfunctory efforts are made to achieve general disarmament agreements and an easing of tension, a group of nations threatened by a common danger is not obliged to disarm unilaterally.

Archbishop Godfrey will get no thanks from those who put their confidence in the humanitarian pacifism of Doctor Schweitzer's latest message. From the limited perspective of the present, it may, indeed, be difficult to discern which of the two stands would be more conducive to real peace—that which urged the lamb to lie down with the lion, or that which preserved intact the inherent right and duty of self-defense. If the past, however, is any guide, no real security can be anticipated where freedom is synonymous with weakness.[6]

I submit that Archbishop Godfrey was speaking in the tradition of papal teaching; I submit that he was speaking not at all as a militarist, but as a worker for peace. I urge that he may well be—probably is—a man deeply persuaded that the case for war grows daily less cogent; that the prospects for a peaceful world grow daily more bright; that the Gospel, the grace of God, the better instincts of mankind and even the dynamic of the future are all entirely on the side of the steady substitution of rule by peaceful law for rule by violent war; that the obligation of every enlightened person, certainly of every devout Christian, is to work for peace and to place every conceivable obstacle in the way of war—but also that there may still come times, please God less often and please God not at all, when moral obligations of justice and charity as well as military necessity, may require us to take up arms for the defense of the common good in a world where not all have accepted either the Gospel or the rule of reason.

Profile of Christ
In the Church of Boston

The Holy Catholic Church is the living presence of Christ in history; it is Christ at work, Christ suffering, Christ sanctifying, Christ gloriously bringing to pass His Kingdom on earth.

So is the Church in every diocese; so has it been in Boston through all these hundred and fifty years since the Vicar of Christ established this mother diocese of all New England and appointed John Cheverus its first bishop.[1]

Christ has worked triumphantly, He has suffered patiently, He has sanctified and pursued His divine purposes in all the five High Priests of this diocese who have succeeded John Cheverus,[2] and something of the way that God has here been glorified by them and by their work in the Church of Boston and in Christ present in that Church is suggested, as by a symbol, in the august, thrilling presence in this resplendent cathedral this morning of two cardinals of the Holy Roman Church, both sons of the Church in Boston, and by the presence among us of shepherds of the five million faithful people in the many dioceses of the area once comprising the single diocese of Boston.

But the mysteries by which Christ has glorified God in this Holy Church of Boston, sorrowful mysteries of suffering, joyful mysteries of divine labors, glorious mysteries of holy triumphs, have not been lived out and exemplified in the lives and works of our prelates alone, as they would be the first to proclaim.

This sermon was preached at the Holy Cross Cathedral, Boston, on December 8, 1958.

"There are different kinds of gifts, though it is the same spirit who gives them, just as there are different kinds of service, though it is the same Lord we serve, and different manifestations of power, though it is the same God who manifests His power everywhere in all of us. . . . [For] the one bread makes us one body [of Christ], though we are many in number. . . ."³

And so, when Saint Paul speaks of the power of God at work in us, he means in all of us, prelates, priests, religious, faithful people, and even some who, in manner akin to certain sages of the world outside His chosen fold of the Old Law and the New, have been the agents of His actual graces and helped us to carry out His purpose beyond all our hopes and dreams, so that He might be glorified as He has been in the history of the Church of Boston and in the Christ at work in that Church.

The profile of Christ as it is manifested in the Church of Boston includes, then, features reflecting the urbane patience of Bishop Cheverus, the forbearance of Bishop Fenwick, the fortitude in the face of adversity of Bishop Fitzpatrick, the mellow wisdom of Archbishop Williams, the Roman dignity of Cardinal O'Connell, the consuming zeal of our reigning Cardinal-Archbishop. But it includes also the reflections of God's power at work in all the devout men and women, even children, who are or have been members of Christ in the Church of Boston. The names of many have become part of the secular as well as sacred history of our part of America; the names of most are lost in the anonymous throng of Christ's people in these parts. A few are recalled on the monuments which perpetuate their glorious part; some lie in unmarked graves, well known, however, to God and His Recording Angel.

The composite profile of Christ in the Church of Boston includes traces of the persevering piety of the Penobscots and Passamaquoddies to whom the first French missionaries preached the faith and who later welcomed Matignon and Cheverus with Latin hymns sung with Indian fervor; of the tenacious hope of the Arcadians still strong among us; of the diverse and divinely appointed virtues of the French from Quebec and from France itself, of the Irish who brought their faith here and the Anglo-Saxons who so often found here their faith; and of the virtues of the Portuguese, the Italians, Poles, Lithuanians, Germans, Lebanese and other Eastern peoples, the Negro, and latterly the Spanish-speaking Catholics, all of whom have brought to the portraiture of Christ among us their respective spiritual characteristics and shadings.

Christ the Divine Teacher has spoken among us in the eloquence of our cardinals, bishops, and priests. But He has also borne His witness to the truth on the lips of laymen learned in reason for the faith that is in them and through the pens of devoted women eager to use the written word to tell of the Word Divine. Echoes of His teachings have reached us through those commissioned to preach and to teach among us, as Virgil Barber, James Fitton, Father James Gillis, the Abbé Hogan, and a host of great priests, but also through laymen who have taken seriously the energies of Confirmation and the wisdom that came with their baptismal salt, and so have written as did John Boyle O'Reilly or Orestes Brownson, or have proclaimed the Gospel in the forum and the market place as did David Goldstein, or have explored and expounded the truth in lecture hall or classroom as have the lay professors, seconding the efforts of our hard-pressed religious and sisters in our schools and colleges, or carrying something of a Catholic Christian love of learning into educational systems all around us, as did Emma Forbes Cary, Louis Mercier, Thomas Dwight, Jeremiah Ford, and as do the growing number of public school teachers and Catholic scholars who serve so valiantly the cause of truth in its many forms and on so many fronts.[4]

Christ the Divine Missionary we see at work in Cheverus, and the later voluntary exiles among the clergy of a score of nations who came here to spread the Sacred Word, but also in James Anthony Walsh who went from here to found the mighty Maryknoll, in the thousands of boys and girls who quit their homes here to herald Christ to the ends of the earth; in Father Jim Hennessey and legions like him.[5] Not less does the ardor of Christ the Missionary glow in the sacrifices and works of the multitudes of laymen and women who have helped so long and so lovingly as promoters of the Propagation of the Faith, or members of the missionary guilds or contributors in myriad ways to Boston's tremendous missionary effort.

The hidden life of Christ has been relived in the secret anxieties and prayers of the shepherds of the Boston flock through the years of temptations that came from persecution and want, and those of the temptations that come from prosperity and power. But this hidden life in which Christ grows strong among us has also been shared by unknown millions, by the nuns in our Carmels and cloisters, by the toiling faithful, typical of the city parishes of New England, who have gone forth for generations to early morning Mass, to novenas, to missions and holy hours, from crowded tenements, three-deckers, and modest homes in the North End, West End, and South End of Boston; in East Boston, Roxbury, Charlestown, and South Boston; in the milltowns of the North Shore and the Merrimack Valley and those along the coast to Plymouth, as those throughout our province. These in their unsung, uncanonized sanctity, fortified by sacraments received regularly but in unrecognized anonymity, have given their silent prayers, their secret gifts, their sons and daughters, their very lives, to strengthen the hidden life of Christ in the Church of Boston.

Nor may we forget, as we reflect on the hidden life of Christ in this diocese, the hundreds of priests whose names show only in the ordination lists, the routine transfers, and finally the necrology, those priests—their name is legion—of whom grateful people are so often heard to say: "I shall never forget how he came in time of sorrow—or how he spoke when I needed such a word—or what he did when I went to him in need!" You know them well, those typical priests of our busy, workaday parishes, and you know how many of the wonderful things that God has done He did through them.

Christ healing through the hands of dedicated doctors; Christ ransoming and consoling through the efforts of compassionate social workers, religious and lay, charitable judges and lawyers; Christ inspiring through our gifted Catholic architects and musicians, our artists and poets; Christ at toil again in the trades and crafts of our working people, always a majority among us and always the sturdy strength of our Church; think how the goodness of God and the glory of Christ have manifested thus in the history of the Church in Boston these many generations!

The profile of Christ in His Passion will reveal the scars and sorrows of those who have here suffered out of love for Him, whether in privation and exile as did those who first came here to profess His faith and spread His glory, or in humiliation at the hands of those who, again knowing not what they did, beat Him in young Tommy Wall, boldly standing up to those who sought to break his youthful faith, who made Him bleed in Father Bapst, outraged for seeking to build His Church; who set fire to His temple at the Convent of the Ursulines or laid snares for His flock in the Broad Street riots.[6] Radiant, too, are the marks of His Passion in His chronic sick at the Holy Ghost Hospital, His orphans and His destitute in so many shelters built by Boston Catholic alms, His crippled children at Kennedy Memorial, Saint Coletta's, and in God only knows how many faithful homes and families; resplendent the traces of His redemptive power in His people faithful to the end in the sicknesses, mental and physical, which have brought

367

them in such numbers to the hospitals of Church and State where so much anguish has been given divine worth by the influence of Catholic spirituality in these hundred and fifty years.

Nor were the purposes achieved by the power of God and to the glory of Christ in the Church of Boston accomplished without the aid and comfort of those outside the household of the faith who in times of suffering spoke the word that consoles, in times of injustice the word that defends, in times of good progress the word that encourages. How can we sketch the profile of Christ in this part of our country without grateful recollection of those who wrote of our heroes and heroines, real and legendary, as did Longfellow, of our missionary priests as did Parkman; of our first bishop as did Channing; of our oppressed peoples, when we were a minority, as did those editors of Boston religious and secular journals who stood apart from the prejudices of their day and spoke up for us when we were few and weak, and therefore helped Christ at work in our humility and need.[7]

All these have their place in the profile of Christ in the Church of Boston, these and a thousand memorable things that each will recall for himself: the glories of Mary in the Mission Church and Notre Dame des Victoires; the graces won through our saints—Patrick for a people who have never wearied of his praise; Saint Anne, Saint John Baptist de la Salle, and the saints cherished by our French; Saint Anthony and Saint Francis so universally loved and invoked among us; the patrons of our parishes, hospitals, schools, and clubs. This majestic Mass is part of the profile of Christ among us, but so are the memories of the crowds who gathered at the news of a miracle at the grave of a priest, so, in another way, are the hushed groups at our wakes, the joyful throngs at our seasons of jubilee, the signs of grief when news comes of tragedy to our brethren in the lands from which our people came, the exuberant exaltation when one of ours is honored, as when our

Father in Christ was given the accolade of the Rome we dearly love by Christ's Vicar, Good Pope John.[8]

Such, in rough sketch, in merest suggestion of detail, is the profile of Christ in the Church of Boston. It is the portrait of a Christ dynamically present and wonderfully at work in head and members, in priest and people, in all the mysteries of the Christ-life of the Church, those of His Hidden, His Public, His Suffering, and His Glorious Life. So has it been from the beginning, so will it be in the future, whate'er befall. For "He Whose power is at work in us is powerful enough, and more than powerful enough, to carry out His purpose beyond all our hopes and dreams; may He be glorified in the Church, and in Christ Jesus, to the last generation of eternity. . . ."[9]

XXIX

The Aims and Ends
Of Catholic Education

In acknowledging the award so graciously conferred this afternoon, I venture to add a little intellectual prestige to my own poor person by responding also for Professor Rogers. I think it is the part of discretion, perhaps even charity, on the part of the Chapter to ask him to give his talk before the awards were made and me to give mine after the presentation. The only way I could hope to win such a distinction is assuredly before, and without reference to the merits of the address of response, and so I am doubly grateful for the consideration that enables me to be honored first and to make my *academic* comments after.

I have been deeply impressed during the conversations at lunch and in this afternoon's discussion by the insight revealed by so many undergraduates into the problems of education generally considered and the specific problems of Catholic education. I wonder, however, whether the discussion and the problem itself are not complicated by our very terminology. For example, the subject assigned for discussion this morning was *Aims of Education*, or *End of Education*, and this afternoon was the *Ends of Catholic Education*. That very word *ends* is a clue to half our embarrassment and much of our difficulty in trying to make our Catholic positions intelligible. It is a word with a slightly specific meaning to us. It is almost technical jargon from our philosophy classes and rings no bell in the minds of

This address was delivered on February 8, 1958, when Wright was inducted (together with Francis M. Rogers, professor of Romance Languages and Literature at Harvard University) as the first member of Gamma Theta, a newly instituted chapter-at-large of Delta Epsilon Sigma.

many of our nonscholastic neighbors, even literate neighbors. I rather suspect that many of those who attend our discussions have to be present for quite a long time before they discover the special meaning in which we are using classroom words like *ends*.

Part of the difficulty in the dialogue between the Catholic and the non-Catholic community starts with the very words which we use and, therefore, involves certain problems of semantics and of definitions. I am fascinated by the changing fortunes of the meanings of words and by the fads which prevail among words. Listening to radio broadcasts, one notes certain words which are apparently enjoying a temporary vogue, but which are almost unintelligible to some of us. Though I, like the fellow on the comic postcard "can't write much reading, but can read lots of writing", still some of the words which I read have entirely new and sometimes peculiar meanings, peculiar at least to me.

One word which shows up at all the educational conventions this season and at most of the symposia on about every subject from coexistence through nuclear fission, is the word *engagement*. I heard it used here this afternoon in apparently one of its current meanings, and I am not at all sure that I have any idea in the world what that word means.

Another word which is becoming beloved by the symposiumists and the commentators is the word *posture*. Now, I remember what the word *posture* meant when I flunked it in grade school. It meant that one should carry his shoulders back, his stomach in, and in those days it was more easy for some of us to carry our stomachs in than it has since developed, but *posture* then referred to physical considerations. The other day in a radio talk, the President used the word *posture* several times, and each time he was apparently referring—though these things are sometimes mystical and difficult to grasp—to certain intellectual relationships of the hour. He spoke of the present military *posture* of the Middle East, which I gather did

371

not mean that the troops were physically at attention or at ease, but meant something about the resources they had, the allies, advantages, difficulties, and plans. Later on he spoke of our present economic *posture*, by which I presume he meant the national economic situation.

So, too, this word *ends* is another sample of the way in which words sometimes divide rather than unite and sometimes conceal rather than reveal meanings. Such a word, I am afraid, is also the other word in today's theme, the word *education*. I have lived for years on the definition of education that is given, or used to be given—I am told it no longer is, by the way, which is significant all by itself—in the catalogue of my own first Alma Mater, Boston College. It is a wonderful definition, a definition that slides readily over your tongue and that by its very eloquence is calculated to silence almost immediately any possibility of opposition or of misgivings of any kind. It defines education as "the complete and harmonious development of all the faculties distinctive of man". Now, who would not wish to have that? *I* certainly did, and I signed up on the basis of it.

But somehow the definition of education, like that of the word *posture* and the word *engagement* and the word *ends*, seems to lack the cogency and clarity in the present moment of history that it had at another. And so, many have been striving in recent months to arrive at a new or, in any case, a more cogent and clear definition of what we are to expect of education and of what we expect education to be.

Going about this problem in a manner somewhat akin to that followed in the panel discussions this afternoon, I have been meeting with different groups to see if I can clarify for myself the answer to the question that you have been facing today: What do you expect a college to do for you? What is supposed to be the *end product* of collegiate education? What precisely has one the right to ask of a specific collegiate system, tradition, or institution?

Recently I spent an exceedingly pleasant evening with a group of parents who are preparing to solve the problem of the college to which they will one day send their sons and daughters. This was a particularly good group with whom to explore the question, because they were, for the most part, themselves the sons and daughters of Catholic colleges and universities. It was a group of about twenty-five couples, most of them of the professional class, all of them *intellectuals* in a fair sense of the word, all of them college and university graduates, all of them devout Catholics, some of them impelled by their love for the Church to be reserved in the expression of their criticisms, but some of them impelled by an equal love of the Church to be exceedingly frank in their expression of opinions, and all of them, in any case, eager to face the questions: What is college education? What should it provide? How much is it worth? Why should we sacrifice for it? What colleges and universities should we choose for those members of the present generation who mean the most to us because they are our sons and daughters?

These particular parents are relatively recently married. Their sons and daughters are still in primary school, so they see things in a greater luminosity than would be the case were their sons and daughters old enough now to have their own say in the matter. There is, of course, a solid probability that they will send the children to the colleges which their daughters, at least, shall pressure them to choose and those for which their sons can qualify. But I did not have the heart to tell them any of that; accordingly, we talked in a quite detached fashion about what ideally a college would do and what ideal considerations would finally determine the decision which, in point of fact, they may never make.

At the end of the evening, the young mother who had been keeping minutes handed me notes containing the characteristics that, they agreed, they expected a college to give their sons and daughters.

Before the discussion began, there had been no little eliminating of things; in fact, all agreed there were certain things that no college should be expected to provide. They agreed, in their innocence, that there were some qualities that the home would have provided by the time young people reach college. They were clearly determined to see to it that any college which would eventually receive *their* sons and daughters would be greatly blessed because of the manner in which they would discharge their obligations in connection with such qualities. I could not help but pray that they would never get tired, and that the colleges of their choice will do as well in playing their parts as these parents will have done in playing theirs if they keep any part of the aims to which they swore the other night!

There were other things that they agreed no college should be expected to do, at least as part of its direct and proper task. These things they thought the Church should be expected to do through the parish, youth programs, retreats, and the like.

But there were many things that they agreed the college should accomplish, and these things I shall review briefly with you. I do so, not because their hopes involve matters that have not occurred to you (many of them have and were said here today), but because I thus will provide you with the consolation of knowing that these ideas are shared not only by the clergy and the hierarchy who must go rushing about patronizing schools, not only by the professors, as they have been represented here today, and not only by the student body, but also by the poor little workaday victims who must foot the bills.

What are the characteristics that these parents, in their idealism, innocence, and very great love, wished our colleges, to communicate to or develop in their boys and girls? Some of them may surprise you. Certainly the order in which they agreed on these qualities is, on occasion, interesting.

The most universal demand of specific college training that

these young fathers and mothers made as they planned, in long-range terms and with great affection, the eventual college and university education of their sons and daughters, was intellectual curiosity, and they were quite explicit about what they meant by such curiosity. Some of them felt that intellectual curiosity, defined in a recent article as *intellectual initiative*, had been somewhat stunted in their own days at college. Frankly, I think that their recollection of their own intellectual state at the time they were in college is no more accurate than is their recollection of one another's faces at the time that they were engaged—*engaged* in the older sense. I think that all of us tend to see our *own* educational system out of focus, out of perspective. It is refreshing to me when someone like Professor Rogers pays such generous tribute to our colleges and campuses as he paid at lunch. I always feel guilty, incidentally—but nonetheless it is refreshing to hear our schools thus praised. So, too, it is refreshing when someone who has been educated on a Catholic campus sees clearly the deficiencies of his educational system. That is as it should be; it would be a sad situation if things were otherwise. So I make no complaint about the slight *amnesia* that makes some of our graduates forget how intellectually alert they really were when they themselves were collegians.

In any case, these parents want the colleges and universities to which they would give their money in exchange for the education of their children to develop in their boys and girls an intellectual curiosity that one of them defined, I think rather felicitously, as a sense of mature quest in relation to knowledge, rather than premature arrival.

One parent was quite outspoken on this point. He said he did not want his college to confirm his adolescent sophomore son in his own all too natural conviction that he knew everything there was to know about any field and, above all, about those fields in which it was extremely improbable that he would know even the beginning of things, let alone the end of them—such fields as theology, for example, or philosophy. He said he found it extremely irritating when boys and girls of college years stood up and said what they apparently intended to be taken as the final word on such problems as the hypotheses respecting the various details of the mystery of Creation, or the ultimate issues of salvation, or what becomes, in God's eternal scheme of things, of whole nations and whole races! He hoped that, as a result of college, there would be a slightly more tentative spirit in their discussion of those things on which the mind of the Church remains tentative, and that they would be possessed of something of the caution, when they come to speak about such things, that he found present in the approach of the Church to its mighty dogmatic definitions. He said he was always impressed by the fact that whereas it sometimes took the Church hundreds of years to get around to a definition, it took many college students only a day or two to get around to an examination and only a second or two to settle exceedingly delicate points in debate.

Now these are things that one must say with a certain reserve, because the implied criticism in such observations as these are easily distorted by hit-and-run reporters who run them out of context—with headings like "Prelate Flays Nuns", or "Bishop Laments College System", or "Cardinal Walks Out on American Catholic Universities". But, nonetheless, that young father's point has a certain merit in its own way, and so let us admit as significant that the first hope these people, at their age and with their own nearness to college and their remoteness from the actual problems of the placement of their children, expressed, probably a little wistfully, was for the college to provide intellectual curiosity, in the sense of the quest that is the scholar's vocation, rather than the premature, precocious, cocksure, and unbecoming sense of finality that sometimes mars certain types of collegians.

Interesting was the next point on which the group of young parents were agreed. They hoped that college would give to their boys and girls a sense of *tradition*. By a sense of tradition, the discussion revealed, they meant a sense of gratitude to all the accumulated work, worry, frustration, searching, and accomplishment, in part or in full, of the centuries of recorded history to which we are indebted for the kind of head start that we have in the direction of the solution of our problems. If it is true that these young Catholic parents were impatient, or thought they were, with their own colleges for giving them, or some of their contemporaries, too great a sense of finality, they were equally critical of other colleges for what they took to be an even more unattractive attitude—that only now are we beginning to recognize the master knots of human fate, and that history needed to wait for our day to learn wherein lies wisdom. We are *the ones*, the people of whom even Job was so impatient; we are *the ones* who know; ours is the age of reason, all other ages were dark.

These parents were impatient with colleges, universities, and textbooks that talk the irritating jargon of the myth of progress, in the nineteenth-century sense, with its pretense that every day, just because it is a day later, we see things a little more clearly than they could possibly have been seen yesterday, certainly more clearly than several centuries ago, say in the days of Plato, Socrates, Aristotle, or the Greek and Latin Fathers! They therefore hoped the college or university would give a sense of quest to their sons and daughters, one that would drive them forward in the search for truth and would make them humble in the acquisition of it; but they also wanted the college or university to give their children a sense of tradition and of their indebtedness to all the fools who have preceded our generation of fools and to all the wise men who have preceded the wise men of our day. One of the parents quoted a phrase for which we are indebted to Raïssa Maritain: "Today's error is at the service of tomorrow's truth!" He wanted his children to have a sense of indebtedness even to those of the past who had been egregiously and unmistakably wrong and

377

who, therefore, had spared us the probability of falling into the same errors and incurring the same condemnations. Surely we who love theology should be exceedingly grateful to those who have arrived at clarity and certainty concerning doctrines revealed by God. But do we not owe a little bow of gratitude to the poor fellows who picked up Denziger numbers along the way and got themselves condemned for propositions that otherwise might have been ours? In the light of such indebtedness, we understand the phrase of Raïssa Maritain about today's error being at the service of tomorrow's truth, and, of course, the application to science and politics is unmistakable!

Closely linked with the sense of tradition was another quality they hoped their sons and daughters would acquire in the college or university of their choice, namely a certain *historical perspective*, an ability to see the evils of one generation in terms of possible blessings to another, or in the shadow of the blessings of another, or as related to those of another, and the good—the blessings and the accomplishments of all periods of history—as related to a total pattern, probably not discernible at a glance, but nonetheless clearly present, if only on the testimony of illumined faith. This perception involves the ability to see what John Donne so wonderfully expounded in one of his sermons, when he spoke of all times as God's times and of all seasons as God's seasons—those of adversity being times of proving and those of prosperity being times of proving no less, though in other forms. In this connection, they hoped that the college or university of their choice would give their children a certain intellectual calm, a spiritual resilience in the face of adverse times. They understood that the Church makes this quality possible for us to acquire by opening up to us the channels of grace and the vision of the glories of the world to come; they thought the family, too, should achieve this quality by functioning as the social unit in which we meet

378

the major crises of life in the wider human communities. But they felt that the college or university should also, and as part of its job well done, communicate a certain intellectual poise and stability. I was happy to hear them repudiate the glib talk of the moment about the need for *emotional maturity*, and to speak as people convinced that if their young people were too undisturbed, they would probably never amount to much. But they did hope that, instead of absolute emotional neutrality and balance, they would have a certain emotional resilience that would enable them to get up again, if cast down, and to resume the battle if thrown back. This resilience college training should assuredly give.

These parents wanted our schools to give their children a *Christian cosmopolitanism*. I was grateful that they emphasized that word *Christian*, too, because it implies roots, whereas cosmopolitanism too often implies running all over the place. The cosmopolitan is not the one to whom home is any place he hangs his hat, but rather he is a person who has roots and loyalties so profound that he can range far and wide among mankind and can profit in depth, not broadmindedness alone, from all that he encounters.

I hope our schools are giving students such a Christian cosmopolitanism, and I wish I could share Professor Rogers' so generous, optimistic feeling that they are. I wish that the adjective *Catholic* were always interchangeable with *Christian cosmopolitan*, but I fear it sometimes is not. When Professor Rogers spoke this noon about how the Catholic *is* this good thing and *is* that good thing, I kept thinking to myself that the student *should be* this, *should be* that, and that such Christian cosmopolitanism should be the characteristic of those who have been educated in a tradition that does span twenty solid centuries and all the seven seas, not to mention the chasm between time and eternity.

These parents asked the college and university to give their sons and daughters a quality that they had a difficult job trying to identify in a single word. They did not wish to use the word that occurs most readily, for that word is *tolerance*, a word that has lost its luster. They did not want, and I was glad they did not, colleges and universities to give their sons and daughters *tolerance* if by tolerance be meant what is almost the same as indifference. But they finally came up with a word for which I was grateful. They hoped that the colleges and universities would give their sons and daughters *patience*: patience with persons, patience with systems with which they disagreed, even systems that they resented or of which they might be victims. By patience they manifestly meant both the longanimity of which the Apostle speaks and that sometimes seems so short-rationed among us and the magnanimity that enables us to be more comprehensive than those who exclude us, more generous than those who, sometimes unjustly and sometimes with good right, find fault with us.

Another quality they hoped the schools and colleges would give their youth was the quality of *discrimination*. They hoped that all the arguments about *segregation*, *democracy*, and *brotherhood* would not destroy the valid and real sense of the word *discrimination*. They thought it would be an unhealthy world in which the capacity to discriminate would be discredited—to discriminate among friends, to discriminate among influences, to discriminate among values, to discriminate among all things that differ. One mother defined what she hoped would be her sons' *discrimination* in what pertains to their sense of values. She said that by a sense of values she meant she wanted her sons to have an ability to use money gracefully when they happened to possess it and to get along gracefully without it when they happened to lack it. Hers is a good definition of one aspect, at least, of a discriminating sense of values.

These parents hoped their sons and daughters would acquire from their college or university education, or, at least, not lose in the process, a salutary *sense of humor*. That, by the way, is almost never mentioned at the education conventions—good reason why, if you listen to the speeches long—but in any instance, these good parents hoped that the colleges and universities would develop in their sons and daughters such a sense of humor. One man was quite spirited in his denunciation of colleges and universities that left no time for nonsense, no time for the pranks that, he argued, had almost as much to do with the refinement and the deepening of the characters of the products of our colleges and universities as anything they learned in class. I have often thought that the boys who put the cow in the belfry at Harvard some years ago learned something in the process or, in any event, got something out of their systems in the course of their stunt as important as anything accomplished the following day in the dean's office. I hope their identity was never discovered, because, if it was not, they will doubtless become overseers of the University and will live to regale alumni banquets with accounts of what they did. In any case, a saving sense of humor is certainly a part of what a college should give or should help to develop.

My group of parents hoped that the colleges or universities would make their sons and daughters useful, competent in some one field, in addition to all these things. But above all, and with all their hearts, the mothers and fathers prayed that education would supplement youthful piety with new motives for certain intellectual and spiritual gifts that are at once the safeguard and the charm of learning. These add up to a sense of awe and reverence, humility before the mystery of truth. They groped all evening for words to describe this particular quality, but no word is better than *humility*.

It brings us back to the qualities the parents first spoke about—the need that the scholar have a sense of quest and the realization that when the college has done its best job, it still has only started the graduate on his way along the road over which the devout life is a pilgrimage, the pilgrimage to which we are called, who, having set forth from God, must one day find our way painfully back to Him.

XXX

Christocentric Humanism

In the Christian Dispensation, the new order of things established in the fullness of time by Divine Providence, everything takes on its ultimate and eternal meaning from Jesus Christ. He it is who makes all things new; from Him all things derive their new creation, both things visible and those invisible. Christ became at the moment of the Incarnation and in fact what He had been in Divine intent from all eternity: Alpha and Omega, the beginning and the end of all creation, the One in Whom all the uncreated divine ideas and the created divine works are summed up and directed to their proper purpose.

All things take on their ultimate, eternal meaning from Jesus Christ. The fact cannot be too often stressed. It is a corollary of the theology concerning Christ, the Eternal Son of God and the Incarnate Word; it is the premise of the Christian humanism that sees in Christ, the apex of creation and the link between humanity and divinity, things created and those which are eternal, not only the object of our cult but also the source of the hallowing of all that God has given us to use in accord with Christ's teaching and example and thus to bring us back to God through Christ, with Christ, and in Christ. It was because a divine Person lived and worked in the atoning Christ that all the acts of His humanity had value so infinite; but it was because His humanity was complete and real—Blessed be Jesus Christ, true God and true Man!—that things human became intimately blended with things divine and the way was opened for us to become, while remaining entirely human, sharers of the divine nature of Him Who had taken on our human lot.

This article was written for and published in the December 1958 issue of *Spiritual Life*.

Wherever there is an anti-humanistic spirit among Christians it is invariably associated with a heresy. In the early Church *docetism*, *gnosticism*, and other heretical doctrinal denials of the fullness and reality of the humanity of Christ invariably were accompanied, on the ascetical and philosophical side, by moral theories predicating the evil of things created and preaching a false repudiation of created goodness, truth, and beauty. The anti-humanistic spirit characterized later heresies which either limited the humanity of Christ or the range of His redemptive influence and atoning power; thus the excessive austerities of the late medieval fanatical cults, the bitter contempt of the world in the preaching of the religious revolutionaries of the sixteenth century, and the classic blending of the restriction of the fruits of the redemption with the anti-humanistic spirit that was the hallmark of Jansenism.

Where, on the other hand, the faith in the fullness and reality of Christ's humanity is unimpaired and truly Catholic, there is a spirit of Christocentric humanism abroad in a generation and even the *profane* arts take on fresh direction and dynamism from the influence of the sacred truths concerning the place in the universe of the Incarnate Son of God.

Even in the direct moments of the Counter-Reformation there was always a strongly Christocentric humanism alive in the Church and breathed in the writing, preaching, and work of those closest to the authentic mind and heart of the Church of the Incarnate Word. Devout humanism was the concomitant of orthodox, integral Catholicism wherever this remained the spiritual force in the cultural lives of individuals or nations. Wherever Catholicism was driven out by heresy or weakened by the influence of heretical concepts, above all in what pertains to the Incarnation, the true nature of the Church, and the doctrine on the Sacraments, there an anti-humanistic spirit grew apace; witness the hacking off of the heads of sacred statues and the smashing of the stained glass in English cathedrals, as well as the eschewing of love, laughter, the ordinary delights of the good life, and the supernatural joys of the Eucharist by the Jansenists and the Puritans alike.

But before these bleak days of the Counter- and Post-Reformation periods, barren in their theology and arid in their spirituality, the theology of Catholicism was at all times and in all places the fruitful mother of those arts and disciplines which are warm with the spirit of humanism. Not without reason do we remember Thomas More as among the greatest of the Christian humanists and among the few of the English intellectuals of his time to stand fast by the ancient Catholic Faith. Not without reason were those who were in any sense humanists in the Christian tradition anxious to remain in some sense Catholics in their theological commitments; one thinks of Erasmus and Colet, as well as those Anglicans who, in the midst of the confusions of Christendom, wanted to think of themselves as still heirs to the ancient beauties of Catholicism even when they had come to uneasy terms with the new errors of Protestantism.

Now that these tensions are beginning to ease and the contribution of polemic to the cause of Christ's truth may be less and must be different, one begins to sense anew the humanistic values in the theology of those Christocentric Franciscan humanists who, like Duns Scotus and Saint Bonaventure, delighted to speculate on the manner in which the whole cosmos, all things created, are caught up in Christ to be brought back to God, integrated and renewed, in Him. Such an emphasis, Christocentric in its theology and humanistic in its philosophical overtones, discovered ties with the Incarnate Word, as well as with the creative God, on every level of being; it saw how all that is, from the tiniest seed to the most remote depths of space, all in time and all in eternity, takes on its true value from its place in the Kingdom of Christ and its part in His work. *Per Ipsum, et cum Ipso, et in Ipso*—thus does every order of creation give its due glory to God and thus also God reveals Himself, in His power, majesty, and beauty, to us that we may know Him, love Him, and serve Him in this world as the condition of our happiness with Him in the world to come. Here is the heart of Christocentric humanism.

All things take on their meaning from their relationship to Jesus Christ. Surely this is true in history; whether sacred history, as recalled in Scripture, the Old Testament and the New, or in secular history as this unfolds before the gaze of one who studies the rise and fall of empires in the light of the central place of the Incarnation in human affairs. Hence the inability of the Christian humanist to draw any sharp distinction between sacred and secular history; hence, too, his lack of concern as to whether there be a true *philosophy of history*, so unmistakable are the evidences of the theology of history in the light of which he studies the traces of the will of God and the signs of the fate of men.

In art, in science, in social doctrine, the influence of Christocentric humanism is not less manifest and unifying. In spirituality it kept the essential difference between the authentic Catholic tradition and all the counterfeit and rival systems, Puritan, secular, or pietistic, which have flourished in and since the Renaissance. This difference reveals itself in spiritual direction and in every form of educational theory; it accounts for the ethical and ascetical views by which Catholicism is distinguished from naturalism and heresy on every front.

The immortal Pope Pius XI highlighted this contention when he pleaded for a sane humanism in every field of education. Christianity, he lost no opportunity to underscore, concurs perfectly with the ideals and content of such humanism; indeed, the intrepid Pontiff considered it among his duties, precisely as Vicar of Christ, to cry out constantly "against whatever is not fully and truly human, and *therefore Christian*, against that which is inhuman, and *therefore anti-Christian*." Of such sane humanism, a Christocentric humanism which sees in men the image of Christ and in Christ the measure of humanity, Pope Pius XI found Saint Albert the

Great, among many saints, to be a patron. A like emphasis recurs frequently in the teaching, not to say the personal example, of Pope Pius XII.

Nor can the student of Catholic theology, in any of its branches, find this surprising. The Christian revelation augmented and elevated nature; it in no way annulled any of the goodness, truth, and beauty present in all being. The humanistic spirit of the Christian attitude toward the goods of nature, even after the coming of the Kingdom of God, is summed up in the line which sings "non eripit mortalia qui regna dat coelestia."

Mere humanism teaches the person "all things are yours"; Christocentric humanism teaches this same principle, but adds, as did Saint Paul, "and you are Christ's, and Christ is God's."[2] In the recognition and ordered love of the hierarchy of being and values implicit in this text of Saint Paul lies the genius and the justification of that Christocentric humanism which, please God, is every day coming more fully into its own.

Abbreviations

AAS   *Acta Apostolicae Sedis* (Rome, 1909–).

ACW   *Ancient Christian Writers*: The Works of the Fathers in Translation, ed. J. Quasten and others (Westminster, Md.: Newman Bookshop, 1946–).

CCL   *Corpus Christianorum*, Series Latina.

CSEL   *Corpus Scriptorum Ecclesiasticorum Latinorum* (Vienna, 1866–).

PG   *Patrologia Graeca*, ed. J. P. Migne (Paris, 1857–66).

PL   *Patrologia Latina*, ed. J. P. Migne (Paris, 1844–64).

Notes

Chapter One
The Religious Inspiration of Massachusetts Law

This address was published as a monograph, *The Religious Inspiration of Massachusetts Law*. The fifteen-page text lacks both date and place of publication.

[1] *The Roman Missal: Sacramentary*. "Votive Mass of the Holy Spirit".

[2] I Cor 12:4–11.

[3] Pope Pius XI, Encyclical *Divini Redemptoris* (March 19, 1937); English trans. *Atheistic Communism* (Washington, D.C.: National Catholic Welfare Conference, 1937), 13.

[4] Decreed by the French National Assembly in the sessions of August 21, 23, 24, and 26, 1789, and accepted by the King.

[5] *Marsellis v. Thalhimer*, 2 Paige 25, 21 Am. Dec. 66 (New York Ch. 1830).

[6] I Blackstone, Commentaries 447.

[7] *Richardson v. Richardson*, 246 Mass. 353, 354, 104. N.E. 73 (1923), quoting from *Smith v. Smith*, 171 Mass. 404, 407, 50 N.E. 933, 934 (1898).

[8] *Reynolds v. Reynolds*, 85 Mass. (3 Allen) 605–607 (1862).

[9] *Mass. Const.* pt. 2, chap. 5, section II (par. 91).

[10] *Pierce v. Society of the Sisters of the Holy Names of Jesus and Mary*, 268 U.S. 510 at 535 (1925).

[11] *Meyer v. Nebraska*, 262 U.S. 390, 399 (1923).

[12] *Holy Trinity v. United States*, 143 U.S. 457, 471 (1892).

[13] *Mass. Const.* art. II.

[14] Ps 144:15.

[15] Rom 8:28.

Chapter Two
The Diocesan Priesthood

[1] Pope Pius XI, Encyclical *Ad Catholici Sacerdotii* (Dec. 20, 1935); English trans. *The Catholic Priesthood* (Washington, D.C.: National Catholic Welfare Conference, 1936), 6.

[2] I Cor 4:1.

[3] Is 61:1–2.
[4] Jn 1:1.
[5] 2 Cor 8:23.
[6] Phil 2:8–9.
[7] Phil 2:9–10.
[8] *Pontificale Romanum*. "De Ordinatione Presbyteri".
[9] *Missale Romanum*. "Credo".

Chapter Three
The Pope and the War

This address was published as a monograph, *The Pope and the War and the Pope and the Peace* (Boston: Archbishop Richard J. Cushing, 1944), 72 pp.

[1] Is 4:6.
[2] St. Ignatius of Antioch, *Epistola ad Romanos* (PG 5, 686): ". . . universo coetui charitatis praesidens."
[3] Dante, *Purgatorio* bk. 32, 102: ". . . di quella Roma onde Cristo è Romano."
[4] Jer 29:11.
[5] *Breviarium Romanum*. Ordinarium divini officii ad Laudes: "Preces".

Chapter Four
Christendom and Heresy

This address was published in *Conferences Delivered at the Tenth Diocesan Congress* (Boston: League of Catholic Women, 1946), 27–34.

[1] Harry E. Fosdick, "One World for Religion Too", *Reader's Digest* 48 (May 1946): 72–74.

[2] Garfield Bromley Oxnam (1891–1963) was the Methodist Bishop of Boston from 1939 to 1944. In 1947, he and others organized the POAU (Protestants and Other Americans United for the Separation of Church and State). See Roy H. Short, *History of the Council of Bishops of the United Methodist Church 1939–1979* (Nashville: Abingdon, 1980), 151–53.

[3] William Thomas Manning (1866–1946) was an early advocate of Christian unity. An active participant in the first and second World Conferences on Faith and Order (1927 and 1937), he was Episcopal Bishop of New York from 1921 to 1946. See "Manning's Bridge to Unity", *Newsweek* (May 27, 1946), 82, and "The Bridge Church", *Time* (May 27, 1946), 57.

[4] Ibid.

[5] Matthew Arnold, *The Complete Works of Matthew Arnold* (London, 1903), vol. 8, *Essays Religious and Mixed*, 331.

[6] This is Wright's own translation of Henri D. Lacordaire, O.P., *Oeuvres* (Paris: Poussielque-Rusand, 1857), vol. 3: *Conférences de Notre-Dame-de-Paris*, 22–23.

[7] Mt 23:9.

[8] Mt 25:41.

[9] Jn 8:32.

[10] William H. Mallock, *Is Life Worth Living?* (New York: Putnams, 1880), 284–85.

Chapter Five
The Holy Father's Historic Appeal to Women

This address was published as a monograph, *The Holy Father's Historic Appeal to Women* (Boston: League of Catholic Women, 1947), 9 pp.

[1] Pope Pius XII, Address on "Woman's Duties in Social and Political Life", *Catholic Mind* 43 (Dec. 1945): 705–16.

[2] Gal 3:28.

[3] Mary R. Beard, *Women as Force in History* (New York: Macmillan, 1946).

[4] Henry Adams, *Mont-Saint-Michel and Chartres*, quoted in Beard, *Women as Force in History*, 215.

[5] James J. Walsh, *The Thirteenth, Greatest of Centuries* (New York: Fordham University Press, 1952), 389–91.

[6] See chap. 4, note 2 above.

[7] Pope Pius XII, op. cit., 714.

[8] Ibid., 708–709.

[9] Ibid., 715.

[10] Dorothy Thompson, "A Woman Says, 'You Must Come into the Room of Your Mother Unarmed' ", *Ladies' Home Journal* 63 (Feb. 1946): 24–25.

Chapter Six
Jesuit Centennial in Boston

This sermon was published in *The Woodstock Letters* 76 (Dec. 1947): 288–98.

[1] *Report of the Trial of McClaurin F. Cooke, Sub-Master of the Eliot School, of the City of Boston, for an Assault and Battery upon Thomas J. Wall, a Pupil of that*

School. With the Arguments of Counsel and the Opinion of the Court Reported in Full
(Boston: A. M. Lawrence, Daily Ledger Office, 1859), 86 pp.

[2] Wright was educated at the Jesuit institutions of Boston College (1927–1931) and the Gregorian University (1932–1935).

[3] U.S. Congress, Senate, Senator George Graham Vest speaking to the Senate of the 56th Congress, April 7, 1900, *Congressional Record* 33: 3884–85.

[4] Cardinal O'Connell died on April 22, 1944. On September 25, 1944, Richard J. Cushing was named the sixth archbishop of Boston. At the time of this sermon, Wright had been auxiliary bishop of Boston for about three months. He was ordained bishop on June 10, 1947.

Chapter Seven
The Historian in the Service of Peace

[1] *Catholic Historical Review* 23 (Jan. 1938): 413–26.

[2] Ibid., 415.

[3] Cf. St. Thomas Aquinas, *Summa Theologica* 1, q.1, a.8 ad 2.

[4] Pope Leo XIII, *Acta Leonis* (Rome, 1881), vol. 3, Brief *Saepenumero Considerantes*, 268.

[5] Pope Pius XI, "Orbem Catholicum", *AAS* 15 (1923): 327.

[6] John E. Harley, *International Understanding* (Stanford, Calif.: Stanford University Press, 1931), xiii.

[7] Ibid.

[8] Carlton J. H. Hayes, *Essays on Nationalism* (New York: Macmillan, 1933).

[9] Ibid., 78.

[10] John J. Wright, *National Patriotism in Papal Teaching* (Westminster, Md.: Newman Press, 1956), 293, note 291.

[11] *American Historical Review* 43 (1937–1938): 321–41.

[12] *Journal of Educational Psychology* 19 (May 1928): 303–12.

Chapter Eight
The Philosophy of Responsibility

This sermon was published as follows: by the League of Catholic Women (Boston, 1949), 5 pp.; by the Advertising Club of Worcester (Worcester, Mass., 1959), 16 pp.; in *Catholic Mind* 58 (Nov.–Dec. 1960): 542–48; and in *The Christian and the Law* (Notre Dame, Ind.: Fides, 1962), 64–75.

[1] Sir 31:10.

² Sir 15:18.

³ Dt 11:26–28.

⁴ Mt 23:37.

⁵ *King Lear*, act I, sc. ii, ll. 113–20; *Julius Caesar*, act I, sc. ii, ll. 140–41.

⁶ Lk 12:20.

⁷ Lk 16:2.

⁸ Mt 8:2–3.

⁹ Lk 15:18–19.

¹⁰ Abraham Lincoln, *Collected Works*, ed. Roy P. Baster (New Brunswick, N.J.: Rutgers University Press, 1953), "Gettysburg Address", p. 23.

¹¹ John L. Spalding, *Opportunity and Other Essays and Addresses* (Chicago: A. C. McClurg, 1900), 8.

Chapter Nine
Monsignor Walter S. Carroll 1908–1950

¹ A priest of the Pittsburgh diocese, Carroll served in the Vatican Secretariat of State from 1940 to 1950. He was the brother of Bishop Howard J. Carroll (1903–1960) and Archbishop Coleman F. Carroll (1905–1977).

² Cardinal Francesco Marchetti-Selvaggiani ordained Wright and Carroll in Rome on December 8, 1935.

³ Archbishop Amleto Giovanni Cicognani, Apostolic Delegate in the United States from 1933 to 1958.

⁴ Jn 11:25–26.

⁵ The text is from Borsi's last letter to his mother, dated October 21, 1915. Borsi died at Mount Zagora on November 10, 1915. Giosuè Borsi, *A Soldier's Confidences with God*, trans. Pasquale Maltese (New York: Kenedy, 1918), 342.

⁶ 2 Cor 11:26–27.

⁷ During the war, in 1943, Carroll went to North Africa to facilitate communications between the Holy See and the local Church, and to further the humanitarian mission of the Pope. He visited the United Nations on behalf of the Vatican several times. In 1947, he was sent by the Vatican to the United States in the interest of relief for the displaced persons of Europe. Pope Pius XII sent Carroll on missions to Austria and Germany, and he represented the Holy See at the meeting of the International Refugee Organization held in Geneva in 1947. Carroll also represented the Holy See at the 1948 International Red Cross Conference.

⁸ 2 Tim 4:7.

⁹ In 1951, Monsignor Giovanni Battista Montini (later Pope Paul VI), while visiting Canada and the United States, went to Pittsburgh to visit with

Carroll's family and to pray at his grave. As head of the English language section of the Vatican Secretariat of State, Carroll had worked closely with Montini for nine years. See John G. Clancy, *Apostle for our Time: Pope Paul VI* (New York: Kenedy, 1963), 75–76.

Chapter Ten
A Clergyman Views Medicine

This address was published in *Journal of the South Carolina Medical Association* 47 (Aug. 1951): 336–44.

[1] James J. Walsh, *The Thirteenth, Greatest of Centuries* (New York: Fordham University Press, 1952), 476–79.

[2] "Medicine, Science and Humanism", *New England Journal of Medicine* (Nov. 2, 1950), 716.

[3] Samuel Butler, *Erewhon, Erewhon Revisited* (London: Dent, 1932), 61.

[4] Ibid., 61.

[5] Ibid., 72.

[6] Institute on Social Medicine of the New York Academy of Medicine, *Social Medicine: The Derivations and Objectives* (New York: Commonwealth Fund, 1949), 114.

[7] George B. Chisholm, "The Re-establishment of Peacetime Society", *Psychiatry* 9 (Feb. 1946): 19.

Chapter Eleven
The Law of God

This address was published in *Catholic Mind* 50 (Aug. 1952): 459–67.

[1] "God's Law: The Measure of Man's Conduct", *Pastoral Letters of the American Hierarchy 1792–1970* (Huntington, Ind.: Our Sunday Visitor Press, 1971), 453–58.

[2] Institute on Social Medicine of the New York Academy of Medicine, *Social Medicine: The Derivations and Objectives* (New York: Commonwealth Fund, 1949), 114.

[3] Robert Frost, *Complete Poems* (New York: Holt, Rinehart and Winston, 1948), 47.

[4] Abraham Lincoln, *Collected Works*, ed. Roy P. Baster (New Brunswick, N.J.: Rutgers University Press, 1953), 332–33.

Chapter Twelve
The Church of the Saints

Beginning in 1948, Wright was the episcopal moderator of the National Retreat Movement for the Laity. See C. Hennessy, S.J., *The Inner Crusade—The Closed Retreat in the United States* (Chicago: Loyola University Press, 1965), v–vi, 156–57, 162–63, and 167–68. Wright also founded the Lancaster Cenacle, in the Worcester diocese. Mother Helen M. Lynch, a Religious of the Cenacle, writes: "In June 1953, a new Cenacle was added to the growing number of foundations with the purchase of the former country estate of the late Bayard Thayer in Lancaster, Massachusetts. This foundation was the direct result of long importuning as His Excellency, the Most Reverend John J. Wright, D.D., had ardently desired a Retreat House for Women since his consecration as the first Bishop of the Diocese of Worcester in 1950. For many years he had been closely associated with the Cenacle of Boston in its apostolate and, as Episcopal Advisor of the National Retreat Movement, he now exercises indefatigable zeal in increasing Retreat consciousness and Retreat centers across the land." See Helen M. Lynch, *In the Shadow of Our Lady of the Cenacle* (New York: Paulist Press, 1954), 247. See also Wright's prefatory note to *Women of the Cenacle* (Milwaukee: Convent of Our Lady of the Cenacle, 1952), ix–xi.

[1] John Henry Newman, *Parochial and Plain Sermons* (London, 1834), vol. 1, 309–24.

[2] 1 Tim 6:11–16.

[3] Eph 2:19–22.

[4] Lk 23:2–3; Jn 18:36–38.

[5] Jn 8:32.

[6] Mk 15:31.

[7] Gen 18:32.

Chapter Thirteen
Pastoral Letter on Sacred Scripture

This pastoral letter was published as follows: *Pastoral Letter on the Five-Hundredth Anniversary of the First Printing of a Book* (Worcester, Mass.: Catholic Free Press, 1952), 18 pp. Portions also appeared in *The Catholic Companion to the Bible*, ed. Ralph L. Woods (Philadelphia: J. B. Lippincott, 1955), 75 and 118–20, as "Gutenberg's Bible" and "Catholic Veneration of the Bible." See also Wright's foreword to that book, 19–22.

[1] Pope Leo XIII, Encyclical *Providentissimus Deus* (Nov. 18, 1893); Pope Benedict XV, Encyclical *Spiritus Paraclitus* (Sept. 15, 1920); Pope Pius XII, Encyclical *Divino Afflante Spiritu* (Sept. 30, 1943).

[2] Thomas à Kempis, *The Imitation of Christ*, bk. 4, chap. 11:5.

[3] Rev 22:20–21.

[4] St. Jerome, *In Isaiam Prophetam* (*CCL* 73, 1–3).

[5] Lk 24:32.

Chapter Fourteen
Education for an Age of Fear

[1] Cardinal Alojzije Stepanic (Yugoslavia) was arrested and jailed in 1946. Cardinal Jozsef Mindszenty (Hungary) was arrested in 1948 and sentenced to life imprisonment in 1949. He was released in 1955 but remained under house arrest until liberated by the Freedom Fighters in 1956. Cardinal Thomas Tienchensin, S.V.D. (China), was impeded from his office and forced to live in exile. Cardinal Joseph Beran (Czechoslovakia), after three years in Dachau, was put under house arrest and banned from Prague. And Cardinal Wyszynski (Poland) was deposed in 1953 and not freed until 1956. See Jozsef Mindszenty, *Memoirs* (New York: Macmillan, 1974), 238.

[2] Tertullian, *Apologeticus* (*PL* 1, 534): "Plures efficimur, quoties metimur a vobis: semen est sanguis Christianorum."

[3] Heb 13:8.

[4] Acts 5:38–39.

[5] John Henry Newman, *Oxford University Sermons* (London, 1909), 282–97.

[6] Mic 5:2.

[7] Theodore Roemer, O.F.M. Cap., *The Catholic Church in the United States* (St. Louis: Herder, 1950).

[8] In October 1854, Father John Bapst, S.J., parish priest at Ellsworth, Maine, was tarred and feathered. Later he became the first president of Boston College. See *The Woodstock Letters* 16 (1887): 324–25.

[9] Virgil, *Aeneid* 1, 199.

[10] Achille Ratti (from 1922 to 1939, Pope Pius XI) was elected to the College of Doctors of the Ambrosian Library, Milan, in 1888. He became prefect of that library in 1907, and in 1912 was appointed vice-prefect of the Vatican Library. See Carlo Confalonieri, *Pius XI, A Close-Up*, trans. Regis N. Barwig (Altadena, Calif.: Benziger Sisters, 1975). See also *Pio XI nel Trentesimo della Morte* (Milan, 1969), 165–75.

[11] John Henry Newman, *The Idea of a University* (Oxford, 1976), 376.

¹² 2 Tim 4:2.
¹³ Is 35:1–8.
¹⁴ Acts 3:6.

Chapter Fifteen
The Nurse's Vocation

¹ 1 Jn 2:16.
² Jn 9:1–3.

Chapter Sixteen
A Good Boy

¹ Mayor O'Brien was elected by the Council after a twenty-day deadlock. He served from 1954 to 1959 and from 1960 to 1961.
² Mayor Holmstrom was in office from 1950 to 1953.
³ *Annual Report of the Several Departments for the Financial Year Ending December 31, 1954*, City Document No. 109 (Worcester, Mass.: 1954), 3–4.
⁴ Ibid., 4.
⁵ Ibid.
⁶ James Keller, M.M., *Government Is Your Business* (New York: The Christophers, 1951).
⁷ Ibid., 31–32
⁸ Ibid., 32.

Chapter Seventeen
Channing and Cheverus

¹ "William Ellery Channing became so fond of Cheverus that when he was called upon to review a new life of Fénelon in 1829 his article became a paean of praise for Cheverus. . . ." Annabelle M. Melville, *Jean Lefebvre de Cheverus 1768–1836* (Milwaukee: Bruce, 1958), 141. See also *United States Catholic Miscellany* 8 (April 25, 1829): 331.
² Josiah P. Quincy, *Figures of the Past* (Boston: Little, Brown, 1926).

³ Walter Muir Whitehill (1905–1978), librarian of the Boston Athenaeum, was a very close and dear friend of Wright. See Walter Muir Whitehill, *A Memorial to Bishop Cheverus, With a Catalogue of the Books Given by Him to the Boston Athenaeum* (Boston: Athenaeum, 1951), iii, and *The Pittsburgh Bibliophiles' Pilgrimage to Italy 1976* (Pittsburgh: Pittsburgh Bibliophiles, 1978), 9–19.

⁴ Quincy, *Figures of the Past*, 261–62.

⁵ Mk 6:8; 2 Cor 11:26.

⁶ Matignon came to Boston to revive, as Whitehill puts it, "a Catholic church that had been established there in 1788. The Abbé de la Poterie, a former naval chaplain who had arrived in Boston with the French fleet in the late summer of 1788, had remained there and became the first resident priest of the town. He took over a chapel in School Street, originally built by the French Huguenots, and although he had the distinction of celebrating the first public Mass in Boston, the Abbé de la Poterie proved to be something less than an upright and edifying character. His successor, the Abbé Rousselet, did not measure up to desirable standards either, while the third resident Catholic priest in Boston, the Reverend John Thayer, a convert, by his lack of tact succeeded in antagonizing Catholics and Protestants alike." Whitehill, *A Memorial to Bishop Cheverus*, vii.

⁷ *The Archives of the Archdiocese of Boston*, 2-N-1(1): "Cheverus to Matignon", July 31, 1797.

⁸ Robert H. Lord, "Jean Lefebvre de Cheverus," *Proceedings of the Massachusetts Historical Society* 65 (1933): 67.

⁹ *The Archives of the Archdiocese of Boston*, from Bishop Tyler's diary, the entry for September 11, 1836. This account is also found in the appendix to Stewart's translation of Hamon's biography of Bishop Cheverus. See André J. M. Hamon, *Vie du Cardinal de Cheverus archevêque de Bordeaux* (Paris, 1837); English trans. *Life of Cardinal Cheverus* (Boston, 1839).

¹⁰ Quincy, *Figures of the Past*, 261–62.

¹¹ Whitehill, *A Memorial to Bishop Cheverus*, xiv.

¹² Melville, *Jean Lefebvre de Cheverus*, 70–72.

¹³ Whitehill, *A Memorial to Bishop Cheverus*, xiv–xv.

¹⁴ Ibid., xvi.

¹⁵ Whitehill, *A Memorial to Bishop Cheverus*, 1–9.

¹⁶ Ibid., xviii.

¹⁷ Ibid., xviii–xix. Whitehill describes Cheverus's gift as: "Louis XVI, King of France. Facsimile du testament de Louis XVI . . . accompagnée d'un notice historique . . . sur le testament du roi Louis XVI, et sur l'origine du testament de la reine, par L.-E. Audot . . . Paris 1816. Given September 25, 1823." *A Memorial to Bishop Cheverus*, 3.

¹⁸ *Boston Monthly Magazine* 1 (1825): 16.

¹⁹ Whitehill, *A Memorial to Bishop Cheverus*, xx.

[20] See note 1.

[21] On January 28, 1950, Pope Pius XII appointed Wright as the first Bishop of Worcester, Massachusetts.

[22] Eph 4:5.

Chapter Eighteen
The Common Good

This address was first preached as a sermon at Saint Ignatius Church, Boston, Massachusetts, on September 30, 1950, on the occasion of the Red Mass. It was published in *The Christian and the Law* (Notre Dame, Ind.: Fides, 1962), 41–55.

[1] Jacques Maritain, *The Person and the Common Good*, trans. John J. Fitzgerald (New York: Scribner's, 1947), 42.

[2] Ibid.

[3] Ibid., 43.

[4] Ibid., 43–44.

[5] Ibid., 44.

[6] Woodrow Wilson, *Selected Literary and Political Papers and Addresses* (New York: Grosset and Dunlap, 1926), 241.

[7] Cicero, *Epist. ad Atticum* Lib. 7, Ep. 11, par. 2.

[8] Mt 13:52.

Chapter Nineteen
Christ, the Divine Intellectual

[1] John Tracy Ellis, "American Catholics and the Intellectual Life", *Thought* 30 (1955): 351–88. See Ellis, *American Catholics and the Intellectual Life*, with a prefatory note by John Wright (Chicago: Heritage Foundation, 1956), 63 pp., and Ellis, *Perspectives in American Catholicism* (Baltimore: Helicon, 1963), 249–50.

Wright further commented on Ellis' ideas in *American Catholicism and the Intellectual Life*, eds. Frank L. Christ and Gerard E. Sherry (New York: Appleton-Century-Crofts, 1961), vii, 156, 186, and 279; and in *The Christian Intellectual*, ed. Samuel Hazo, prefatory note by John J. Wright (Pittsburgh, Pa.: Duquesne University Press, 1963), vii-viii.

[2] John Lancaster Spalding, *Means and Ends of Education* (Chicago, 1897), 220.

[3] John Ireland, *The Church and Modern Society* (Saint Paul, 1905), vol. 1, 92.

[4] Pope Pius XII, *Discorsi e Radiomessaggi 1939–1958*, 20 vols. (Vatican City, 1958).
[5] *The Litany of the Most Sacred Heart of Jesus*.
[6] Ibid.
[7] Jn 1:14.
[8] 2 Tim 2:9.
[9] Thomas à Kempis, *The Imitation of Christ*, bk. 1, chap. 1:3.
[10] *The Litany of the Most Sacred Heart of Jesus*.

Chapter Twenty
Youth, the Hope of Christ and the Church

[1] Is 6:1–8.
[2] 2 Cor 8:23.
[3] Cf. Is 6:1–8.

Chapter Twenty-One
The Isaiah Thomas Award

[1] Mt 20:1–16.
[2] Mt 20:12–13.
[3] Mt 20:15.

Chapter Twenty-Two
Christian Charity and Intellectual Clarity

[1] John Henry Newman, *Lectures on the Doctrine of Justification* (New York: Longmans, Green, 1924), 268–71.
[2] See Wright's introduction to *The Church Today, The Collected Writings of Emmanuel Cardinal Suhard* (Chicago: Fides, 1953), xiii–xvii.
[3] Alfred O. Mendel, ed., *The Living Thoughts of Tom Paine* (New York: Longmans, Green, 1940), 89.

Chapter Twenty-Three
Interview with John Deedy, Jr.

This interview, "The Church in the Sputnik Age", was published in *Ave Maria* (April 5, 1958), 5–8. *Ave Maria* prefaced the interview with these words:

"What is the Church's attitude toward science? Is science something to be feared, something hostile to religion? What do the latest developments mean for man's soul? These are questions that are interesting many a Catholic today, but they are questions which not everyone is equipped to answer satisfactorily. When *Ave Maria* decided to have someone answer them for our readers, we looked long and hard for a mind which was learned in not just one field but many, a person who would be fully able to give the human and Christian attitude toward our rapidly unfolding knowledge of the universe. We found him in Worcester's Bishop John J. Wright. Here are his answers, which, it will be noted, are profoundly optimistic."

Chapter Twenty-Four
The Roman Spirit

[1] Lk 22:32.

[2] St. Ignatius, *Epistola ad Romanos* (PG 5, 686): ". . . universo coetui charitatis praesidens."

[3] Ralph L. Hayes (1884–1970) was born in Pittsburgh, Pa., on September 21, 1884. Ordained to the priesthood on September 19, 1909 and to the episcopacy on September 21, 1933, he was rector of the North American College (Rome) from 1935 to 1944.

[4] St. Paulinus of Nola, Carmen XVII (CSEL 30, p. 93): ". . . per te barbari discunt resonare Christum corde Romano placidamque casti vivere pacem." P. G. Walsh, in his translation of *The Poems of St. Paulinus of Nola* (ACW 40, 112) renders the text as: "In this mute region of the world, the barbarians through your schooling learn to make Christ's name resound from Roman hearts, and to live in purity and tranquil peace."

One time in his student days, Wright came across this text, and it deeply impressed him. He included it in his thesis, and—when ordained bishop—selected it as his motto and included it in his coat of arms.

Cardinal Wright's personal coat of arms is composed of the shield and its charges, the motto beneath the shield, and the external trappings around the shield.

Arms: a cauldron in silver resting upon a fire, or rising from the fire, and an eagle of gold between two fleurs-de-lis. The Cardinal's arms are based upon those sometimes attributed to his patron saint, St. John the Evangelist, in allusion to the Roman tradition of St. John before the Latin Gate and the miraculous escape of the saint from the cauldron of boiling oil prepared for him under the Emperor Domitian.

The fleurs-de-lis are taken from the arms of the Archdiocese of Boston, where Wright was born and served as auxiliary bishop before being named to the See of Worcester and subsequently to the diocese of Pittsburgh. These fleurs-de-lis also appear frequently on arms associated with the name *Wright*.

The Cardinal's Motto: The words, "Resonare Christum" are from the above-quoted passage in the writings of St. Paulinus of Nola: ". . . per te barbari discunt *resonare Christum* corde Romano, placidamque casti vivere pacem." Wright's translation reads: "Through you the heathens of our world's unheeded parts / Have learned *to echo Christ* with Roman hearts / And live a life of chaste and stable peace."

The external ornaments are composed of the scarlet pontifical hat with its fifteen scarlet tassels on each side, arranged in five rows with the episcopal gold cross indicating his Sacred Congregation. These are the presently accepted heraldic trappings of a prelate of the rank of Cardinal-Bishop. Before 1870 the pontifical hat was worn at solemn cavalcades held in conjunction with papal functions. The color of the pontifical hat and the number and color of the tassels are signs of the rank of the prelate. This custom is preserved in ecclesiastical heraldry.

The arms were designed in 1947 after Wright was named an auxiliary to the Archbishop of Boston and titular bishop to the See of Tegea. These arms were designed by Dom William Wilfred Bayne, O.S.B., of the then Portsmouth Priory—now Portsmouth Abbey—in Portsmouth, Rhode Island.

The shield has a tint rose red. The cauldron is, as mentioned, silver, with the eagle and the fleurs-de-lis of gold.

This description and explanation of Wright's coat of arms is based—with my additions and corrections—on the text published on page 12 of the booklet entitled: *The Pontifical Liturgy in Memory of John Cardinal Wright* (Pittsburgh: Saint Paul Cathedral, Aug. 20, 1979).

See John J. Wright, *National Patriotism in Papal Teaching* (Westminster, Md.: Newman Press, 1956), xii; also, *Classica et Iberica, a Festschrift in Honor of the Reverend Joseph M.-F. Marique, S.J.*, ed. P. T. Brannan, S.J. (Worcester, Mass.: Institute for Early Christian Iberian Studies, 1975), 417–25.

⁵ William H. O'Connell, *Recollections of Seventy Years* (Boston: Houghton Mifflin, 1934), 134.

⁶ Gilbert Keith Chesterton, *The Collected Poems* (New York: Dodd, Mead, 1932), 257.

⁷ Dante, *Purgatorio* bk. 32, 102.

⁸ Acts 5:34–39.

⁹ Lk 22:32.

Chapter Twenty-Five
Interview with Donald McDonald

This interview, "Conversations With Bishop John J. Wright", was published in *The Catholic Messenger* (July 9, 1959), 4–6. In 1960, McDonald again published it in his volume *Catholics in Conversation* (Philadelphia: J. B. Lippincott, 1960), 13–32. In the introduction, McDonald wrote: "Witty, profound, scholarly, Bishop Wright is acknowledged as one of the most brilliant members of the Church's hierarchy in this or any other country. Though his interests range widely, he has spoken out and written most frequently on two subjects: the condition of intellectual life among Catholics and the problem of international peace and world order."

[1] See "Christ, the Divine Intellectual", 248–57.

[2] John Tracy Ellis, "American Catholics and the Intellectual Life", *Thought* 30 (1955): 351–88.

[3] Pope Pius XI, Encyclical *Mens Nostra* (Dec. 20, 1929), *AAS* (1929), 689–706.

[4] Alfred Noyes, ed., *The Golden Book of Catholic Poetry* (Philadelphia: J. B. Lippincott, 1946), 249.

[5] Benjamin L. Masse, S.J., ed., *The Catholic Mind through Fifty Years 1903–1953* (New York: America Press, 1952), 239–45.

[6] In 1955, Wright hosted the Liturgical Week in Worcester, Mass. At that time he delivered the address, "The Mass and International Order". This address was published in *Worship* 30 (Feb. 1956): 172–80. It was also published by Dan Herr and Clem Lane, *Realities—Significant Writings from the Catholic Press* (Milwaukee: Bruce, 1957), 187–97.

Chapter Twenty-Six
Our Patriotic Debt to Our Dead

This address was published in *Annals of Saint Anthony's Shrine* 11 (1959): 12–20.

[1] Acts 21:39.

[2] Pericles (c. 500–429 B.C.) delivered the funeral oration at the commemoration of the Athenians who fell in the first year of the Peloponnesian War.

[3] Thucydides, *History of the Peloponnesian War*, trans. C. Foster Smith (New York: Putnams, 1929), 333–35.

[4] Ibid., 335.

[5] Is 2:4–5.

[6] Mt 5:9 and Lk 11:21.

[7] Thucydides, *History of the Peloponnesian War*, 337.

Chapter Twenty-Seven
Peace, the Work of Justice

[1] Pope Pius XII had died on October 9, sixteen days before Wright's address.

[2] Ps 118:8–9.

[3] Dante, *Paradiso* bk. 3, 85: "E'n la sua volontade è nostra pace."
[4] Lk 11:21–22.
[5] "Dr. Schweitzer vs. Archbishop Godfrey", *America* (May 10, 1958), 188.
[6] Ibid.

Chapter Twenty-Eight
Profile of Christ in the Church of Boston

This sermon was printed by Sullivan Brothers of Lowell, Mass., and published as a pamphlet: *Profile of Christ in the Church of Boston*: Sermon of the Most Reverend John J. Wright Bishop of Worcester, Holy Cross Cathedral, Boston, December 8, 1958, 8 pp.

[1] The See was erected by Pope Pius VII on April 8, 1808.

[2] Jean Cheverus (1808–1823), Benedict J. Fenwick (1825–1846), John B. Fitzpatrick (1844–1866), John J. Williams (1866–1907), William H. O'Connell (1906–1944) and Richard J. Cushing (1944–1970). Cardinal Cushing was born in South Boston, Mass., and Cardinal Spellman was born in Whitman, Mass.

[3] 1 Cor 12:4.

[4] Virgil Barber (1782–1874): convert, Jesuit priest, missionary to the Indians in Maine, and founder of New Hampshire's first Catholic parish at Claremont.

James Fitton (1805–1881): New England missionary, pioneer in Catholic education, and founder of Mount St. James Seminary, Worcester, which became Holy Cross College.

James Gillis (1876–1957): Paulist priest, author, editor, and radio orator.

John Hogan (1829–1901): first president of St. John's Seminary, Brighton, Mass. (1884–1889). He again served as president from 1894–1901.

John Boyle O'Reilly (1844–1890): poet, novelist, journalist, patriot, and editor of *The Pilot*.

Orestes Brownson (1803–1876): convert, scholar, and philosopher.

David Goldstein (1870–1958): convert, pioneer of street preaching and Catholic Evidence Guild work. In 1917 he organized the Catholic Truth Guild of Boston.

Emma Forbes Cary (1833–1918): convert, author, worked on behalf of prison inmates. From 1867–1892 she was a member of the Prison Commission of Massachusetts. She also founded the Radcliffe Catholic Club.

Louis Mercier (1880–1953): educator, professor of modern languages, and humanistic scholar.

Thomas Dwight (1843–1911): anatomist, professor, and from 1873–1878 editor of the *Boston Medical and Surgical Journal*.

Jeremiah Ford (1873–1958): educator, author of numerous Spanish grammars and literature texts, president of the American Catholic Historical Association (1935).

[5] James A. Walsh (1867–1936): bishop, co-founder of the Maryknoll Missionaries.

James Hennessey (1905–1945): missionary to the South Pacific. He was killed when the United States forces torpedoed and sank the Japanese prison ship, Montevideo Maru.

[6] On March 14, 1859, a young Catholic boy, Thomas J. Wall, was beaten for refusing to read the Protestant Bible and to recite Protestant prayers at Boston's Eliot School.

In October 1854, Father Bapst, S.J., parish priest at Ellsworth, Maine, was tarred and feathered.

The Ursuline convent at Charlestown, Mass., was sacked and burned by an anti-Catholic mob on August 11, 1834.

[7] Henry Wadsworth Longfellow, *Complete Poetical Works* (Boston: Houghton Mifflin, 1926); Francis Parkman, *The Jesuits in North America in the 17th Century* (Boston: Little, Brown, 1867); *United States Catholic Miscellany* (April 25, 1829): 331.

[8] Here Wright refers to Father Patrick J. Power. Born in Ireland on October 20, 1844, Power came to the United States as a young man. Sent to the seminary by Father James Fitton, he was ordained to the priesthood in 1867 and assigned to a parish in Chicopee, Mass. (at that time a part of the Boston diocese). Father Power soon became ill and returned to Boston where he died on December 8, 1869. Miraculous cures were attributed to his grave at Holy Cross Cemetery, Walden, Mass.

[9] Eph 3:20–21.

Chapter Twenty-Nine
The Aims and Ends of Catholic Education

This address was published in the *Delta Epsilon Sigma Bulletin* 2 (May 1958): 5–12.

Chapter Thirty
Christocentric Humanism

This article was written for and published in *Spiritual Life* 4 (Dec. 1958): 282–86.

[1] John J. Wright, *National Patriotism in Papal Teaching* (Westminster, Md.: Newman Press, 1956), 298.

[2] Semaines Sociales de France (Nice), *Ordre Sociale et Education* (Paris: J. Gabalda, 1934), 151.

Index

411

Hamon, Abbé: 225
Harley, John E.: 101
Harrington, Timothy: 118
Harvard College: 222, 224
Harvard University: 131, 305, 321
Hayes, Carlton: 102
Hayes, Ralph L.: 296–301
Heflin, Thomas: 70
Hennessey, James: 366, 407n
Henry VIII: 75
Herberg, William: 331
heresy: 54–70, 91–92, 252–53, 384
Hesburgh, Theodore: 306–8
Hildebrand: see saints: Gregory VII, Pope
historians, Catholic: 98–104, 196, 307
Hogan, John B.: 365, 406n
holiness: 156–65, 273, 366
Holmes, Oliver W.: 337
Holmstrom, Andrew: 211–15, 264, 399n
Holy Cross Cathedral, Boston, Massachusetts: 363n
Holy Cross College: 121, 406n
Holy Name Society: 39
Holy Spirit: 9, 254, 288
hope: 288–90, 291
hospitals: 122–23, 135, 367
human rights: 26–27, 28
humanism: 56, 100–101, 146, 290
humanism, Christian: 93, 101, 253, 323–27, 383–87
humanities: 186, 285–86
humility: 381
humor, sense of: 118, 381

illness: 203–10
Immaculate Conception Church, Boston, Massachusetts: 21n
Ingunda: 72
intellectuals, Catholic: 187–202, 250–57, 270–82, 302–7, 373
internationalism: 49, 97–99, 101–2, 328–35
interracial relations: 99, 103
Ireland, John: 250
Isabella of Spain: 73
Isaiah Thomas Award: 264–69, 264n

Jesuits: 68, 87–96, 284
Jesus Christ: 36, 52, 86, 160, 161–63, 178, 254–55, 295, 364, 366–69, 383–84; authority, 67–68; and the Church, 162, 272, 369; Divine Intellectual, 254; Divine Missionary, 365; Divine Physician, 210; Divine Teacher, 365; Incarnation, 36, 325–26, 383; King, 254–55; laborer, 254; Logos, 254–55; Lord, 54; obedience, 39; passion and death, 161–62; priesthood, 35–37, 39, 254; Prince of Peace, 348; Savior, 54; teacher, 255
John XXIII, Pope: 117, 369
John Paul II, Pope: 117
Joliet, Louis: 291
journalism and journalists: 79, 94, 167, 188, 189, 193, 195, 197, 251, 252, 253, 278, 284, 300, 304, 332, 334
joy: 290

412

413